D0906579

SHARED SECRETS

SHARED SECRETS

THE QUEER WORLD

OF NEWBERY MEDALIST

CHARLES J. FINGER

Elizabeth Findley Shores

THE UNIVERSITY OF ARKANSAS PRESS

FAYETTEVILLE

2021

Copyright © 2021 by The University of Arkansas Press. All rights reserved. No part of this book should be used or reproduced in any manner without prior permission in writing from the University of Arkansas Press or as expressly permitted by law.

ISBN: 978-1-68226-155-2
eISBN: 978-1-61075-736-2

Manufactured in the United States of America

25 24 23 22 21   5 4 3 2 1

Designer: April Leidig

∞ The paper used in this publication meets the minimum requirements of the American National Standard for Permanence of Paper for Printed Library Materials z39.48-1984.

Library of Congress Cataloging-in-Publication Data
Names: Shores, Elizabeth Findley, author.
Title: Shared secrets: the queer world of Newbery medalist Charles J. Finger / Elizabeth Findley Shores.
Description: Fayetteville: The University of Arkansas Press, [2021] | Includes bibliographical references and index. |
Summary: "Biography of the British expatriate Charles Joseph Finger (1867–1941), known primarily as an award-winning author of children's literature. Finger's allusive and suggestive short fiction won some critical acclaim during his lifetime, but the Newbery Medal that made him famous ended his development as an author of serious queer literature. His insistence on forging a life on the secret byways of queer culture offers a rare example of gay community at a time when openly lived identities were prohibitively difficult to actualize"—Provided by publisher.
Identifiers: LCCN 2020023356 (print) | LCCN 2020023357 (ebook) | ISBN 9781682261552 (cloth; alk. paper) | ISBN 9781610757362 (ebook)
Subjects: LCSH: Finger, Charles Joseph, 1869–1941—Relations with men. | Authors, American—20th century—Biography. | Gay authors—United States—Biography. | Homosexuality and Literature—England—History—19th century. | Homosexuality and Literature—United States—History—20th century.
Classification: LCC PS3511.I557 Z86 2020 (print) | LCC PS3511.I557 (ebook) | DDC 813/.52 [B]—dc23
LC record available at https://lccn.loc.gov/2020023356
LC ebook record available at https://lccn.loc.gov/2020023357

For my husband, Finos Buford Johnson Jr.,
and our sons, Findley Shores Johnson and Layet Spigner Johnson,
adventurers all.

CONTENTS

ACKNOWLEDGMENTS

MY FIRST AND DEEPEST thanks are to my husband, Buddy Johnson, for joining me in discovering the life and times of Charles J. Finger. My next thanks must go to Leland Razer and the staff of the Interlibrary Loan Department, the staff of the Adolphine Fletcher Terry Library and Maumelle Library, and the entire Central Arkansas Library System, because a public library is as crucial as a university press for an independent scholar. They made this project possible.

The following archivists and institutions also were important resources: the Special Collections staff of the University of Arkansas Libraries, particularly Timothy G. Nutt, Geoffery L. Stark, and Joshua Youngblood; Suzanne Campbell, Shannon Sturm, and Brittany Wollman, West Texas Collection, Angelo State University; Charles Wommack, Special Collections, University of Arizona Library; Kaye Lundgren and Michael Stotts, Arkansas Studies Institute; Lisa Perry, Northeast Arkansas Regional Archives; Tamara Shkundina, Leo Garza, Deborah Orellana, and Jeffery Thivel, Harold Washington Library Center, Chicago Public Library; Kylie Lewis, Special Collections and Archives, Emporia State University; Kathy Makas, Ford Research Center, the Henry Ford Museum of American Innovation; Evelyn Lemons, Fort Concho National Historic Landmark; Aaron M. Lisec, Special Collections Research Center, Southern Illinois University; Kathy A. Lafferty, Spencer Research Library, University of Kansas; Bryan Whitledge, Casey Gamble, and Erin Hensbergen, Clarke Historical Library, Central Michigan University; Maurice Klapwald and Tal Nadan, New York Public Library; Lily Birkhimer, Ohio History Connection; Olivia Diamond and Iris Chin, Special Collections and University Archives, University of Oregon; AnnaLee Pauls and Brianna Cregle, Rare Books and Special Collections, Princeton University Library; Joanne Spruce, Local History Centre, Walsall, England; Mike Glasson, Walsall Leather Museum, Walsall, England; Julie Brown, Linda Davies, and Stephen Snoddy, the New Art Gallery, Walsall, England; Alison Gibson, Union Township (Ohio) Public Library; Anne

Causey, Albert and Shirley Small Special Collections Library, University of Virginia; and Dolores Colon, Beinecke Rare Book and Manuscript Library, Yale University.

Findley Shores Johnson and Layet Spigner Johnson good-naturedly listened to stories about Finger for several years. Dick and Julie Johnson of Fayetteville, Arkansas, provided a home away from home. Steve and Kiki Dreyer Burke were kind hosts in Fort Thomas, Kentucky, and Steve accompanied Buddy and me to Ripley, Ohio. Anneke Wambaugh of Seattle performed archival research in New York and helped review key primary sources in Arkansas. Adrienne Ames of Nashville, Tennessee, shared her impressions of Patagonia. The following shed light on crucial points: Wendell Hall and John Helmkamp of Little Rock on the risks of the male gaze, Dave Hoffpauir of Little Rock on sexuality, Dieter Huppenkothen of Vienna on an obscure term in the German language, Layet Johnson on the artistic relationship of Frank Brangwyn and Paul Honoré, William B. Jones of Little Rock on Robert Louis Stevenson, and Nigel May of Bexleyheath, Kent, England, on Henry Somerfield.

I am immeasurably indebted to D. S. Cunningham of the University of Arkansas Press for his patience, advice, and encouragement, to the anonymous reviewers for their helpful comments, and to Denise Logsdon for her sensitive and thorough copyediting. My thanks also to Robert B Leflar and Sarah May Leflar of Fayetteville and Scott, Arkansas, for generously allowing me to explore Gayeta on numerous visits and to Charles Joseph Leflar of Fayetteville for permitting me to examine additional materials that were saved by the Leflars' mother, Helen Finger Leflar.

At a time in American history when the dangers to immigrants, dreamers, and everyone who is different seem greater than ever, it is a privilege to tell the story of C. J. Finger's quest.

SHARED SECRETS

INTRODUCTION

A BRIEF SERIES OF odd columns appeared in the weekly newspaper of a small west Texas town in late 1902 and early 1903. The author, who wrote under the byline Jack Random, described being in a saloon a few nights before Christmas, wishing his readers a happy New Year and wondering why he was "to Comfort . . . ever a stranger." The writer was an Englishman, a handsome, theatrical, young music teacher named C. J. Finger. His pseudonym alluded to Roderick Random, the protagonist of a hugely popular British picaresque novel of the eighteenth century, and to Finger's childhood literary hero, Jack Harkaway. Rhythmically it resembled the name of one of Finger's role models, Jack London.

Describing sitting beside a "warm stove . . . amidst my . . . boon companions," Finger-as-Random alluded to Walt Whitman's poem "A Glimpse." Mentioning that he was "reading my Walt Whitman," he referred slyly to one of the literal signs—carrying a copy of Whitman's *Leaves of Grass*—that gay men used to identify themselves to each other during Finger's youth in London.[1] For understanding readers, these Whitman references conveyed that Zenker's Saloon was a safe cruising ground and hinted that Finger was interested in meeting men. In another column Finger subtly outed himself by extolling the book *Ioläus: An Anthology of Friendship* by Edward Carpenter, declaring "every book and *man lover* will place this work among his most cherished volumes [emphasis added]."[2]

For nearly a century, the British expatriate Charles Joseph Finger (1867–1941) has been known primarily as the fourth recipient of the Newbery Medal, a prize awarded by the American Library Association (ALA) for an outstanding work of literature for children.[3] The story of Finger receiving the medal in 1925 for *Tales from Silver Lands* is an interesting look at the interworkings of librarians, publishers, book reviewers, and booksellers during the early years of publishing for children in the US, and particularly the efforts of one editor, May Massee, who commissioned Finger to write a set of ostensible folktales set in Patagonia.

There is another story about Finger, however. As a youth and young man, he reveled in the easy homosociality of the Regent Street Polytechnic Institute in London.[4] Finger enjoyed most of the activities at the "Poly" but was happiest at meetings of the Literary Society, his own version of London's ubiquitous private men's clubs, which he started with his closest friends. One night in 1889, Finger led the club in a discussion of Whitman's concept of "manly friendship" between "comrades," and someone, probably Finger himself, commented that "humanity ever seeks . . . a fancied Paradise, when the Golden Age of Love and Peace and Joy will be the heritage of every child of man."[5] Finger searched throughout his life for comrades who would occupy that paradise with him. He wanted to share his love of literature within a friendly and understanding circle of gay literati, exchanging books, discussing books, inviting friends and visitors into his personal library as if it were a shrine, literally describing the juxtaposition of various writers on his shelves, even writing one entire book about his love of books—all of this a lifelong practice of what the scholar Natasha Hurley, in *Circulating Queerness: Before the Gay and Lesbian Novel* (2018), calls "queer sociability and textual circulation."[6] Finger was more than a queer bibliophile, however. He was a highly enterprising, prolific writer who studied the publishing opportunities of the day and used every publication means available to him to express his twin loves, literature and men. His literary accomplishments cannot be understood apart from his colorful and adventurous life in South America and Texas, nor from the thirty-seven years he spent unhappily married and "a slave to duty," nor from his lifelong attempts to recreate the camaraderie he enjoyed at the Poly in London.[7]

Despite the rich, participatory education he was receiving at the Poly and opportunities to write for London newspapers, Finger left England in 1890 under pressure to either contribute to his family's household income or stop being a drain upon it. At the time a major scandal involving gay men was sending waves of fear through London's gay subculture. As Finger later had an autobiographical character muse, "It's *queer*, when you come to think of it, but there must have been some men born out of their time [emphasis added]." He went first to South America, a continent known by readers of the notorious editor Sir Richard Francis Burton as a region where male homosexuality was accepted. He was looking for "friends, real friends"—as one acquaintance put it in a short story with a character evidently based on Finger—friends who were "a queer medley."[8]

Working occasionally as a reporter in South America for British newspapers and as a columnist and reporter for the newspaper in San Angelo, Texas, launching men's clubs wherever he went, Finger found friends and readers who communicated via literary exchanges. After a long, self-guided education as a writer, during which he supported his family by managing small railroads in Ohio, he experimented with ways to reach two primary audiences: editors who would pay him to write and gay readers who would appreciate his veiled writing. He produced an enormous body of work, thanks to editors including Henry Louis (H. L.) Mencken, the vast capacity of middlebrow book publishers, and what the literary historian Sarah E. Gardner calls "book review culture." Gardner demonstrates that a "public discourse" among "authors, publishers, reviewers, and readers" determined how the nation understood the American South in the years between the World Wars. Such discourse enabled Finger to draw two concentric circles of readers: an outer circle of middlebrow literati and an inner circle of "understanding" friends who saw through the veiled messages and allusions in much of his work and shared his vision of a world where men could be free to love whom they wished.[9] Art colonies—communities where artists worked, taught, and communed—were important sites in the American literary and art world, and Finger tried to establish his own Arcadian retreat on a farm in Arkansas that he called Gayeta, with a library at the center of his house that served as a rural salon for the local intelligentsia and visiting writers and artists.[10] To gather a larger circle in their conversations, he published a highly idiosyncratic literary journal, *All's Well*, which became a virtual social network for him.

His small body of allusive, suggestive short fiction—which appeared in *Reedy's Mirror*, the *Century*, Mencken's magazine the *Smart Set*, and the *Double Dealer*—won some critical acclaim, but the Newbery Medal that made him a famous writer ended his development as an author of serious gay literature. From 1925 on, Finger's erratic financial success depended upon perpetuating his reputation as a wholesome and fatherly writer when, in truth, he loved his children but loathed his marriage and longed to leave Gayeta. He worked constantly, hoping that someday his book royalties would be enough to support his wife so that he could move away without leaving her impoverished. Grasping at every freelance opportunity arguably compromised his principles, and his scheme to make his youngest child his professional collaborator permanently damaged his relationship with her.

Close readings of Finger's articles for *Polytechnic Magazine* and his Jack Random columns, later fiction, pseudo-autobiographical stories, and nearly two hundred book reviews, combined with a reconstruction of his travels on four continents and an inventory of his large personal library, reveal his persistent attempts over a lifetime to replicate the camaraderie he enjoyed among his literary fellows at the Poly. His signaling through code and double entendre are examples of what the scholar Richard R. Bozorth calls a "game of knowledge" and Hurley calls a "distinctly literary model of queer world-making." Finger's oeuvre is significant today not for its literary quality, which was uneven, or simply for the innumerable clues that he was a closeted gay man, but as evidence that he used the enormous expansion of middle-brow publishing in the interwar years to travel on what Hurley calls "the complex ... routes and paths" of "queer traffic in literature," finding his readers at the intersection of veiled writing and mainstream publishing. Hurley suggests that "virtually no scholarly work takes up and explores ... the history of reading and writing queer literature beyond the work of canonical writers," that there has been "no study of what we might call queer book history," but Finger's life and work are an example of that history. For fifty years he persistently, creatively, and shrewdly talked and wrote about books to reach readers who would understand his deepest longings and share his secrets.[11]

Caroline Wigginton's study of early American women's various means of expression and message exchange as "relational publication" provides additional theoretical support for this interpretation of Finger's work. Wigginton found women "serially circulated ... original texts in person and in letters" to define and reinforce their ties of friendship and shared interests. Similarly, the poet George Sterling gave Finger a photograph of himself, possibly taken by Jack London, which Finger later gave to his friend and benefactor Fielding P. Sizer. Sizer pasted a clipping of Finger's published review of Sterling's *Selected Poems* (1923) inside a copy of the book and added the photograph, tracing the transmission of this gift in notes at the top and bottom edges of the picture: "Sterling to Finger" at the top, "Finger to Sizer" at the bottom.

Wigginton's understanding of the reading aloud of elegies as another type of relational publication is like Hurley's sense of "performative acts of reading and collecting" as a form of "queer traffic"; both remind one of Finger's ceremonial toasts on New Year's Eve. Through Wigginton's view of networks of writers and readers as "neighborhoods" or "virtual spaces—traced through the circulations of texts, objects, and people" like "the itinerancy of a preacher, the crossroads of a trading post, and the serial passing on of a letter"—one sees Finger's vision of the "social circle that sits at the sign of All's Well."[12]

Gardner shows that the American book-buying public of the 1920s and 1930s wrote "lots and lots of letters" to their favorite writers.[13] It probably was in a fan letter that Finger found the friend who became the greatest love of his life. A highly secretive man who had a distinguished career in the United States Army, George Washington Maddox was Finger's muse and the object of his dreams. Together and individually, they enjoyed decades of association with prominent men in journalism, publishing, literary criticism, book collecting, and the visual arts—most importantly with the editor Robert Hobart Davis and the artist Paul Honoré. Some of their trips and parties are traceable in Finger's work, their social circle another example of Hurley's "queer world-making."[14]

After accepting the Newbery Medal in 1925 in Seattle, Finger did not go straight home. Instead, he went south by steamer to San Francisco to meet Sterling, who was one of the contributors to *All's Well*. Still mourning for his close friend Jack London, who died nine years earlier, Sterling was depressed, alcoholic, and possibly suicidal. He talked to Finger about London, took him to meet some of his other close friends, and gave him one of his most private and personal belongings, a death mask of London. As they walked late at night up and down the steep streets of Russian Hill, Sterling could have told Finger about one of the saddest points in their relationship, when London declined an invitation to build a house next to Sterling's in Carmel, a free-loving community of writers and artists on the coast just south of Monterey Bay. London wrote to Sterling that their dream of living side by side in literary and romantic partnership was a dream "too bright to last," that gentle rejection foreshadowing the greatest heartbreak of Finger's life.[15]

[**1**]

HARK, AWAY!

WALT WHITMAN WAS the subject at the meeting of the Polytechnic Literary Society in London on May 31, 1889. Whitman envisioned "a fancied Paradise" where, as one of the club members put it, every man could enjoy a "Golden Age of Love and Peace and Joy." "Manly friendship" between "comrades," the American poet had proclaimed, was even the foundation of democracy and freedom. Leading this discussion of one of his favorite writers, with his best friends beside him and a circle of other appreciative young men around him, twenty-one-year-old Charles Joseph Frederick Finger was as close to that paradise as he had ever been. Books and book talk were a primary means of communication for closeted gay men in Victorian London, and sharing a work of Whitman was a symbolic gesture, one of the secret signs that such men exchanged. Young Charley Finger reveled in literature—from the penny dreadful tales about young Jack Harkaway to the works of H. Rider Haggard and Robert Louis Stevenson—and organized the literary society just before his twenty-first birthday as a support group for fellow aspiring writers.[1] Presiding that spring night over his club of like-minded friends in the reading room at the Regent Street Polytechnic Institute, with comrades who understood his desire to find a "golden" paradise—that word *golden* evoking a gay utopia—Finger was, for the moment, in just such a place.[2]

The oldest child in a large family, Finger was restless, with a strong distaste for domestic life, a tendency to be starstruck, and secrets. One secret was the matter of his birthday. He was born on Christmas Day in 1867, more than a year before his parents were married on January 14, 1869, a fact that he seems never to have acknowledged publicly and tried to disguise by giving various inaccurate years for his birth. His parents were Julia Connolly, a daughter of a laborer, and Charles Henry Christian Martin Finger, a German-born tailor.[3] Their other children were Mary Phillipina, born in 1870, George Leonard Francis (1873), Ellen Alice (1876), Julia Emilie, who was born in 1878 and died within a year, and Emil William Henry (1880) and Lizzie Emilie Florence (1883), the last two both named in memory of the daughter who died in infancy.[4] For a while, during Charley's early childhood, the family was fairly prosperous and lived in Mayfair, a fashionable area near Buckingham Palace. His parents sent him to Frankfort-on-the-Main, Germany, to live with relatives and receive music lessons. Finger later referred repeatedly in fiction and memoir to a mild flirtation with a girl there, sometimes indicating she was a cousin; these stories are some of the many tangled threads in the vast, embroidered version of his life that he wrote for mainstream readers. However, when Martin suffered a business reversal, the family called Charley home to contribute to the household income. He found part-time work as a church organist and an apprentice teacher at a parish school but longed for more adventure.[5]

When he was eighteen, he joined the polytechnic institute to learn shorthand, a necessary skill for jobs writing for newspapers. Thousands of working- and middle-class youth paid modest tuition to take classes and join clubs at the Poly. Precursor of the contemporary University of Westminster, the institute was an enormous combination of trade school, social hall, and uplift charity on a beautiful thoroughfare lined with mansions, shops, and galleries that was one of the city's most popular nighttime cruising grounds for gay men and adolescents. The Poly's six-story main building buzzed with activities for boys and young men all day and evening. (Classes and meetings for girls and young women took place in a separate building on the same street.)[6] An expansive yet sheltered setting where young men could find friends without the fear of social rejection, the Poly combined the appeal of London's many gentleman's clubs—homosocial retreats for elite men—with a missionary image.[7]

The institute's founder was usually in the building, greeting many boys by name, occasionally sitting in on club meetings and making notes for the *Polytechnic Magazine*, which he edited. Quintin Hogg (1845–1903) was a wealthy sugar merchant and member of the London County Council. Social work programs in London in the 1880s could be meeting grounds for closeted gay adolescents and men, but Hogg brilliantly deflected suspicion by claiming that the institute's swimming pool and gymnasium cultivated "muscular Christians." He addressed every Poly member as "my dear Boy" and preached that because "God is Love," anyone who could "touch the chord of love in the heart of a man" would unite that man "with his Maker." Hogg wished that Christians might unite "in one great, grand desire to show their fellow-men that God is Love." He spent every free moment with his "boys," even taking one on his honeymoon, and after purchasing a house beside the institute for his family, he had a covered passage built between his home study and the gymnasium so that he could slip into the gym without being observed. Eventually he added a room adjacent to that passage to use as his private bed-chamber. Seemingly a sexual predator, he ruled the Poly as his homosocial fiefdom. When Hogg died suddenly a few years later, there was a rumor that he committed suicide because he was about to be exposed.[8]

Although there is no hint in Finger's journal or elsewhere that he was seduced by Hogg, Charley Finger did want "to belong to everything, to try everything, to know everybody[,] to be one in [the] buoyant companion-ship" at the Poly. He enjoyed swimming, gymnastics, wrestling, and boxing and spent many hours in the institute's reading room. He played the piano for various club meetings, and his Poly mates were friendly audiences for his musical and theatrical efforts, giving him the confidence for a lifetime of performances. He and his best friends belonged to the Mutual Improvement Society, which met weekly to discuss articles in the newspapers and hold debates on political questions. Such clubs were common in England as ventures in cooperative self-education, and many members went on to jobs in journalism.[9] Finger's closest friends were Henry "Harry" Somerfield, a strongly leftist artist, aspiring architect, and voracious reader—they might have met at Somerfield's father's newsstand in Marylebone; and Charles James "C. J." Peer, a tall, passionate young man who seemed to Charley "like some strong animal crashing through underbrush, intent on a course."[10] Inspired by Peer's activism, Finger participated in the Polytechnic Parliament and adopted "C. J." as his own nickname. Accompanied by one or both of these friends, he went on long rambles around the city and countryside, spent hours browsing in reading rooms and at newsstands, and attended leftist meetings and rallies. He began writing articles for the institute's magazine and letters to the editors of newspapers and even sold a few articles.[11] He may even have written an article for the *Times* of London.

A lengthy article about the Poly, by an anonymous writer, appeared in the *Times* in April 1888. Anonymous newspaper reports were not unusual, and when an American building trades magazine reprinted the article in November, it gave the author the pseudonym "Britannicus." Certain details suggest that Finger was Britannicus: The writer mentioned the reading room and the Mutual's debates on "the Irish question," a subject that Finger had addressed in a "fierce debate." There was an audience in Victorian London for suggestive articles about homosocial and homoerotic scenes, and the *Times* article was studded with signifiers of gay club culture: the swimming pool—the image of men bathing or undressing instantly recognizable as representing the Hellenic man–man love—and the "much gayer sight" in the gymnasium of young men performing synchronized dances and exercising on the parallel bars and trapeze. The word *gay* did not yet connote homosexual for the general public, but it was in use as a code word; thus, Britannicus signaled to knowing *Times* readers that the Polytechnic was an amenable place for homosocial encounters. "Nothing [at] the University gymnasiums can . . . compete with . . . these young men, these auctioneer's clerks, these tailors, these carpenters of London," Britannicus boasted. "It adds a new dignity to the draper's counter to reflect that the young man who stands behind it and measures you a yard of ribbon, may, when he is stripped among his fellows in the evening," display a "fine" figure.

The young man behind "the draper's counter" could have been Finger himself. A draper was a merchant who sold cloth and dry goods, in the same general business as Finger's father the tailor, and a few years after the *Times* article appeared, Finger described a pseudo-autobiographical character, London Johnny, as an "ex-draper's assistant."[12] If Finger wrote the anonymous article about the Poly, it is the earliest example of his using veiled language to reach man-loving readers.

When he decided to start his club for aspiring writers, Finger wrote to Walter Crane—a protégé of William Morris and an artist with a lavish style who illustrated R. L. Stevenson's travel books—for advice. Crane replied, recommending "members . . . study a work simultaneously, making abstracts or notes," and meet to compare them.[13] Finger probably attended an exhibit that Crane organized, the opening in September 1889 of the second annual show of the Arts and Crafts Exhibition Society at the New Gallery, down the street from the Poly—and probably had a passing encounter with Oscar Wilde there. Wilde had reported for the *Pall Mall Gazette* on the society's first show and Crane had illustrated Wilde's forthcoming book *The Happy Prince and Other Tales*, so it seems likely that Wilde attended the 1889 opening.

Wilde's interest in pederasty was in the open—he was known to frequent a pornography shop on Coventry Street with young male friends and had been in a relationship with an adolescent boy for two years. "The Portrait of Mr. W. H.," his conjectural story about Shakespeare's relationship with a boy actor, had appeared in *Blackwood's Edinburgh Magazine* three months earlier. In Finger's first recollection of seeing Wilde, the famous author "stopped suddenly when he noticed, hanging on the wall to his right, a piece of embroidered silk" and "fell to stroking it as a woman might a child's hair," his "woman-like caress of the silken fabric" like "a fondling touch, that careful down stroking of the silk with extreme finger tips." (Wilde did have a special affinity for draperies. Three and a half years earlier, he wrote to a friend that he thought Morris should work more on "textures which hang in folds" and less on wallpapers.)

Finger emphasized that he was not attracted to the effeminate aesthete. "My beau ideal was a man of the physical type of [William] Morris," who, despite being a wallpaper designer, was "rugged and strong." In Finger's subsequent version of his encounter with Wilde, Finger was chatting with Halliday Sparling, an associate of Morris's, when Wilde approached them. Again Wilde "fell to stroking . . . some hanging stuff of beryl-blue and there seemed . . . a desire to be noticed as one noticing." Finger's lines about Wilde, on the surface just two of the hundreds of instances of name-dropping in his writings, contained hints to knowing readers that he caught Wilde's eye and perceived Wilde's "desire to be noticed," that he knew how to read the glances and body language of a gay man.[14]

The literary society became the focus of Finger's activity, and other Poly men began calling him "Literary Finger."[15] One of his presentations was on a mystery involving the authorship of *The Loving Ballad of Lord Bateman* (1839), a bawdy little illustrated book involving two muscled, wasp-waisted dandies wearing tights, hats with giant feathers, and slippers with pompoms. Some critics and admirers maintained that Charles Dickens wrote the anonymous ballad; others attributed it to Dickens's friend William Makepeace Thackeray.[16]

———

MARTIN FINGER IMMIGRATED to New York in 1888, leaving Charley at the crowded family home, where he gave piano lessons to friends to earn a little money and tended to his mother, Julia, when she was ill. The Fingers intended for the entire family to move to New York, but Finger "did not wish to be imported."[17] He wanted to see the world, find places where men were safe to be jolly fellows, and write about them.[18] As Stevenson observed in *Travels with a Donkey in the Cevennes*, a book that Crane illustrated, "the best that we find in our travels is an honest friend. . . . We travel, indeed, to find them."[19] Finger wished he could go to the United States, not to join his father but to meet up with Dan Cauthorn, a friend he had met through Peer. Peer went to New York in 1889, possibly on Hogg's behalf to explore employment prospects or tour destinations for young Poly men, and met Daniel Armistead Cauthorn, an American sheep rancher, on the return voyage.[20] Cauthorn wanted someone to accompany him on some sightseeing trips, so Peer introduced him to Finger, who joined Cauthorn on several jaunts around England. The American rancher was a symbol of independence, and Cauthorn, a rugged bachelor, seemed like "a new type of man" to Finger. One evening, they talked at a coffeehouse "until long after midnight." Finger confessed that he felt little interest in women, and Cauthorn encouraged him to remain single if he wished and to leave England for a life of freedom. Writing his memoir forty years later, Finger remembered this conversation as a turning point.[21]

Finger and Peer went on a two-day ramble around the city in January 1890, walking to Hampstead Heath, a large park in northern London where city dwellers enjoyed lounging on the grassy slope of Parliament Hill and taking in the view across the city and all the way to the South Down. Spending the night at Peer's boardinghouse, they "tried gymnastics in the bedroom . . . between 12:30 and 2," Finger noted in his journal.[22] During this extended period together, the two young men must have talked over career prospects. Peer had gotten a job with William Thomas Stead, an enterprising editor who had just left the *Pall Mall Gazette* to launch a new magazine, *Review of Reviews*.[23] With twenty-one daily newspapers in London, there was ample opportunity for Finger, who could write quickly and clearly and was not afraid to go to unfamiliar places or talk with strangers. Stead later gave Somerfield some freelance work designing covers for the *Review*, so he probably would have given Finger freelance assignments.[24] However, the biggest news in London journalism that week was that a newspaper editor had been sentenced to a year in prison for exposing the clandestine gay activities of prominent London men. This turn of events was a reminder, if Finger needed one, that London was not a paradise for gay men.

The conviction of Ernest Parke was a consequence of a shocking series of articles about underage call girls that Stead had written for the *Pall Mall Gazette* a few years earlier. Public uproar prompted Parliament to raise the age of consent for girls from thirteen to sixteen and establish more regulation of brothels. The 1885 law, known as the Labouchere Amendment, also made sexual relations between men a crime punishable by as much as two years in prison with hard labor. This made blackmail a real danger, and encounters between men became much more secretive. The incident that led to Parke's imprisonment began when a fifteen-year-old messenger told police that men who frequented a brothel at 19 Cleveland Street, less than a half mile from the Poly, had paid him for sex. Parke, editor of the radical news weekly the *North London Press*, identified two of the men as the earl of Euston and the eldest son of the Prince of Wales, and the earl responded by suing Parke for libel. Parke's conviction was the beginning of a panicked period in London's gay world.[25]

Leaving London for the US would cost more money than Finger had.[26] He could, however, run away to sea like the character of Jack Harkaway, an English boy who left school to become a sailor, enjoying thrills and comradeship in exotic places—free, as Finger reminisced decades later, and "unyoked by woman."[27] Many working-class men were immigrating to South America to work on sheep farms, and Finger had gone on a few multiple-day treks with Harry Somerfield and other friends, giving him some experience living outdoors. He could even get paid to make the trip by signing on as a seaman on a coal ship. A week before the ramble with Peer, he paid one pound to an immigration agency to secure a job on the steamship SS *Gulf of Akaba* that would depart Antwerp, Belgium, in February for Valparaiso, on the western coast of Chile.[28]

Three of Finger's other friends decided to go with him. Arnold Fox, a year younger than Finger and a fellow member of the Poly Parliament, frequently spent the night at the Finger house.[29] Alfred Edward Hyde read Whitman and relished a good debate.[30] S. Charles Saxby was a member of the Mutual and the Radical Party.[31] Finger sold books and old newspapers to pay for travel gear, and two Poly fellows gave him a copy of *Voyage of the Beagle*, Charles Darwin's 1839 account of exploring the coasts of South America. When the literary society presented him with a gift of four pounds, Finger was overcome by emotion. Saying goodbye to Peer was the hardest part of leaving. The two friends went to a photography studio to have portraits made for each other and awkwardly shared their feelings in notes, the contents of those messages a mystery but the effort the two young men made evident in Finger's diary: He mailed a letter to Peer on February 11, went to Peer's room the next day to see him, and was disappointed to find him away. He left but returned later in the day, when Peer told him he had mailed a reply to his letter. The next day, Finger mailed another letter to Peer.[32]

On February 19, after bidding farewell to his mother and siblings, Finger set out with Fox for Liverpool Street Station and the Great Eastern Railway "boat train" that would take them to Harwich, where they would take a boat to Antwerp. Peer met them somewhere en route and carried one of Finger's boxes. At the station Finger let out a loud whoop when he saw below him about "50 fellows" who came to see the four adventurers off. Wearing a large hat and carrying a banjo, he descended the steps at the station, and the young men surged around him. The gang was so rowdy that another passenger quickly yielded his seat to find a quieter compartment. With a few minutes before the train would depart, Finger launched into a farewell speech through the open window of the car, his friends loudly taunting him with "Anarchism!" "Coercion!" and even a pun: "Peerless!" The whistle blew at eight, and their jeers turned to cheers as the train steamed out of the station, taking Finger away from the security of his home, family, and friends at the Poly and toward a new life of adventure.[33]

A HIGH AND SPLENDID SECRET

THE *GULF OF AKABA* MADE its first stops at Las Palmas on Grand Canary Island, Spain, where Finger noticed "the Spanish young men are fully poised," and St. Vincent in the Cape Verde archipelago, which became the basis for his later claims that he "went to Africa on a sailing [*sic*] ship." As the *Akaba* steamed south, he worked as a cook and used his free time to write in his diary and read. One of his books was a copy of *Arabian Nights*, the set of Middle Eastern tales ostensibly told by a woman who is to be executed but persuades a king to postpone her death by telling him a new story each night for one thousand and one nights. The outer story of the woman tricking the king was a frame narrative, a device Finger eventually used in much of his fiction. There were several editions of the tales at the time, including R. L. Stevenson's retellings and Sir Richard Francis Burton's sixteen volumes of translations. Burton's translation, and particularly his essay "Pederasty" in the tenth volume (1887), was part of a subversive British literature celebrating man–man love. Comparing sexual practices in various historical periods and cultures was a ruse for fairly explicit descriptions of homosexual acts, and Burton's version was notorious for its homoerotic passages. He also put forth the theory of a "Sotadic Zone," encompassing South America, where male homosexuality was accepted. *Arabian Nights* was immensely popular—so popular, in fact, that someone aboard stole Finger's copy.[1]

The *Akaba* entered the Strait of Magellan, a passage between the islands at the base of Argentina and Chile, in a region known as Patagonia on April 6, 1890, anchoring some distance off Punta Arenas, or Sandy Point, Chile.[2] Half a lifetime later, Finger remembered the chilly scene he and his friends regarded from the deck: A "long spit of sand thrusting into cold green-gray waters, a pale amethyst sky with scurrying clouds, a background of snow-crested mountains."[3] Sick of ship life after five weeks on board and not eager to work off their passage by unloading coal at Valparaiso, Finger, Arnold Fox, and Charlie Saxby slipped off the *Akaba*, leaving most of their luggage with Ted Hyde. By helping row a tugboat that was pulling a barge through the heavy surf, they made their way to the pier.[4] Punta Arenas was a Chilean military base and a lively expatriate community of families and single men from Britain, Europe, and Argentina. There seemed to be a saloon for every ten residents. Sailors, shepherds, cowboys, and gold diggers up from the streamside claims on Tierra del Fuego spent their earnings on liquor and prostitutes, carousing until late at night. A direct gaze at the wrong man could result in a beating, but Finger, dark-haired and handsome, outgoing, and always ready to entertain on the piano or with a dramatic reading, made friends quickly, and he soon met the leading British and European settlers.[5]

While Fox and Saxby found jobs on a ranch close to town, Finger signed a contract to help establish a new ranch across the strait on "Tierra del," as locals usually shortened the name for the archipelago between the strait and the southern tip of the continent. His new employers were a Scotsman, John Farquhar MacRae—one of the most powerful ranchers in Chile—and the British consul, Rodolfo Stubenrauch. MacRae and Stubenrauch had leased a large tract on Tierra del Fuego from the Chilean government. Finger's first assignment was to help the English crew boss and a Scottish shepherd, Robert B. Gillies, tend MacRae's flock on the plain near Rio Pescado, or Fish River, north of Punta Arenas.[6] The men occupied a "comfortable little log house with a stove" near the river, slaughtering sheep for food and cutting wood for fuel. Emulating his friend Harry Somerfield, Finger drew a sketch of the shanty in his diary, showing a small house with three windows and mountains in the background. The country was rural but not wild, and the shanty was a convenient stopping place for people traveling between Punta Arenas and the interior. Finger met natives as well as British and European ranch hands who passed by. He rode the boundaries of a section of the property each day, herded the sheep, scanned them for signs of scab—a parasite that burrowed into the animals' flesh—and watched for vultures, foxes, and wild dogs that might attack the sheep and natives who might steal them.[7] For a novice shepherd, the biggest problem was getting lost. It was monotonous but grueling work, and the wind on the pampas was so fierce it burned one's face a dark red.[8]

In May Finger helped to herd a flock of rams to Cape Negro and load them on the schooner *Julieta* for transport down the coast and across the strait to the big island. From the first night aboard the *Julieta*, Finger heard frightening stories about the Ona people, whose cookfires inspired the name Tierra del Fuego, or Land of Fire. Ranchers had no clear understanding of where or how these indigenous people lived. Guards on the Stubenrauch ranches were expected to shoot Indians they suspected of cutting fence wire to steal sheep and horses; some shepherds shot Onas on sight. Called *Sorto*, meaning "devil," MacRae was known as "an intrepid rider and an unerring shot" who had personally killed as many as sixty Indians.[9] At the new ranch near the village of Porvenir, or Yet to Come, on Chilota Bay, the men took turns on overnight watch, "keeping . . . a sharp look out for Indians," but the only things they spotted were shooting stars and a wild dog. Once the men finished building a corral, Gillies departed, and Finger, now the cook, laundry man, and carpenter's helper, was soon bored and lonely again. As the men drank and joked about women, he read and wrote entries in his journal and letters that were picked up by the *Chilota*, a small steamboat that made regular runs between Punta Arenas and Porvenir.[10]

He met a storekeeper named Cosmos or Cosme "the Greek" Spiro, one of the original European settlers at Porvenir. Spiro had searched the island's canyons for gold and other minerals for nearly twenty years. He told Finger about a placer, or alluvial gold deposit, a few miles away on the Santa Maria River that probably belonged to the well-known, Ona-killing, Austrian engineer and gold mine operator Julius Popper, with whom Spiro had prospected. The customary arrangement for gold diggers was to share expenses and proceeds after giving a percentage to the claim's owner. Some diggers thought the Santa Maria takings were poor, but optimism about new strikes was perennial. Finger pawned his watch with Spiro to buy supplies and joined three other freelance gold diggers at the claim.[11] The crew spent their days sifting and washing gravel to find small particles of gold—some the size of peas and most much smaller—and the occasional nugget, weighing their findings at the end of each day, cooking in a wooden shack, and sleeping in a tent. "Drink, Gold, Horses and Murders are the general and favorite subjects," Finger dolefully observed. "I sadly miss the luxury of . . . conversation . . . with my friends."

When Fox turned up, the two left to work a claim on their own, huddling in a shack during a late snowstorm and taking turns hiking to Porvenir for supplies and mail. Exploring a steep cliff overlooking the Santa Maria, they found a magnificent view, the strait "a broad band of bright silver" with a steamer passing slowly from right to left. The thrill Finger felt was memorable a quarter century later: "When I . . . saw spread out as in a map the deep gash glacier-fringed which is Admiralty Sound, the green stretch of Bahía Inutil, and snow-crested Mount Sarmiento," it was "as if I had uncovered some high and splendid secret."[12] Standing on the edge of a precipice became a recurring image in Finger's writing.

Ready for an indoor job, he returned to Punta Arenas to deliver some documents from MacRae to Stubenrauch and heard that Gillies had recently survived a shipwreck. Finger learned the details after tracking Gillies down, and the incident became grist for several stories that he wrote as a freelancer in Chile and later. After leaving Porvenir Gillies had joined the crew of the *Seatoller*, a three-masted sailing ship on a stopover in the Falkland Islands. When its captain attempted to sail around Cape Horn (sailing ships could not go through the strait), the *Seatoller* struck rocks and sank. Eight or nine men died in the disaster. Five others, including Gillies, survived by swimming a mile to tiny, mountainous Staten Island. Someone else had sent an initial report to the *Times* in London, but Finger interviewed Gillies, the other survivors, and Stubenrauch for a follow-up report that he sent to several British newspapers. The Glasgow *Standard*, the London *Daily Telegraph*, and the London *Star* published his account, and the newspaper at the Poly proudly noted his journalistic coup. Finger's report probably also was the basis of a long, unsigned article in the *Times* on December 8, 1890, that specifically mentioned Gillies and the "kind treatment" the survivors received from Stubenrauch and misspelled the name of an Argentine transport ship (*Villaino* instead of *Villarino*), just as Finger did in his journal.[13]

Patagonia was an open field for journalists, so Finger could have used his acquaintances in the power structure of Punta Arenas, his quick pen, and his newspaper connections in London to write more colorful news features for British newspapers.[14] Instead, he moved almost constantly from one low-level job to another—carpentry work and sign-painting as a day laborer, clerking in a general store, piano instruction for children—and spent his wages on drink and gambling. He lost money at billiards several times, despairing in his journal, "I am undone," but enjoyed the "jollity and companionship" he found in the town's saloons so much that none he found later in life compared.[15] At the same time, he made a show of entertaining young women, serving one champagne and cookies at the counter in the general store and giving silk handkerchiefs to another. He sketched a young woman on the pier at Punta Arenas in January and wrote coyly in his journal that a "young lady, who shall here be nameless, very broadly hinted that I should agree to marry her." This probably was Mary Ann Cameron, the fifteen-year-old daughter of John Cameron, a Scottish widower with five children who managed Pecket Harbor Ranch. "To imagine myself married," Finger wrote, "in the words of Shakespeare . . . 'would be argument for a week, laughter for a month, and a good jest forever.'" When a friend teased him about going to hotels to meet women, Finger replied, "Do you think so? I can assure you I do not."[16]

Bored by clerking in the store and hoping to find another job that would pay enough for him to buy a pianoforte and open a music hall, he resigned in February. Mary Ann's father offered him a "good, easy job" at Pecket Harbor Ranch, but Finger was motivated to save as much as he could and took a job farther from the pool tables, this time working for an English pioneer, Henry Leonard Reynard, who leased Elizabeth Island in the strait for a sheep ranch. Eight miles long and two miles wide, the island was primarily grassland.[17] Finger's job was, once again, tending sheep: shearing them, herding them on horseback, castrating the rams, skinning dead ones—sometimes in pouring rain or snowstorms. For variety, there was hoeing potatoes, digging wells, and operating the wool press, which made Finger's right hand hurt so much he was "hardly able to hold a pen." Meyrick MacLean, the ranch manager, and his wife were kind, encouraging Finger to relax and write letters in their house and sometimes inviting him in for a "musical evening." Although it required an entire day to sail over and back, Finger went to Cape Negro or Punta Arenas whenever he could to see friends and collect his mail.

Probably hoping Finger would begin courting Mary Ann, the Camerons encouraged him to visit their ranch, but he resisted, thinking "'tis no use bemoaning . . . my nature." Still hopeful, Mary Ann and her sister visited the MacLean family on the island for the entire month of June 1891, teasing Finger by calling him "Papa." He made sketches of Mary Ann but felt "melancholy" and wrote in his journal that when he saw the *Gulf of Akaba* steam past the island, he wished he were on board, not explaining whether he longed for a few hours of sociability with the ship's passengers and crew or a trip home to London. When Cameron arrived on the three-masted schooner *Martha Gale* to retrieve his daughters, he again offered Finger a job, which he declined. Nonetheless, when he accompanied the Camerons on the smaller schooner *Rippling Wave* out to the *Martha Gale* for their voyage back to Pecket Harbor, something happened with Mary Ann. "I am rather afraid," Finger wrote in his journal, "that I'm somewhat susceptible to the influence of the other [sex]: is it worthwhile to cure myself I wonder."[18] He next saw John Cameron on October 13, when he made a heroic solo trip through a heavy storm to get medical help for the seriously ill MacLean family. With the wind at his back, he had rowed to the mainland and rushed to Pecket Harbor Ranch on foot. Cameron "rode back at full gallop" with Finger—who was no longer a novice on horseback—to help him row to the island against the wind. "It blew half a gale but we fetched Hook Point in safety at 1:30" in the afternoon, Finger wrote. The MacLeans survived but left Elizabeth Island soon after this dramatic event.[19]

Finger also quit the island job to launch a "concert room" in Punta Arenas. He missed the kind of companionship he'd enjoyed at the Poly, he wrote to a friend in London. "I believe it is this longing . . . that has caused me to change my occupation so often the last two years." Meyrick's brother Colin Fraser MacLean, a hotel proprietor, lent Finger some money, so his "Moral Public House" may have been a bar in Colin's hotel. Finger "provided free literature; gave away journals, [and] sang comic songs," but his refusal to serve men who he thought were drinking too much was a fiasco because the men who filled the town after riding boundary fences or dredging for gold wanted to drink to excess. The pub failed, and Finger was "stunned by the shock" and felt friendless. Fox had left Chile to work as an electrician on British ships. Saxby had taken a job four hundred miles away at St. Julian Bay in Argentina. Hyde was a contented store clerk in Coronel, 1,600 miles away on the western coast. When Reynard offered Finger another contract to return to Elizabeth Island and run the sheep farm, Finger agreed to work for six more months but wrote, "it's impossible to realize the loneliness—the terrible loneliness."[20] Alone in the island house, he wrote letters and made sketches, one day drawing a careful picture of Charles Peer, probably copying the photograph Peer had given him. He quit the Elizabeth Island job for good in May 1893, and Reynard gave him a letter of recommendation, praising him as "thoroughly steady, honest, and zealous in the discharge of all his duties."[21]

Finger's activities over the next year are not clear because no journal for the period survives, but he evidently took a temporary job as a guide for some touring scientists. Scientific expeditions in Patagonia were not unusual. He may have accompanied Fernande Lataste, a French zoologist who led a survey of birds on the strait in 1893. Perhaps Finger met the Lataste group at St. Julian Bay and escorted the men down the coast and on horseback on Tierra del Fuego.[22] He also may have traveled with another young English expatriate, Richard Bevil Molesworth, whom he later mentioned in a letter. They had several mutual acquaintances in Punta Arenas, and Molesworth also was a writer; his short story "A Ghost of the Pampas" appeared in an English magazine in April 1893. Its narrator tells a friend named Charley the story of his life in Patagonia where he "got some friends, real friends." They were "a *queer* medley [emphasis added]," Molesworth wrote, using an emerging slang word for homosexual, and included a gaucho named Doroteo who "wound himself around my heart."[23]

Out of money by June 1894, Finger finally accepted Cameron's offer of a job as secretary, paymaster, and boss of the woolshed at Pecket Harbor Ranch. That summer, he reconnected with twenty-four-year-old Ernest Schumacher, a German immigrant he'd first met at Fish River, and they ran errands for Cameron on the *Martha Gale*.[24] When the Camerons moved to Lake Romero Ranch, Finger and Schumacher went with them, and Finger became the manager of the ranch *boliche*, a combination of hotel, commissary, saloon, and gambling hall. It was the "kind of grog-shop about which potential trouble generally hung like a threatening cloud." Schumacher later recalled how a gaucho, James Radburne, stabbed a romantic rival to death and "then got on his horse and went to the wide open spaces." A biographer of Radburne captured a sly joke about Finger's saloon. As Radburne was telling a story to the biographer, Radburne's wife interrupted to say he "was always . . . very bad with the girls." Radburne replied, "'*Que, che!* . . . I was just talking about Charlie Finger's boliche. There were no girls there. Remember him?' The Senora answered with a solemn, 'Ah, *si*,' and nothing more was said."[25]

Mary Ann Cameron married a cousin of Meyrick and Colin MacLean in October 1894, and Finger helped throw a party for them, inviting "campmen and shepherds from all neighbouring Estancias" to attend. A newspaper published an account of the event that he clearly wrote. There were horse races—a popular complement to gambling—a banquet, a concert, and a dance. Finger probably provided the music on piano, as he often did at gatherings and ceremonial occasions. At the end of the evening, as the moon rose and the visiting ranchmen began to saddle their horses, he made a toast "to the health and happiness of the bride" and led the crowd in singing the Scottish poet Robert Burns's song: "For auld lang syne, my jo, for auld lang syne, we'll tak' a cup o' kindness yet, for auld lang syne."[26]

He did not stay at Cameron's ranch much longer. In a letter to the Poly, Finger was vague about his "sundry reasons" for leaving Lake Romero Ranch, but thirty years later, in reviewing the biography of Radburne, he offered details considerably more colorful than those in his journal. The belated story is an example of how Finger sometimes revised his stories to obscure discrepancies and gaps in his life. Now the boliche was a "sanctuary to fleeing outlaws." Finger rode down from the Andes with a herd of twenty horses and met the boliche's owner, who asked him to run the business while the owner went into hiding. Finger agreed, and for two weeks, he and acquaintances named "Jack and Joe" conducted horse races, boxing matches, shooting competitions, and cribbage games "with horses for stakes." At last, "fidgety to be away," he put the boliche in charge of someone named Swinhoe; this final detail matched Radburne's biography.[27]

By the summer of 1895, Saxby reported in a letter to the Poly that Finger was clerking in a store 120 miles north of the ranch where Saxby worked.[28] Assuming Saxby still worked near St. Julian Bay, that puts Finger at Port Desire, a small colony on the coast of Argentina. Sometime after that, he returned to Punta Arenas, paid some debts, bought some horses, and went wandering, having "a free and happy time." Hyde referred to Finger as "nomadic," and a writer for the Poly magazine called him a "roving spirit," comparing him to R. L. Stevenson. Perhaps Finger made a horse-trading expedition with Schumacher, who later told him "sometimes I dream . . . about the horses I used to [own and] when I wake up, for a moment I feel disappointed that I am not really the free rover I used to be when as you say we were all young and beautiful."[29]

A letter from Finger's sister Alice, who now lived in New York, reached him some time during his wandering. He wrote nothing of its contents in his journal but resolved "to go home" because of it.[30] Their brother George was planning a trip back to England, so Alice may have suggested that C. J. go to London to see him. He bid Schumacher farewell "on the hill behind San Julian Bay," and decades later, he recalled the vivid figure Schumacher cut on the day they parted. Ernest was "a young man riding in pride, his horse-gear a thing of beauty[,] a blue poncho with scarlet lining fastened at the neck by brass chain and clasps, his hat with broad brim saucily cocked on the side." Schumacher left Chile for California, married, and had a family, but in 1926, he wrote to Finger that he wished he could "once again . . . feel the gentle west wind blow through poncho, coat, shirt, and singlet and cool off your skin and occasionally try to lift you out of your saddle." "In spite of the fact that . . . I am happily married," Schumacher confessed, "whenever I think of the south I regret the day I was such fool as to leave there."[31]

At Buenos Aires, a little more than six years after arriving in Patagonia, Finger boarded a ship bound for England. He was twenty-eight years old. His friends in London received him "with eager friendliness"—one thought,

"Charley is looking a very picture of health, bigger, broader, and more muscular than when he went away"—but Finger sensed he was no longer "indispensable."[32] Harry Somerfield had moved to Walsall for a job as an architectural draftsman. C. J. Peer, always as interested in social work as in journalism, now worked full-time for Quintin Hogg's institute, directing a bureau that helped young people from rural England find jobs in London. He occasionally wrote articles for an American periodical, the *Altruistic Review*. He had married, and he and his wife, Helen Faithful, had two children.[33]

Peer gave Finger an anthology of poetry that contained Whitman's brief poem "For You O Democracy." The poem was a distillation of Whitman's entire vision of a gay utopia, like the Greek god Pan's mythical kingdom, in a few hopeful lines about an America where "the manly love of comrades" was "as trees along all the rivers."[34] The city of London, by contrast, was more dangerous than ever to men who preferred the company of men. Wilde had become a successful playwright with four plays that reflected the anxiety about blackmail and double lives—the most recent *The Importance of Being Earnest*—but was arrested for having a homosexual encounter at the Hotel Savoy. At his trial in 1895, he defended himself with the famous words "the love that dare not speak its name" but was convicted under the Labouchere Amendment and sentenced to two years of hard labor. Now male homosexuality was so scandalous and dangerous the editor W. T. Stead feared "the freedom of comradeship" was at risk.[35] Just two weeks after reaching London, Finger joined his brother on a voyage to New York. Although there would be a reunion with his family, he was thinking ahead to the wide, open plains of the Southwest, where Dan Cauthorn had a sheep ranch.[36]

[3]

JACK RANDOM

FINGER'S MOTHER and all his siblings had joined his father in New York. Martin and George were tailors, Alice was a stenographer, Phillipina had married Arnold Fox—who had moved to New York—and Emil was an electrician, like Fox. When Finger rejoined the family, he found that George and Alice were kindred spirits—George because of his interest in reform politics and Alice because of her professional ambition. During his brief stay in New York, Finger introduced the family to two other ambitious immigrants: Herbert St. John Brenon, a young Irishman he had met on the voyage to the US, and Robert Wilhelm Bergmann. Brenon wanted to find work as an actor or stage manager and explored New York with Finger, who later recalled that they were together when they met twenty-year-old Bergmann, a German immigrant who dreamed of painting backdrops for stage productions. Finger also went on dates with two young Englishwomen, but if the Fingers hoped he would remain "en famille," as he put it, by marrying one of them, they were disappointed.[1] After spending most of his proceeds from selling horses in Argentina, Finger left to find a job in Texas. Later he used his brief acquaintance with one of the young women to cruel effect in a short story: "I was glad that I had broken my word and had not been a slave to duty and the girl at Hoboken. . . . To have slept in the same bed with her night after night, would have been hell."[2]

In a letter to the Polytechnic magazine, Finger disguised his straightforward trip to Texas as a wandering journey through exotic locales, embroidering a brief stopover at Key West, Florida, by claiming he offered to enlist in the military to serve in Cuba and later claiming he actually went to Cuba, thus bolstering his identity as a writer-adventurer. In reality he went to Galveston, Texas, and stayed a few days to play piano in a music hall and ride "bronchos" in "a Wild West show," adopting the stage name Patagonian

Pete. The interlude in Galveston remained vivid in Finger's memory: He reminisced in 1927 about meeting a man on the dock who "took me to a saloon" and "places of common resort where men drop in and out." By 1931 he wrote that he carried his "belongings in a sailor's bag" and "spent a great deal of . . . time in one of those *queer* shops [with] books on navigation, telescopes, revolvers, watches, knives [emphasis added]." These were suggestive images; sailors were commonly understood to be open to gay encounters, and manly men used weapons. Finger stayed in a boardinghouse room "with dingy wallpaper, a bed that creaked and groaned, [and] two or three or four men in a room."[3] Leaving Galveston, he continued westward across Texas, stopping in each railroad town but finding no work. When his money ran out at Ballinger, Finger slipped into a freight car on the Gulf, Colorado & Santa Fe Railway for a ride to San Angelo, the last stop on the line. Alighting at the adobe depot shortly before midnight on October 8, Finger was hungry, cold, "flat busted," and seventy miles short of reaching Sonora, the town nearest to the Cauthorn ranch. He probably spent the night in one of the town's many wagon yards.

The wide, unpaved streets of San Angelo were crowded with wagons and carriages, men on horseback, and a few automobiles. A barbershop, bathhouse, and photography studio beckoned at the intersection of Chadbourne and Concho Streets. Ranch hands "cantered into town circumspectly," Finger observed, and "squatted on their heels outside saloons." Inside the Arc Light, men stood at the massive oak bar, some making eye contact in the large mirror behind the bartender.[4] A stage ran regularly between San Angelo and Sonora, but Finger apparently did not find Cauthorn, who was still unmarried at forty-seven and rarely seen. Instead, he found a job on a sheep ranch in Buckhorn Draw, part of the Devils River basin, about eighty miles from San Angelo. Sudden fall storms out there could last twenty-four hours, with powerful gusts of wind shrieking across the prairie, so Finger, with six years of experience around sheep ranches on the pampas in South America, probably seemed like a good choice for a new hand. Christopher Ferguson, the English ranch owner, also could have seen Finger as a prospective husband for his sixteen-year-old daughter, as John Cameron had in Chile. He hired Finger for the familiar work of hunting for lost sheep, shooting predators, and cutting firewood. Finger thought his new employer was "a man of vast sympathies and a wholesome sense of humor."[5] He soon met Boyd and Louise Postel Cornick of Knickerbocker, a busy village on the road between the ranch and San Angelo. Boyd was a physician who treated tuberculosis patients and was interested in economic reform; Louise was "a creature of wide sympathies, with an abiding sense of justice, of breadth of view and sanity." The Cornicks had five children—the oldest thirteen-year-old Philip—and liked Finger so much they treated him almost like another son. While the Fergusons gave Finger a financial foothold in Texas, the Cornicks seemed like the family he had always wanted, interested in literature and progressive politics and tolerant of his odd inclinations. For a while Knickerbocker felt like his spiritual home.[6]

Within weeks of taking the job on Ferguson's ranch, Finger launched his American writing career with an article on "South American sheep prospects" for the weekly *San Angelo Enterprise*.[7] Over the next few months, he drafted a piece he called "Dream-seer," now lost, that received "some faint editorial praise." Next, he sold a short story to the *Youth's Companion*, an illustrated weekly with a national circulation. "How Lazy Sam Got His Rise: A Story of Patagonia" involved a ranch hand and a plan to blow up lava caves where sheep-killing pumas hid.[8]

Something, perhaps this new literary success, made Finger leave the Ferguson ranch in 1897 and return to New York. The record of this period is blurry. Perhaps he went to New York simply in hope of finding work as a writer, but the gap in his journals could indicate he left Texas suddenly to escape harassment or even arrest. While Finger was in New York, a newspaper in El Paso, Texas, reported gossip that a local businessman had been engaging in the kind of crime "for which Oscar Wilde served two years" but that attempts to "catch the man in his acts" had been foiled.[9] After wandering from New York to Ontario and down into Mexico for several months, Finger returned to Devils River country and began a program of serious reading, copying excerpts into a kind of journal known as a commonplace book. Some entries hinted at unrequited love, such as this by Henry David Thoreau: "Between two by nature alike and fitted to sympathize, there is no veil, and there can be no obstacle. Who are the estranged? Two friends explaining."[10] He wrote another Patagonian story, "London Johnny and the Claim-Jumpers: A Story of Tierra-Del-Fuego," that involved a young "ex-draper's assistant, hailing from London City," who foils a pair of claim jumpers. The Polytechnic magazine published the story in two installments and noted Finger was "temporarily encamped" in Texas again "while he gained his living as a story-writer and newspaper correspondent."[11]

The Fergusons' daughter Eleanor Barbara, or Nellie, had become a quiet, dreamy young woman who loved to roam the ranch, observing birds and the wildflowers that burst into bloom after a spring rain to create vast scenes of pastel beauty. She rarely ventured into town or met potential suitors.[12] Hoping to keep Finger nearby, her father secured a federal postmaster appointment—a valuable position that provided a part-time income—in January 1899 and gave the job to Finger, but sorting the mail did not hold C. J.'s interest for long, and Ferguson relinquished the postmaster appointment in October.[13] Finger had met a young German musician, Ferdinand J. Haberkorn, in San Angelo.[14] Just as in Punta Arenas, middle- and upper-class parents in small-town Texas saw musical ability as an important social skill for children, so the two immigrants decided to establish a music school.[15] The need for startup money was the impetus for Finger's next departure from west Texas and the Fergusons. Telling Haberkorn, "I shall go away somewhere and get [money for a school] if you hold on awhile," Finger left for a temporary job in Canada, probably on a crew that helped survey rivers in northern Ontario.[16] During his absence Haberkorn took a room in Ballinger in order to give violin lessons to local children and commuted on the railroad to teach classes at Brownwood and Fort Worth.[17]

Finger rented a room in Ballinger when he returned in January 1901 and began giving piano lessons to children, including eight-year-old David Guion, the son of John Guion, a lawyer from Mississippi. Finger and Haberkorn held a children's recital at the courthouse in Ballinger that spring.[18] They established another studio for music lessons in second-floor rooms in the M. C. Ragsdale Building in San Angelo, calling it the San Angelo Music School and using the space as Finger's living quarters as well. The photographer McArthur Cullen Ragsdale had his studio and family home in the building, and he and his family befriended Finger. Ragsdale made publicity photographs of the town's new music teachers, one showing Finger posing with a book, violin, clarinet, banjo, and figurine of Shakespeare arranged beside him.[19] Now the parents of little David Guion sent him on the train from Ballinger to San Angelo for piano lessons, and the Cornicks, who had moved to town so that Boyd could establish a tuberculosis sanitarium, enrolled their daughters.[20] Fifteen-year-old Amelia Ferguson and her eleven-year-old brother, George, also took piano lessons, so the Fergusons may also have moved into town. To meet and impress more of San Angelo's upper-crust parents, Finger became director of the Episcopal choir and opened his apartment for meetings of local clubs.[21]

He and Haberkorn produced a concert series in December 1901 and January 1902 that was both the crescendo and the finale of their collaboration.

Suffering from typhoid fever, Haberkorn moved temporarily to Iowa before spending two years in Illinois studying and teaching violin. There may have been more to Haberkorn's departure than the physical strain of teaching and performing in locations from Fort Worth to San Angelo. Finger told Cornick in a letter that he tried to help Haberkorn get "on a solid financial basis," and Pinckney E. Truly, the editor of the *Ballinger Ledger* and the *San Angelo Press*, alluded to the mysterious nature of the "Finger–Haberkorn Affair," commenting, "What the real cause of their separation was, was never publicly made known."[22] Haberkorn returned to Ballinger in 1904 to marry the daughter of his former boardinghouse landlord. They had one son, and Haberkorn had a long career as a performer, instructor, and conductor.[23]

Finger's attention to Haberkorn and their music school had been sporadic since he took a part-time job with the *San Angelo Standard* in the summer of 1901.[24] Then, at the same time as the winter concert series, Truly took over the *San Angelo Press*, giving Finger a desk in the *Press* office and paying him to write articles for the *Ledger* and the *Press*. Like newspapers in towns and small cities everywhere, the *Ledger* and *Press* were virtual town centers, in effect open-air stages where Finger could experiment with fashioning an image as an erudite adventurer and, at a casual glance, a ladies' man. Truly encouraged him to write controversial material that made the weekly *Press* a topic in saloons and parlors, but after a reader mocked Finger with a series of fabricated quotations—"Haberkorn was Haberkorn. I have said all I have to say on his playing long ago" and "I am the reincarnation of Mozart, Liszt, Mendelsohn, and Wagner"—Finger vowed "to make no more divergencies from the *straight* path of the Art Melodious [emphasis added]."[25] He occasionally flirted with women, at least in print: "We hope ere four months have passed," he wrote, "to be riding on the front seat of a horseless carriage with some fair San Angelo girl by our side." His female partner in a game of High Five at a party was "vivacious and charming."[26] These ruses did not deter local gossip, however. Finger joked in a letter to Philip Cornick, now an eighteen-year-old student at the University of Tennessee, about a rumor that Finger was "celibate and a human oyster" (oysters being hermaphroditic and not engaging in sexual reproduction). To counteract the rumor, he escorted two different women on dates and joked to Philip that the new story around town was that he was a Mormon.[27]

Philip had become a special friend. They shared a love of literature and journalism and corresponded about Shakespeare. It probably was Philip who gave Finger a volume of experimental journalism, writing in it "To my friend '*Temeraire*'"—a French adjective meaning bold, daring, foolhardy, or headstrong—"with the best of all good wishes, and many happy returns of the day, Dec. 25th, 1901."[28] After Philip's sister Sophie died, Finger addressed him as "my dear Boy," in Quintin Hogg fashion. Philip may have resisted feeling an attraction to men—what Finger called, in Victorian London queer code, "the Grecian habit of thought upon physical beauty." He observed that Philip's "sense . . . of double dealing" led to "much needless self-torturing." When Finger suspected that Philip felt "a soupçon of jealousy" about something, he acknowledged Philip's "faithful" friendship but encouraged him to become more independent and abandon "piety" and "hypocrisy."[29]

Young Cornick may have been jealous of Thomas Spencer "Deacon" Sharpe Jr., an amateur actor Finger's age in San Angelo. Finger and Sharpe vacationed together in August 1902 at Cloudcroft, a popular summer resort in the Sacramento Mountains east of Alamogordo, New Mexico, where they entertained guests on the lodge stage—Finger called himself "Angelo Charlie, the famous cowboy pianist." Waking in his tent at Cloudcroft beneath the "arched green glory of the lofty trees," he felt the "security of comradeship" and told readers of the *Press* he heard the "great god Pan himself," his pipes resounding "through leafy arches dim, deep in the woods."[30] Here he evoked for observant readers the mythical Greek god of Arcadia, half man and half goat, often depicted with an erect phallus, who wooed young men and women with music. Pan had been a significant part of the aesthetic life in London: Stevenson declared "Pan is not dead [but] survives in triumph." In the frontispiece of Stevenson's *An Inland Voyage*, the illustrator Walter Crane depicted Pan lounging in the reeds beside a river, discreetly hiding his phallus with his panpipe as two men rowed by. Oscar Wilde pleaded with Pan to "leave the hills of Arcady! / This modern world hath need of Thee!"[31]

Although Finger imagined hearing Pan's music at Cloudcroft, he was not in love with Sharpe. That fall, he considered going to New Mexico to join Dan Cauthorn, whom someone at the *Press*, probably Finger, called a "bachelor capitalist"—the word *bachelor* vague enough to mean an unmarried straight man yet with a Dickensian hint at homosexuality. Cauthorn moved about quite a bit and may have talked to Finger about moneymaking opportunities in New Mexico; Finger wrote to ask his brother George to go with him to New Mexico, but George declined. Cauthorn later moved to the small town of Porter, Oklahoma, where he lived alone in a rented room, relying on income from the family businesses. As he grew older, he sometimes spent summers in Duluth, Minnesota, taking rooms at the YMCA as many men did to seek discreet lodging for same-sex partners.[32]

Finger continued to juggle music lessons and newspaper work. Columns were a significant step in a writer's career, and Truly permitted Finger to launch an experimental column under the pseudonym Jack Random. Random introduced himself on December 10, 1902, as a "ne'er-do-well and literary hack" who traveled from New Orleans to Ballinger in a boxcar to report on the Azelia Club's ball. Finger concluded this piece with a typical Finger flourish, a toast wrapped around a sly gay wink: "to you, young ladies. . . . Long may you dance in the *golden* light of the sun of happiness [emphasis added]."[33] Finger's invention of a literary double at this point in his life demonstrates his deliberate effort to create a controversial public image, his deep concern for the double lives that writers and gay men led, and his longing for that "golden light" in a world where secrecy was unnecessary. As a literary persona, Jack Random had something in common with Oscar Wilde, who used an outlandish public image to promote his work. The name had further layers of significance, echoing that of Finger's childhood literary hero Jack Harkaway. The combination of "Jack" with the two-syllable heft of "Random" evoked the rising American writer-adventurer Jack London. The last name alluded to Roderick Random, the protagonist of a hugely popular eighteenth-century picaresque novel by another British writer-adventurer, Tobias Smollett, that is considered the earliest treatment in English literature of gay identity. Finger read *The Adventures of Roderick Random* as a young man in London and knew that it was a significant influence on Dickens and Thackeray; his adoption of Random as a name suggested the height of his literary ambition.[34]

The second Random column appeared on Christmas Eve, the day before Finger's thirty-fifth birthday. Finger situated his alter ego "in Zenker's saloon reading my Walt Whitman." In comes "the Judge," a reference to Finger's friend John Guion, who slaps him on the shoulder and urges him to "quit your shifty habits and settle down." Random sits "by the warm stove in the lighted saloon" wondering "Why to Comfort was I ever a stranger?" Finger's plug of Zenker's saloon worked on three levels. On the surface he was simply recommending Charles W. Zenker's new bar, the Orient, to his readers, not surprisingly, since Zenker advertised in the *San Angelo Press* and his daughter took music lessons from Finger.[35] However, gay men in some cities circulated lists of favorite bars, and with its reference to Whitman, the column signaled to knowing readers that in a town with so many saloons, Zenker's

was a safe choice for men seeking men.[36] Finally, the specific detail of the
"warm stove" echoed Whitman's poem "A Glimpse": "of a crowd of work-
men and drivers in a bar-room around the stove late of a winter night, and
I unremark'd seated in a corner, / Of a youth who loves me and whom I
love, silently approaching and seating himself near, that he may hold me by
the hand."[37] Given that Jack Random called himself "a stranger" to comfort, this seems to have been a plea for someone to join Finger at the bar.
In case these allusions to Smollett and Whitman were not enough to alert
any gay men reading the *San Angelo Press*, Finger dedicated the column to
"Edward Carpenter—the True Man." Carpenter was a British reformer who
promoted "homogenic love," openly discussing the reality of gay and lesbian
attraction. Dedications like this, to persons whom Finger admired, became
an important part of Finger's writing process. Truly published the piece with
an enthusiastic editorial endorsement, but some readers found Finger preten-
tious. Smarting from some kind of ridicule, Finger placed a small advertisement in the December 31 issue, extending "heartfelt good wishes" that "in
the New Year . . . music and kindness [would] disperse the cloudy fumes
of care."[38]

There were no more Jack Random columns, but Truly published five
pieces in early 1903 that hinted at Finger's true nature. The first was entitled
"Mollie Random"—*Mollie* was an eighteenth-century British slang term
for a gay man. Ostensibly a letter from Random's mother, this piece teased
readers with the possibility that Random was a real person. "Mollie" wrote
that her son was a "wayward boy" and "night wanderer" whose ramblings
"have been taken up and woven into such forms of beauty by the writer who
[']personated my poor Jack."[39] Next, a letter to the editor from "A Bachelor
Friend, Lule Harper," described reading an old letter "written during a
sojourn on the pirate Isle of Galveston" that envisioned a loved one riding the tides "as if a beautiful pearl had risen to the surface from the ocean
caves . . . to show to the surface world that the purest and sweetest things
come from the depths of nature," a reflection of the Hellenic idea of man–
man love as natural.[40] An anonymous report of a masquerade ball, clearly
written by Finger, used the word *gay* twice to describe the scene and reproduced a conversation with a matron who called the ball "a picture of life
[where] each would pass for what he or she is not," to which he replied "not
always, perhaps."[41] Finally, Finger returned to the topic of Carpenter twice in
articles below his own name. He had sent a copy of the December 24 column
to Carpenter, who responded by sending Finger his new book, *Ioläus: An*

Anthology of Friendship. A small, elegant volume with red initials and side notes, *Ioläus* was a collection of excerpts demonstrating that male homosexuality was accepted and even celebrated in ancient and medieval cultures. Finger was thrilled by this gift. "A more pleasing book it would be hard to find," he wrote. "Every reading man, every book and *man lover* will place this work amongst his most cherished volumes [emphasis added]."[42] For anyone who noticed the words *man lover* in Finger's closing, the message was clear.

JUDGE GUION'S ADVICE to "settle down" was distinctly unappealing, but Finger spent the first months of 1903 contemplating how to make something more of himself, like his ambitious siblings. (Alice had become a notary and was in a serious relationship with the scene-painter who now went by Robert Bergman. George had married a woman named Minnie Bergman, possibly Robert's sister, and followed Bergman into the painting trade.)[43] Finger read biographies of Dickens and Samuel Johnson and devised a chart for teaching literature that he sent to various authorities, seeking endorsements.[44] He joined a fraternal organization with the Fergusons' older son, Albert, and gave music lessons to their younger children. When he gave a music school party in January 1903, Nellie, who was twenty-two and rarely appeared in lists of guests at social events in San Angelo, was there.[45]

Nellie became pregnant in March, evidently by Finger since he married her after a few months of indecision and erratic behavior. Perhaps he had succumbed to Guion's advice. Perhaps Chris and Bejata Ferguson offered him a financial stake in their ranch if he married Nellie. Perhaps he was genuinely, if fleetingly, attracted to her, as he was to Mary Ann Cameron on Elizabeth Island in 1891, or to the idea of being a family man. Once Nellie was pregnant, however, Finger balked at marrying her, like the character of Roderick Random when confronted by a servant with the news that she is pregnant, and perhaps like Finger's father, Martin, in 1867.[46] The Fergusons could have sued Finger—to seduce an unmarried woman below the age of twenty-five years was a crime in Texas punishable by a prison sentence—but there was no way they could remain in San Angelo without Nellie's reputation being ruined.[47] Instead, Ferguson took a job with the El Paso & Northeastern (EP&NE) Railroad. He and Bejata moved to Alamogordo, a company town created by the railroad, leaving twenty-five-year-old Albert in charge of the ranch and Nellie to follow them with the younger children.[48] Finger dallied, accepting the position of "sachem" in the fraternal organization and opening the Concho Club with a reading room, game rooms, and a punching bag and mitts on the second floor of the Lasker Building in San Angelo.[49] As Nellie and the children left for Alamogordo in July, Finger went to El Paso, where he wrote travel pieces for the *Press* and thought about opening another men's club. After more wandering, he finally relented in August and married Nellie at the Methodist Episcopal church in Alamogordo.[50]

With his reporter seemingly gone, Truly resigned from the *Press*. The new editor barely disguised his attitude toward Finger. "Simple is the announcement, and simple was the quiet church wedding, but great was the surprise [among] Prof. and Mrs. Finger's many friends here," he wrote. Implying that Finger took advantage of Nellie, the editor observed she was "of a quiet, sweet nature and . . . held in high regard by all her acquaintances" while he was "a man of extensive travel, wide experience and learning."[51] Despite this snub, Finger returned to San Angelo, moving with Nellie into his rooms in the Ragsdale Building and beginning a new period of unproductive indecision. He made the high bid on a residential lot in town.[52] He tried to restart his music school but soon dropped some pupils.[53] With Sharpe considering a return to El Paso, Finger inquired about jobs there, but then Sharpe left to go "prospecting" in New Mexico—like Cauthorn, Sharpe made frequent trips out of state, sometimes with other men, and never married.[54] The Concho Club fizzled.[55] About the time Coleman National Bank sued Finger for not paying for the residential lot, Nellie, at least seven months pregnant, left for Alamogordo. Still, Finger remained in San Angelo.[56] The child was born December 1, 1903, and they named him Hubert Philip, spelling the middle name with one "l," as Philip Cornick did, rather than two, as Finger's sister Phillipina did.[57] Still, Finger stayed put. On January 7, the *Press* reported that he had sold his furniture and planned to leave town. Asked where he was going, Finger would not be pinned down: "He anticipates . . . traveling, not having decided just where he will locate permanently." He left without paying for the real estate.[58]

Finger eventually moved to Alamogordo, taking a job in the boiler shop of the EP&NE, corresponding with Cornick and meeting him in El Paso from time to time. Little Hubert was "a bright fellow and of good physique[;] I love to play with him," he told Cornick. Nonetheless, Finger planned to send Nellie, her sister Amelia, and the baby to spend the summer in a tent at Cloudcroft. He closed, "Phil old man, please let me hear from you more often. I really care to hear from no one else."[59] The railroad superintendent, Dennis

Sullivan, promoted Finger to a clerical position in June 1904 and let him lease and furnish space on the second floor of First National Bank as quarters for the Railway Club of Alamogordo, with a gymnasium, dressing rooms, and library. Finger again presided as a Hogg-like impresario and formally opened the club by playing a piano march.[60] He conducted nightly debates, booked touring musical companies, showed movies, held a dance twice a month, and produced a gigantic ball on New Year's Eve—the railroad provided a special excursion train for El Paso residents to attend.[61] Praising Finger as a "delightful" writer "of originality, impudence and common sense," the editor of the Alamogordo newspaper asked rhetorically, "What would Alamogordo be without . . . C. J. Finger[?]"[62]

The Fingers' second child was born in June 1905. They named her Julia Louise, for Finger's mother, and called her Kitty. Within three weeks Nellie and her mother took the children to spend a month at a cabin or lodge while Finger arranged to add bathtubs to the men's club.[63] Then came the news that the EP&NE had been sold. No longer needed, Sullivan found a new job out of state, and Finger agreed to go with him. Leaving the Railway Club and Nellie's parents behind, he, Nellie, Hubert, and two-month-old Kitty moved with Nellie's sister Amelia to southern Ohio.[64] Even though he and Nellie had five children in all, for the rest of his life, Finger expressed a hatred of marriage and a belief that he had been entrapped.

[4]

FINGER'S LIBRARY

FINGER LIVED IN OHIO from 1905 to 1920, first working for Dennis Sullivan with the Ohio River and Columbus Railway Company (OR&C)— a small freight railroad in Brown County—and renting a modest frame house on the east side of the town of Ripley.[1] The Fingers had three more children: Charles Joseph Jr. in 1907; Helen Grace—named in honor of Finger's sister Ellen Alice, who by that time used the name Helen—in 1912; and Herbert Eric in 1915.[2] When the OR&C merged with the Cincinnati, Georgetown, and Portsmouth Railway (CG&P) in 1912, Finger became secretary and auditor of the combined Ohio Southeastern System and worked in the company's office in downtown Cincinnati. The family moved to Fruit Hill, a suburban community on the Ohio Pike, and he commuted via the CG&P.[3] There were complicated developments and setbacks for the company, and in 1914 the Ohio Southeastern System went into receivership, meaning a court took over its operation, and Finger began two years as its court-appointed receiver, or manager.[4] The family moved back to Ripley and bought the spacious Gilliland house, named for an abolitionist minister.[5] The court relinquished control of the railroad in 1916, and Fishel and Marks, a scrap metal business in Cleveland, bought the company and kept Finger on as manager. The Fingers moved to Cleveland in 1917, occupying a crowded four-bedroom house on a tiny lot during their last years in Ohio, while Finger traveled frequently on company business. By mid-1918 he was manager of Fishel and Marks and president of another railroad the company owned, the Columbus, Magnetic Springs, and Northern Railway. That railroad was not profitable and also went into receivership for a brief period; Finger, again a court-appointed receiver, oversaw its sale. He continued to work for the scrap company through the first half of 1920, traveling around Ohio to gather information about potential mining enterprises.[6]

Working in dull jobs to support his growing family, Finger sought the same social and creative outlets as in Punta Arenas, San Angelo, and Alamogordo. He joined men's clubs, gave piano lessons, played the organ for lodge meetings and churches, and led the choir at a Presbyterian church.[7] He was friendly with small-town newspaper editors and other leading men in Ripley and in Maysville, Kentucky, a ferry ride across the Ohio River,[8] occasionally writing a letter to the editor or a poem over the name Jack Random.[9] He got to know Claude Meeker, an investment broker in Columbus, Ohio, with whom he could talk about literature and England—Meeker was an aficionado of the Brontë sisters and had been the US consul to the city of Bradford, England, for four years.[10]

Nellie and the rest of the Fergusons remained as close as possible. Her sister Amelia married Emil Finger, C. J.'s brother.[11] Her sister May lived with their parents in Tucumcari, New Mexico,[12] before moving to Kansas City to live with Amelia and Emil.[13] Nellie took the children on a month-long trip to Tucumcari and Kansas City in 1910. While she was gone, Finger and a friend bought a motorboat and went on river jaunts.[14] Gazing across the broad, flat Ohio, he could see the Kentucky hills, where slaves had slipped through the woods and down to the riverbank on dark nights. Ripley had been a crucial point on the route for many African Americans who escaped from slavery, those crossings to freedom inspiring the crucial scene in Harriet Beecher Stowe's *Uncle Tom's Cabin* where Eliza crosses the icy river with a babe in arms.[15] Finger probably was not moved by those other wanderers' search for freedom, however; he told Boyd Cornick in a letter that he and Nellie found the racially integrated public school in Ripley "repugnant" and had sent their children to a parochial school.[16] He may have visited Philip Cornick, who was an assayer for a mining company in the state of Sonora on the west coast of Mexico, during the summer when Nellie was gone. Wrestling with the responsibilities of family life, he wrote to Philip, "I preach the repudiation of duty."[17] Nonetheless, he kept the railroad job and met Nellie and the children in Kansas City to escort them back to Ripley.[18]

In Texas Finger had collected volumes in the series English Men of Letters, in which different authors wrote introductions for classic works.[19] Continuing the self-guided study of literature that he had begun on the Ferguson ranch, Finger now carried a satchel of books and magazines for reading in railroad cars and hotel rooms and looked for bookstores as he traveled.[20] He bought books in three categories: classic and recent British, European, and American literature; leftist political works, some focused on gay and lesbian identity; and popular and prolific contemporary writers, particularly in the genre of travel and adventure, with many titles fitting in two or all three categories. Browsing a college bookstore in Delaware, Ohio, in 1919, he bought *The Story of a Round House and other Poems* by the British poet John Masefield and *A Miscellany of British Poetry* and began reading them that night at the Allen Hotel.[21] A decade younger than Finger, Masefield had sailed around Cape Horn and worked in the US for several years before returning to England. His poem "Biography" conveyed the same restless searching that propelled Finger and the same loneliness for friends left behind: "Towns can be prisons where the spirit dulls / Away from mates and ocean-wandering hulls . . . / I miss that friend who used to walk / Home to my lodgings with me, deep in talk." Finger eventually owned eight of Masefield's books.[22]

Wanting to tell adventure stories, he studied Kipling. Wanting to promote himself as an authority on exploration in Patagonia, he reread Darwin's *Voyage of the Beagle*, other nonfiction accounts of the region, and William Henry (W. H.) Hudson's anticolonialist novel *The Purple Land* (1885) in a 1916 edition with an introduction by Theodore Roosevelt.[23] He studied Hilaire Belloc and G. K. Chesterton—very popular British authors who were friends and prolific writers in several genres—collecting at least twelve books by Belloc and sixteen by Chesterton. Finger's most battered volume by Belloc was a collection of newspaper essays, *On Everything* (1910). Chesterton's novel *The Club of Queer Trades* (1905) explicitly described the gay subculture in London and reflected the deep unease he felt as a young man attending art school during the period of Oscar Wilde's trial and conviction. Finger later likened the two to Oscar Wilde: "Filled with a burning desire to be admired," they "loved to show off."[24]

Wilde had become a "protomartyr to freedom," in the words of the critic Edmund Gosse, and although Finger professed disdain for Wilde, he studied two works that Wilde wrote in prison: "The Ballad of Reading Gaol," a poem, and "De Profundis," a lengthy letter to his lover.[25] Finger also plunged into the work of George Sylvester Viereck, a German-American writer who often celebrated pansexualism and was widely associated with Wilde,[26] and continued his study of William Morris. He already had read Morris's *News from Nowhere* (1891), a vision of London transformed into a rural Utopia, and acquired four more of the socialist leader's works plus at least three books by Morris's associate H. M. Hyndman, noting Edward Carpenter's description of Hyndman as "filled with a kind of revolutionary anticipation."[27]

He bought Carpenter's memoir *My Days and Dreams* (1916) and carefully tucked a photograph of Carpenter, clipped from some publication, inside it. This was the work in which Carpenter revealed himself to the entire reading public as a gay man, breaking through what he called the "double veil" of reserve and ignorance.[28] Finger also became deeply interested in the work of Carpenter's associate Havelock Ellis, a British physician roughly Finger's age, whom he first read in London.[29] Ellis collaborated on a groundbreaking book about homosexuality, *Sexual Inversion* (1897), and described his vision of a rural Utopia in *The Nineteenth Century: A Dialogue in Utopia* (1899).[30] Ellis also edited two literary anthologies that Finger collected while he lived in Ohio.

Finger focused on the prolific American book reviewer James Huneker, collecting thirteen of his books, and Joseph Conrad, the writer of sea and adventure fiction who was the subject of the first essay in Huneker's 1915 collection *Ivory, Apes, and Peacocks*. Huneker praised Conrad as "an aboriginal force," borrowing Whitman's exclamation "this is no book, who touches this, touches a man."[31] In Conrad's *Heart of Darkness* (1899), a narrator recalls hearing a seaman, Marlow, tell a story of traveling upriver in Africa to find and arrest a renegade company employee named Kurtz. Small details matched Finger's life: Marlow sees "a man-of-war anchored off the coast," and Finger saw one in Punta Arenas. Marlow finds a damaged but intact book at an abandoned campsite; Finger found several books in an empty house in the gold region of the Santa Maria River. Marlow gets to know Kurtz "as well as it is possible for one man to know another." Such stories reminded Finger of his "own South American days." He absorbed Conrad's use of narrative frames, adopting them as his own main strategy for implying that he drew suggestive, fantastical, scandalous stories from personal experience. He recognized the gay subtext that Conrad scholars later interpreted, observing Conrad's characters "knew and were true to their knowledge . . . that on the whole, with *active* ardent spirits, romantic love has little place [emphasis added]." Finger frequently used *active* as a synonym for "fit," the latter word connoting virility and recognizable by 1900 as code for being gay: The men Finger knew in Patagonia were "active in adventure" and uninterested in women; the young hero in one of his stories "thanked his lucky stars that he had escaped monotony and could be vivid and active in a glorious world." "It is the truth and nothing but the truth," Finger declared in his memoir, "that in my very active life I had felt no desire for the company of women."[32]

He bought the 1912 edition of Jack London's *Revolution and Other Essays* at a bookstore in Cincinnati.[33] He also read London's *The Star Rover* (1914), a novel with the theme of imprisonment and a hero who escapes by entering a trance; Finger later used a trance in *The Magic Tower* as a device for transporting a character to a better world. He identified with London, calling himself "one of the odd type, blood brother to other literary wanderers, to . . . Jack London[,] a restless soul, keen . . . to know men as they are." This sly line was a signal that he knew the rumors of London's sexual interest in men. Like Finger, London was born to an unmarried mother and had little formal education but read widely. He went to sea in the early 1890s, working on a three-masted sealing schooner and seal hunting in the Bering Sea. *The Sea-Wolf* (1904) had a plot that could have been lifted from reports that Finger wrote of the *Seatoller* disaster in Patagonia. *Martin Eden* (1909) had a protagonist who gives up gold prospecting to reinvent himself as a writer, sounding like Finger himself. Unlike Finger, however, London had become the highest-paid writer in the world.[34] London's huge success was inspiring but frustrating. Finger asked Philip Cornick, "Are there not many men who have all the London requisites and who yet have been unable to achieve fame? Modesty forbids me to mention the most potent example."[35]

ONE OF THE MAGAZINES Finger routinely read was the *Public*, a progressive journal that promoted the tax reform philosophy of the activist Henry George, who was a hero for Finger's brother George as well as Boyd and Philip Cornick. Turning the pages of the January 1912 issue, Finger could have recognized the photograph of Herbert Seely Bigelow, minister and newly elected president of the state's Fourth Constitutional Convention, as a regular passenger on the CG&P commuter train. A handsome man with thick hair and large eyes, Bigelow lived with his wife and children in Fruit Hill. His office in downtown Cincinnati was only a block from Finger's, so they probably rode the same train.[36] When they met, Finger felt he was "eating out my own heart because of a lack of congenial company." Bigelow was "square-shouldered, well-muscled and bright-eyed, intensely alive in discussion" and "a man of generous emotion." Becoming good friends, they "sat together[, rode] together and argued together"—Britain and Germany were at war and British losses had been monumental, but Bigelow opposed the

US going to Britain's aid.[37] Bigelow and his wife separated the next year, and he moved into a downtown hotel.[38] Finger's days of working downtown ended when he moved back to Ripley in 1914, but his friendship with Bigelow continued. The Fingers named their youngest child, born in October 1915, Herbert Eric.[39] Finger later recalled how a Ku Klux Klan gang abducted Bigelow, tied him to a tree, and whipped him as punishment for speaking out against the military draft. Bigelow was "pale of face and on the verge of nervous prostration, bruised and beaten, tired about the eyes and unable to speak above a whisper." The American Civil Liberties Union—then known as the National Civil Liberties Bureau—and a few newspapers condemned the attack on Bigelow, but no one was prosecuted. Bigelow continued to speak out against the draft and later served one term on the Cincinnati city council and one term in US Congress. He remained a clergyman into old age, and after his wife died, he married his secretary.[40]

Magazines were the most important field for aspiring writers and the greatest source of income for many throughout their careers.[41] With the family's housekeeper, Margaret Germann, as his typist, Finger contributed at least thirty-three book reviews plus several topical articles and at least one letter to the editor to the *Public* between 1915 and 1919.[42] Two gaps in the appearance of his *Public* articles indicate when he had conflicting demands on his time, the first in 1916, when he was the receiver for the OR&C, and the second between June 1917 and July 1919, overlapping the period when the scrap metal dealership purchased the OR&C and Finger began working for that company.[43]

Several events were reminders that as a family man and small-time executive, Finger would never become free or even a full-time—much less famous—writer. First, Philip Cornick visited the Fingers in Ripley. Following a coup in Mexico in 1914, he had spent time in Arizona and California and even gone to Patagonia. He returned to the US in February 1916 and came to Ripley in October.[44] A few weeks later, Jack London's death was news across the country, shocking Finger with the idea that he might die before proving that he was a writer. He later had a character exclaim in a short story over "the waste of . . . Jack London going out with his best work undone!"[45] A third reminder was a reunion with his old transatlantic acquaintance Herbert Brenon, who now was a famous movie producer. Brenon passed through Ohio in April 1917 and stopped to see Finger. They must have talked about the US declaration of war against Germany two weeks earlier. They also probably chatted about Finger's sister Alice, who had married Robert

Bergman. With Alice working as a court stenographer, the couple had moved into the city, and Berg was on the brink of his own great career as an artist.[46] Contemplating Brenon's and Bergman's successes had to intensify Finger's longing to change careers. Trying to promote himself as a potential author of true-life adventure, he wrote to the editor of the *Public* to comment on an article about Porvenir. The town, in his memory, was a sort of Utopia. "Frankness was so extant that everyone had certainly put away lying[.] I had a good time there."[47]

Hints that he had startling stories to tell became one of Finger's tactics for promoting himself as a writer. His most brazen attempt to attract an editor's attention was an overture that he made to Frank Harris, the editor of *Pearson's Magazine* and a friend of the late Oscar Wilde. Finger wrote to Harris in March 1919 that he sometimes bought a dozen copies of *Pearson's* and gave them away "in Pullman smokers, hotel lobbies and cars, to casual acquaintances," a line echoing London's about talking "in hotels and clubs and homes and Pullmans and steamer-chairs with captains of industry."[48] In a rough, first-draft style that became typical of his first-person reminiscing, Finger wrote, "Listen, Mr. Harris, I read your 'Bomb' under strange conditions. I was alone in South America on Isla Isabel, when a Chilean war vessel, El Almirante Blanco, anchored in the Straits. . . . A young officer [gave] me Shaw's Cashel Byron, your 'Bomb' and 'Sartor Resartus.' . . . Later, I wrote an appreciative review of the 'Bomb' for a Chilean newspaper." This story was garbled fiction. Finger may have had a real conversation with a Chilean naval officer in 1891—he wrote in his journal that he received a job offer from an officer of the *Admiral Lynch*—but in the letter to Harris, he conflated the name of the *Admiral Lynch* with another Chilean ship, the *Blanco Encalada*.[49] Worse, Harris's novel *The Bomb* was not published until 1908, twelve years after Finger left South America. Coming to the point, Finger closed, "If there is any way, Mr. Harris, in which I can help Pearson's, let me know."[50] Harris published Finger's letter, giving him a bit of exposure as an eyewitness to the socialist dramas in London in the 1880s, but did not invite him to write for the magazine.[51]

Finger also began modeling himself as an authority on problems in the railroad industry, contributing several articles on the subject to the *Public*, actually naming the men he blamed for the downfall of the OR&C,[52] but burning bridges in the railroad industry did not seem risky because Finger had a new vision of an Arcadian ranch life in Arkansas. He often revised his story of how and why the family moved, saying it was to escape the cold winters in Ohio, or that it was "by chance," or that he decided to buy a farm only after losing a newspaper job in St. Louis.[53] One consistent element of these stories was the omission of Nellie and his father-in-law, Christopher Ferguson. However, the idea to acquire a sheep farm was, in some part, a Ferguson plan. After Bejata Ferguson died in 1913, Christopher evidently gave Nellie money to buy the Gilliland house, so he may have intended to move to Ripley, but Nellie wanted to live in the countryside.[54] She also may have been angry over an affair that Finger had—perhaps his relationship with Bigelow—and threatened him if he did not agree to move; Finger later hinted that his wife threatened divorce and referred to his employer Fishel standing by him during some kind of "social scandal."[55] On the other hand, after Ferguson sold his property in Tucumcari, Finger may have suggested using the proceeds to start a sheep farm in northwest Arkansas.[56] The region was a back-to-the-land destination for some American writers and artists thanks to the writer-farmer William R. Lighton, who wrote about it in the *Saturday Evening Post* in 1910 and in two books, *Happy Hollow Farm* (1914) and *Letters of an Old Farmer to His Son* (1915).[57] Perhaps Finger passed through Fayetteville, Arkansas, on a mission to buy scrap metal and was tempted by advertisements for farms in the local newspapers. After all, a vision of the manly Anglo-Saxon squire at the center of a rural world imbued the ideas of William Morris and Edward Carpenter.[58] Jack London was another example of a writer-farmer. He spent the last part of his life at Beauty Ranch, a farm in California, and made a ranch the setting for his final novel, *The Little Lady of the Big House* (1916).

In December 1919, two days before his birthday, Finger joined Nellie and Ferguson in purchasing a hillside farm three miles west of Fayetteville, apparently without seeing it first, and mused optimistically that agriculture could be the means of "a peaceful and happy life."[59] Nellie, her sister May, four-year-old Herbert, and Christopher Ferguson all moved to the farm by April, with Germann left to run the household in Cleveland while Finger continued working for Fishel and Marks and the older children completed the school year.[60] London often admitted that he wrote in order to afford his ranch. Likewise, Finger realized a sheep farm would not fully support his family, but perhaps he thought it would placate Nellie while freeing him from wage slavery.[61]

[5]

DARING DISCOURSE

WRITING INTENSIVELY during his off hours once Nellie moved to Arkansas, Finger found his most important literary mentor in a St. Louis editor, William Marion Reedy, who published a weekly journal of his observations on local and national politics. *Reedy's Mirror* also was a platform for new fiction writers and poets—Reedy was one of the first editors to publish Carl Sandburg, Edgar Lee Masters, Sara Teasdale, and Fannie Hurst.[1] At one time the *Mirror* had a national circulation of 32,000, almost three times that of the *Nation*.[2] When Finger submitted a short story about his alter ego, Jack Random, in 1916, Reedy immediately saw potential in this unusual new writer. Over the next several years, he gave Finger several priceless gifts: encouragement, his first fiction publication since 1898, a connection to an even more influential literary editor—H. L. Mencken—and a job editing the *Mirror*. At the same time that Finger's family began a new life farming in the Arkansas Ozarks, Finger's long-range dream of a literary life suddenly came true.

He probably employed an overly complicated narrative frame in that first submission to the *Mirror*. Reedy rejected the story, commenting, "the story in it is too much subordinated" but as "a straight story [it] would be very effective and excruciatingly funny." Reedy actually apologized for being unable to accept the submission and added a handwritten postscript in which he joked that he was "Sherlock Holmes" to recognize that the character of Jack Random in the story was Finger himself. "No relative of Roderick, I hope." He recommended that a character named Ascher demonstrate "physical prowess" in a prizefight so that his "manliness" would "sweep all the fantastic cobwebs out of the brain of Enid." Reedy recognized that Finger's treatment of marriage was ironic: "My dear Finger, this is the damnedest almost-est ms. that has come my way in a long time. It is full of all kinds

of developmental possibilities [in] the way of satirical and ironical fiction."
With enough revision the story would "sell someday for more money than
I owe." It appears that Finger didn't succeed in revising this early attempt
at fiction. Nonetheless, by 1919 *Reedy's Mirror* succeeded the *Public* as his
primary outlet for book reviews and opinion pieces.[3]

Most importantly for Finger's long-range ambitions, Reedy published
"Canassa" and "A Good Time," stories set in Patagonia and seemingly autobiographical, and suggested Finger approach Alfred A. Knopf in New York
about publishing a collection of stories. "If Knopf won't have it . . . Boni &
Liveright"—another publishing house in New York that published many
daring writers of the 1910s and 1920s—"will surely take it." "Tell Liveright,"
Reedy wrote later the same month, "I think . . . your short stories have a quality of directness and vivid truth not to be found elsewhere."[4] He probably
also encouraged Finger to approach Mencken. As coeditor with George Jean
Nathan of the magazine *Smart Set*, Mencken was the leading example of
what a self-taught essayist and critic could achieve in the US. Like Finger, he
received his formal education at a polytechnic school and was highly scornful
of academia. Also like Finger, Mencken was proud of his German ancestry.
He had a wide circle of friends who were writers and artists and made a glorious living as a pontificator. With Mencken so widely respected, *Smart Set*
was the most important magazine in the US for new writers hoping to attract
the attention of major literary critics and get their first book contracts.[5]

Mencken did not particularly like Reedy but took him seriously as a scout
for new literary talent. He too declined Finger's first submission but, like
Reedy, was encouraging. "The writing is undoubtedly very good and the
two men are drawn capitally," he wrote. Mencken asked Finger to spice up
the story with more "romance." Finger sent a second draft but apparently
went too far with the romance; Mencken regretfully rejected that draft in
January 1920, finding it "very risky for a magazine" because of Anthony
Comstock, a morality crusader who used federal postal regulations to sup-
press distribution of publications he considered pornographic. (Mencken's
caution demonstrated the crucial importance of mail delivery to the publishing world. He rejected something by Theodore Dreiser for the same reason.) He explained to Finger that with an anthology, a publisher could "take
chances with the Comstocks but in a magazine," Finger's story "would lead
to almost certain difficulty, particularly in view of the general anti-Christian
tone of the thing." He added ruefully, "I am genuinely sorry to lose the story,
and hope that you have another as good." Mencken underlined "genuinely

sorry" and asked, "What else are you doing? I surely hope that you let me see everything you complete."[6] Finger responded quickly with the story "Incongruity," which Mencken and Nathan published in January 1920 along with a short story by John McClure, a one-act play by F. Scott Fitzgerald, and an essay on none other than Havelock Ellis by an avant-garde critic in New York, Carl Van Vechten. This was Finger's breakthrough.[7]

"Incongruity" had a Conradian double narrative frame and, as Mencken requested, romance. A railroad executive meets a retired ship's captain who tells the story of rescuing Carl, a former gold prospector, and Agnes from a small boat during a storm. The character of Agnes reflects not just Finger's female cousin in Germany and Mary Ann Cameron, the rancher's daughter in Chile, but Ferdinand Haberkorn, his violinist friend in Texas, and even female characters in Conrad's popular novel *Victory*, in which, as James Huneker discussed in one of the collections of essays that Finger read, one woman is a violinist and the other a "most buoyant and attractive girl" named Freya.[8] Carl and Agnes played duets on piano and violin and planned to marry until a rival named Hyde—for Finger's friend Ted Hyde—wooed her. In the end, the captain recalls, Carl admitted "she was too *straight* for me and my mind [emphasis added]." "I'm just a natural born scallywag, I guess."[9] Reedy praised "Incongruity" as "good Finger and good Conrad" and published Finger's story "Ma-Ha-Su-Ma" in March. That story began with an awkward note to the reader to establish Finger's firsthand experience, explaining he had given Reedy "proof," in the form of diary pages, that "I lived for a time with the natives." The queer literature scholar Natasha Hurley traces this kind of "first-person accounts of 'going native claiming to be true stories'" to Melville's *Typee*. Derivative of H. Rider Haggard, J. Fenimore Cooper, and Edgar Rice Burroughs, Finger's story involves a man who attempts to sleep with a naked woman but is clumsy and repulsed. "'I cannot,' he protested. . . . 'My God. My God. What shall I do?'"[10]

Next, Mencken published "Some Mischievous Thing" in April. In this story Finger merged his narrator and an autobiographical character into a lightkeeper, who says, "It's queer, when you come to think of it, but there must have been some men born out of their time." The lightkeeper tells another version of an unconsummated flirtation with a woman. "Not more than a year ago I was studying harmony . . . in Frankfort-on-Main," he begins. "Well, I met a girl." He extricated himself from the relationship by inviting an officer to join them on outings. Finger used details from South America: the shipwreck of the *Seatoller* and the three-masted schooner *Martha Gale*.

Someone fell or jumped into the sea and disappeared—a detail matching the end of Conrad's story "The Secret Sharer." There is another mishap, and the lightkeeper is rescued. He says, "Sometimes it looks to me as though the affairs of men are run by a Spottgeist, a Rubezahl—some mischievous Thing."[11]

Finger had become deeply frustrated by the ties of middle-class marriage and fatherhood and made vehement declarations against the institution of marriage in "Odd Thoughts," a new column for the *Mirror. Odd* was one of the more secretive code words for being gay, and Finger sometimes used it in combination with *crooked* as an antonym for *straight*. He later wondered "whether I was born with a crooked streak, or whether much travel in odd corners of the world and living with odd people has given me a kind of twist [that] places a bar between me and my fellows more often than not."[12] In the first installment of the column, he warned "young unmarried men" not to believe that "so-called 'art' pictures" of women were accurate. In the second column, he praised James Branch Cabell's controversial novel *Jurgen: A Comedy of Justice* for erotic scenes that were "subtle and delicate, odd and original." That some of those scenes hinted at man–man love Finger did not need to acknowledge because the readers he wanted to reach already knew.[13]

Despite his estrangement from Nellie, when he received literary encouragement from William Rose Benét, an editor of the *New York Evening Post*, and the novelist Theodore Dreiser, Finger wrote a rare long letter to her.[14] Benét had written, "Your work is great stuff and I want all you will let me have." Dreiser encouraged Finger to send a collection of short stories to his publisher, Boni & Liveright, and mention his name. "He says," Finger told Nellie, "quite simply 'I like the way you work things out and your manner of expression.'" Newly inspired, Finger quickly wrote a story called "She Turned Things Round." "This new tale would make a cat laugh," he told Nellie. He planned to resign from Fishel and Marks by May 1 but wanted to visit "Reedy and a few of the St. Louis fellows" before joining her in Fayetteville. "I'm close to them at heart." He closed "Ever Thine, Respectfully, CJF."[15]

REEDY PUBLISHED one more story by Finger, "Ebro," running it in June 1920 beside a positive review of new work by Conrad. "Ebro" was packed with autobiographical elements, allusions to other writers, disguised messages, and material for an extended discourse with the inner circle of understanding readers Finger hoped to draw around him. One man relates how he listened to a second man, Ebro, tell a third man, Percival, a story while they shared a railway car. The narrative frame placed Finger at a remove from the action of the story, teasing the reader with whether it was true, but Reedy, who "had a genius for understanding everybody," recognized that Ebro was autobiographical.[16] The likely inspiration for the name "Ebro" was the writer W. H. Hudson, who left Argentina for England on the ship *Ebro* and with whom Finger was corresponding as he wrote the story.[17] Ebro "was just an ordinary looking man with manner somewhat defiant . . . He might have been an engineer or a manufacturer in moderate circumstances."[18] He was "a square built man who might have been forty or sixty. It was hard to tell." The name "Percival" was a joke at the expense of Percival Chubb of St. Louis, an Englishman who, ironically, collaborated with Edward Carpenter in founding the Fellowship of the New Life in 1883 but became an object of ridicule after criticizing local newspapers.[19] Capturing the discreet drama of gay men's eyes meeting, Finger has Percival "flinch" when Ebro, whose "eyes were bright and keen," looks straight at him in a scene resembling one in Bayard Taylor's classic homoerotic novel *Joseph and His Friend* (1870). As the literary historian Roger Austen distilled that scene, Joseph gazes upon Philip Held, "a twenty-eight-year-old with 'all the charm of early manhood,' and Philip answers his gaze with a look implying 'We are men, let us know each other!'—Taylor adding that this sort of look 'is, alas! too rare in this world.'"[20]

For Finger, who spent so much time traveling by rail, the encounter by strangers on a train was a familiar starting place. His story also was the newest homage to Leo Tolstoy's notorious novella *The Kreutzer Sonata* (1889), in which a narrator describes a conversation by four men on a train with one eventually revealing, "I am telling you how I killed my wife."[21] An anonymous short story had appeared in the *New York Sun* in 1897, and in several other newspapers around the country in 1898, in which a stranger tells three other men in the smoking compartment of a train he had a "narrow escape . . . from being a married man."[22] A Russian playwright had adapted Tolstoy's story for a play set in the US, and Finger's friend Herbert Brenon had adapted that play for a popular film in 1915.[23] John Galsworthy, an English essayist and short-story writer, also used the device in a book that Finger read in Ohio. Galsworthy's narrator, on a train, meets a "wife-insurance agent" who sells policies that protect men who want divorces.[24]

Ebro confesses that he "dodged . . . the girl at Hoboken" but does not feel guilty about it because marriage "would have been hell," this line a striking insult to Nellie. He joined "a Franco-Russian ornithological expedition" and had a passionate sexual affair with a native in Patagonia, nicknaming the woman "Gayeta" because, he says, when she asked him for "galleta, meaning biscuit," he thought she was saying "welcome." Finger's reference to native Patagonians crying *galleta* was true. A travel writer who stopped in Punta Arenas within weeks of Finger's arrival in 1890 described native people approaching the ship in canoes and calling out "Galletas, galletas."[25] "It was through my mistake that I came to call her Gayeta," Finger wrote, implying to general readers that Ebro's spelling of his lover's name was a mistake, but this was an inside joke. While *gay* connoted prostitution in the straight world, it was a recognizable code word. Huneker, for example, in one of the collections of essays that Finger read, called Walt Whitman "a gay old pagan who never called a sin a sin when it was a pleasure." Gayeta was "a dandy name," Ebro comments, one that "calls up a picture of merriment and light-heartedness"—hinting again that Finger was joking with the reader. His juxtaposition of "Gayeta" with *dandy* was another signal that the native with whom he had a passionate affair was not a woman. Not only was "dandy" the name of a certain homosexual type in Victorian London, it had a subtle but significant meaning as the personification of mythical figures that could change form and occupied a world outside binary, heterosexual society.[26]

Ebro and Gayeta lived together for a while, having "rare fun." He dressed her in black stockings, red garters, and French shoes. "I can see her now as she stood up and, bending over slightly, looked with pride at her legs." The sudden, provocative image of a nearly nude South American woman posing before an American man is a shocking turn in the story. "Heels together, sir—heels and knees touching. Slim ankles, the curve of the calf and the thigh, the sinuous graceful lines to the waist. She was well worth looking at." Here Finger perpetuated a running joke with the novelist Frederick O'Brien. He had reviewed O'Brien's book *White Shadows on the South Seas* a month earlier, making the provocative comment that women's naked legs would make men recoil. O'Brien responded in a letter that ran in the same issue of the *Mirror* as "Ebro": "Oh, naughty Finger! You have poked fun at me, but you have scratched the escutcheon of the lovers of Mimi and Fifi," using a phallic pun to subtly joke that Finger was the opposite of men who loved women. It was "a warm argument," Finger later recalled, "both of us flashing falchions bright."[27]

After Gayeta had a child, Ebro lost interest in her. His dismissal was perfectly cruel, his use of "revulsion" rhyming with Edward Carpenter's phrase "positive repulsion," but when a man named Hyslop murdered Gayeta and her baby—a reference to Sam Hyslop, a resident of Tierra del Fuego in 1890 who was believed to be a contract killer of Onan Indians—Ebro "took careful aim at the back of Hyslop's head and pulled the trigger." "Whenever I broke the moral code," Ebro said, "it was in search of happiness."[28]

With "Ebro" and the stories that preceded it, Finger joined writers who used innuendo, double entendre, and code to signal that some of their characters, or they themselves, were gay or lesbian. His word play and the intertextual relationship of the story to O'Brien's joke are examples of what the literary scholar Richard Bozorth called "coterie discourse."[29] They reveal that Finger sought, among the readers of *Reedy's Mirror* and *Smart Set*, friends with whom he could communicate and freely be himself. Continually corresponding with other writers and editors to promote himself, Finger sent a copy of "Ebro" to Hudson, who mentioned it to his friend Robert Bontine (R. B.) Cunninghame Graham. Finger also sent a copy of the July 22 issue of the *Mirror* to Hudson, pointing out his positive review of John Masefield's new collection, *Enslaved*, and Hudson passed that review on to Masefield.[30] Finger further promoted "Ebro" in a prolonged bit of mockery in the *Mirror*. To ridicule Percival Chubb, Reedy had created a persona named "Elmer Chubb, Ph.D., L.L.D.," publishing occasional letters from Elmer Chubb that were actually written by Edgar Lee Masters, Reedy himself, or perhaps Finger.[31] Now Finger reported that Elmer Chubb canceled his subscription to *Reedy's Mirror* because he was offended by "Ebro" and then published a letter by Masters, in the guise of Elmer Chubb, who denied reading "Ebro" because "I do not pollute my mind with . . . vile literature."[32] Reedy joined in these high jinks, writing from San Francisco "Percival Chubb was out here two years ago and disapproved of [earthquakes] as sternly as he disapproves of 'Ebro.'"[33]

Reedy, his assistant Alma Meyer, and Finger had become good friends. While Reedy recovered from a serious eye disorder, Finger assumed a long-distance, part-time role on the *Mirror*'s staff.[34] Then Reedy asked Finger to take over the *Mirror* while he went to San Francisco to report on the Democratic National Convention. Although Nellie would have to wait longer for Finger's help on the farm, this was a thrilling opportunity. He resigned from Fishel and Marks, delivered the children to Fayetteville, and moved to St. Louis. Beginning on July 8, he edited eight issues, struggling to match Reedy's command of politics in what was effectively a high-pressure, two-month course on how to produce an idiosyncratic periodical.

———

IT PROBABLY WAS DURING this exhilarating period that Finger met the man who became his closest reader and greatest comrade, one with a "knightly spirit" with whom he shared "the scarlet and gold of remembered happiness."[35] Lt. Col. George Washington Maddox was a Kentuckian and a 1905 graduate of the US Military Academy at West Point. He served in the Philippine Islands, Cuba, and at various posts in the US before World War I. Posing with other officers for a photograph shortly before shipping out for France in 1918, he looked much younger than his thirty-seven years, with something of a dancer's poise. He became fourth in command of two divisions in France, helping lead the Saint-Mihiel and Meuse–Argonne offensives.[36] One month after the war's end, he received a promotion to lieutenant colonel. Back in the US, he was an assistant inspector with the Reserve Officers Training Corps near New York and then commander of the Twenty-sixth Infantry at Camp Zachary Taylor outside Louisville, Kentucky. He commanded an occupation of Lexington, Kentucky, in 1920 when the governor declared martial law because of Klan activity.[37]

Maddox loved literature and read widely in fiction and poetry, sometimes writing to authors he admired. Any of Finger's stories in *Reedy's Mirror* or *Smart Set* could have inspired him to write to Finger.[38] Perhaps they began a correspondence and planned to meet in St. Louis when the army staged athletic championships there over Independence Day weekend in 1920; some of Maddox's troops participated, so he may have escorted them there. Maddox was still handsome, with a straight nose, full mouth, heavy dark brows, and eyes that turned down at the edges, but the war had aged him. His hair was streaked with gray and fully white at the temples. His expression seemed to combine friendliness with weariness. If he and Finger attended the army boxing matches together, it would not be a coincidence that Finger briefly mused on boxing in the *Mirror* on July 22.[39]

The prospect of giving up the *Mirror* job to join Nellie and his father-in-law had become loathsome to Finger. In the same issue as the boxing thoughts, he published a diatribe against marriage under his own name. It was "a mere partnership for the raising of children" who were "the accidental results of an indulgence in the sexual appetite." This was the view held by John Addington Symonds, coauthor with Havelock Ellis of *Sexual Inversion*. "Someday . . . people will throw off the intolerable burden of trying to [be] a loving devoted couple," Finger went on. He returned to this theme in August, referring to "the slavery known as married life" and writing "in the home . . . there is no cessation to the dull, dreary round."[40]

In San Francisco Reedy worried about being away from the *Mirror* but thought Finger was doing a good job. "Dear Ebro," he wrote on July 28, "you're doing splendidly." He continued to encourage Finger's fiction efforts and mentioned friends whom he wanted Finger to meet but confided, "I'm not feeling so damned good, but for Christ's sake don't tell [Meyer]." He died of angina shortly after laying aside this letter. The news reached Finger in time for him to add a small announcement beneath the masthead of *Reedy's Mirror*: "It is with feelings of deepest grief that I have to announce the sudden death of William Marion Reedy."[41] He quickly conveyed to the *St. Louis Post-Dispatch* that he would continue to put out the *Mirror* and devoted the August 5 issue to Reedy, creating a touching and dramatic cover by reproducing part of Reedy's last handwritten manuscript and filling the issue with columns and poems by Reedy's friends and black-bordered display advertisements in Reedy's memory. It had been "a high privilege," he wrote, to fill in for Reedy and work alongside his "brave little office partner, Miss Alma Meyer."[42] Then Finger made a quick trip to Arkansas, "to the little farm in the Ozarks which absorbs my surplus earnings," and returned to put out more issues of the *Mirror*.[43] He and Nellie may have had words; he referred in the August 19 issue to "women applying for divorce."[44] The trade newspaper the *Fourth Estate* reported that Finger "has succeeded Reedy as editor," but Margaret Chambers Reedy, his widow, decided on August 21 to sell the business and told Finger he could put out one more issue.[45]

For his last number of the *Mirror*, Finger wrote a Conradian short story about the death of his alter ego, Jack Random, using a narrative frame, an intertextual allusion to his earlier "Odd Thoughts" columns, a salute to his old friend Harry Somerfield, and a reference to Random as "a civil engineer" in a nod to Philip Cornick, who was an officer in the US Army Corps of Engineers during World War I.[46] "Many readers will recall the name of Jack Random," the narrator begins. "News came telling of his death the other day" from "Somerfield, the well known book illustrator." He quotes Somerfield's account of Random drowning "near the little town of Jack Fish on the north shore of Lake Superior," drawing here upon his memory of

Ontario. After telling a friend "I'm through with life," Random waded into the water. "So long, old scout," he shouted before climbing on a boulder. He "poised a moment erect, hands high above his head and thumbs locked, then dived." Random "struck out strongly," Somerfield went on. "I saw his hands go up and his head disappear. That was the last I saw of him." Random's suicide resembled a scene in Conrad's short story "The Planter of Malata" and the final gesture of a ship captain's secret lover in "The Secret Sharer."

This background leads to the main story, as told by Random in a conversation that the narrator recalls, about the character of Rowe, "a decent young fellow: a Second Lieutenant," the rank that Maddox held while he was in France, who shared a secret with Random, that "he prayed . . . it might never fall to his lot to take human life." The story occurs in the trenches somewhere on the Western Front during the Christmas truce of 1914. When a German soldier named Meyer—this detail a gesture to Alma Meyer—stands up and sings for the enjoyment of German and English troops, an English officer named Carson orders Rowe to shoot him. Random saw Carson as "incarnate evil" who, "having found a violet"—that flower and color a bit of queer code—"deliberately besmirched it." Realizing "what had to be done meant less to me" than it did to Rowe, Random seized the rifle and shot the young German himself. "I have borne the yoke of self-contempt ever since," he told the narrator. Concluding this story within a story, Finger commented, "The demon of remorse from which [Random] saved Rowe evidently fastened itself upon him. His soul was incurably wounded. There are thousands like him. That is a by-product of the war which we do not count."[47]

Margaret Reedy published a final issue of the *Mirror* without Finger on September 2, filling it with pieces Reedy wrote over the years and a short farewell, "Finis," by Meyer. With his position on the *Mirror*, Finger had plunged from the edge to the mainstream of the literary world, but upon Reedy's death, he had no alternative but to join his family on the farm.[48]

[**6**]

ALL'S WELL

THE SMALL RURAL PROPERTY in Arkansas where Finger spent the last twenty years of his life became a locus of intense ambivalence for him, a financial millstone that forever tied him to Nellie yet the setting for his happiest times with his children and wife—holidays and birthdays, amateur theatricals, long literary conversations beneath the trees or before one of the fireplaces, and many occasions for entertaining visiting friends as well as stars in the publishing galaxy. The farm was a property of about 115 acres, partly planted in apple trees, on the northeastern slope of Kessler Mountain fronting the road between Fayetteville and Farmington.[1] A branch line of the St. Louis–San Francisco Railway ran through the valley at the bottom of the hill, providing mail and passenger service. Finger named the farm Gayeta for the character in his story "Ebro" and with eighteen-year-old Hubert built a house he called Gayeta Lodge. The family gradually added an office building, two or more guest cottages, and smaller outbuildings.[2] Finger hoped Gayeta would become a destination for his friends, like Elbert Hubbard's famous art colony in New York, Roycroft Inn, where Reedy had been an annual summer resident. C. J. and Nellie even established a Gayeta guest book like the one that Hubbard kept.[3]

He designed four small bedrooms for him and the boys across the south side of the main house and two bedrooms for Nellie and the girls on the north side. Unheated and with exterior doors, these bedrooms were in effect sleeping porches like those of Jack London's autobiographical protagonist Dick Forrest and his wife in *The Little Lady of the Big House*. Like Forrest's house, Gayeta also had French doors, a pergola, a goldfish pond, and a library.[4] The house did not have electricity or running water, so to cook or do laundry, the Fingers and Fergusons had to cut wood, haul it, chop it, build a fire, and draw water from a well. The work was constant, and everyone pitched in. "To feed the creatures we [ate,] there was wagon after wagon load of miscellaneous feed, of hay, bran, shorts, corn chops and other incidentals, with ton upon ton of feed for the horses that hauled the stuff, that plowed the land," Finger wrote. Each child "had to work with [their] hands; this one at farm work and carpentering; this one at poultry and the sheep; the girls at housework." The children attended schools in town, Hubert riding a mare and Kitty driving a buggy with the other children.[5] The library was the center of Gayeta; Finger thought of it as a "temple" and the fireplace as an "altar," like London and like Henry James—for whom, the scholar James Gifford observed, the library was "the center of any 'vision of Arcadia'" and the "center of James's homosexual utopia."[6]

Inspired by Reedy, in December 1920 Finger launched his own periodical as a vehicle for promoting Gayeta as an art colony in the manner of Hubbard's periodical *Roycroft*. He promoted *All's Well* as "the *Mirror* repolished," but it was no news magazine, and as a literary magazine, its greatest emphasis was on writing by Finger himself. It was an outlier in the genre known as "little magazines" because of their small circulations, which tended to be avant-garde and concentrated on publishing little-known, promising writers who were happy for the exposure.[7] Years of skimming periodicals in reading rooms from London to El Paso, followed by his immersion in books and writing book reviews in Ohio, had prepared Finger well for this project. He understood that American readers chose from the enormous variety of daily, weekly, and monthly periodicals according to their affiliations and thus were part of far-flung communities of shared interests and values.[8] The *Public* catered to progressives; *Smart Set* appealed to physicians, lawyers, and businessmen, standard-bearers of middle-class society who regarded writers as social and cultural leaders.[9] Thanks to the daily or even twice-daily mail delivery that was available in most of the country, Finger could create a network of interacting, overlapping, one-to-one relationships with writers and readers, a network that he called the "social circle that sits at the sign of All's Well." He wanted "busy men and women who . . . have time for a literary hobby" as an outer circle with whom he could "talk . . . about Hudson and Conrad and D'Aurevilly and Carl Van Doren and [Oswald Garrison] Villard and [George] Gissing."[10] His readers would be like the safe circle of friends he had in the Polytechnic Literary Society, his short-lived private salon in Punta Arenas, the Railway Club in Alamogordo, and the Discussion Club in Ripley.[11]

He also envisioned an inner circle, what John Addington Symonds thought of as a community of homosexual readers. *All's Well* would be like Henry James's concept of books as "meeting-places, borders of osmotic transcendence [or] 'lovers' embraces,'" the kind of network that the literary scholar Gregory Woods later termed a "transnational . . . powerful collectivity."[12] Every January, Finger offered readers his best wishes for the New Year. In January 1927 he wrote, "Here's a toast to the indestructibility of friendship! Here's to a wider and fairer vision!" Although *All's Well* lost money, he reflected in 1928, "it is a mighty fine link that binds friends" and the little magazine was "the best asset that I have." Thanking a friend for renewing his subscription, Finger wrote the renewal felt like "the light of a friend saying 'All's Well'" and added, in a striking turn of phrase, "one cannot lose touch with friends and be gay."[13] His daughter Helen became bitter and sardonic because her father created *All's Well* as a way to find friends. "He may have lost money on all of that, but he just loved it. The thing is that he made so many good friends, just life-long friends, out of that thing, so that was worthwhile, wasn't it?"[14]

The journal's name mystified some of Reedy's friends. Theodore Dreiser and the poet George Sterling disliked it. Vincent Starrett of Chicago commented, "Where Finger got his title—'All's Well'—heaven knows. Is it Browning [or] Shakespeare? That is part of the mystery."[15] To answer their questions, Finger had letterhead printed with a watchman holding up a lantern—"All's well!" was the announcement that watchmen on steamships proclaimed at night.[16] A shadowy scene in "The Secret Sharer" had the same line, as one man whispers, "All's well so far" to another while they secretly share a bed and clasp hands. (Conrad considered "The Secret Sharer" his best work so far because it had "no damned tricks with girls.")[17] Thus, Finger's name for his new magazine could have been a smile and a wink to his readers, conveying that they shared a secret, the dream of an Arcadia where men could be free to recognize, know, and love one another. More than that, the title was a declaration that he was creating that Arcadia, if not yet on a physical plane, at least between the lines in *All's Well* for readers who understood the subtext. The journal's main department was a long column of personal comments similar to Reedy's "Reflections" and Michael Monahan's "Side Talks by the Editor" in a defunct small magazine known variously as the *Papyrus* and the *Phoenix*. Comparing this department's collections of anecdotes and observations to free-form musical compositions, Finger called it

"Free Fantasia," a phrase he used as early as 1901 and could have first seen in 1888.[18]

The first issue contained the short story "The Lizard God" over Finger's name and another story by "Ebro" as well as a posthumous column by Reedy and a piece by Starrett, one of the *Mirror*'s former contributors.[19] A conversation between the curator of a natural history museum and a stranger, "Lizard God" is a fantastic story about a dangerous adventure in an exotic locale with a photographer named Somerfield who worked in South America to support "his family in Ohio [because] he was mighty fond of his family." Somerfield photographs a local ritual in which pregnant women parade past native men in a celebration of fertility but is unmoved by female nudity: "I never saw a stark woman that looked beautiful yet. That's all bunk." The vivid, detailed descriptions of flora and fauna and the weird and violent events in the story were striking; the offhand nature of the storyteller's comments gave it an arch, slightly scandalous quality. The magazine *Current Opinion* republished the story in May 1921.[20]

Finger sent sample copies of *All's Well* to literary editors at newspapers and placed an advertisement for the magazine in a national monthly, the *Drama*, promising, "people who hanker after . . . convention will not like it."[21] Carrying on his practice of courting local newspapers for publicity, Finger cultivated the editor of the *Fayetteville Democrat* and often shared news of his literary achievements, which the newspaper reported.[22] He contacted past subscribers and contributors to the *Mirror,* the *Phoenix,* and the *Public,* asking them to subscribe, contribute articles, or both. James Branch Cabell was one of his first subscribers.[23] By the time Finger asked H. L. Mencken and George Jean Nathan at *Smart Set* to subscribe, Mencken's derisive take on the American South, the essay "The Sahara of the Bozart," was well known, making Finger's outreach from Arkansas a gamble, but Mencken subscribed and even promoted *All's Well* in *Smart Set* in August 1921. He joked that Finger's journal came out of "trackless, unexplored Arkansas, a state still almost fabulous" but noted Finger "is not actually a Southerner" and linked *All's Well* to the *Double Dealer* and the *Reviewer,* other Southern little magazines, adding that Finger had "written some excellent short-stories."[24]

THE MOST IMPORTANT early visitor to Gayeta was Carl Sandburg, the famous journalist and poet who was a central figure in what became known as the Chicago literary renaissance. a group including Sherwood Anderson, Ben Hecht, and Edgar Lee Masters that produced gritty, realistic fiction and poetry. Sandburg and Finger probably had corresponded during the last weeks of the *Mirror* since Reedy was one of Sandburg's first publishers and the poet shared Finger's sense of deep indebtedness.[25] In April 1921, when Sandburg was on a five-week, cross-country speaking tour that included a lecture at the University of Arkansas, Finger invited him to Gayeta and then alerted the local newspaper, which reported that Sandburg would be calling on him. "Mr. Sandburg is a personal friend of Charles J. Finger and family of this place." After the lecture a journalism instructor at the university, Murray Sheehan, escorted Sandburg to Gayeta, where the poet sat on a slippery horsehair sofa in the Finger living room and played a guitar and sang a few folk songs.[26] Finger methodically used this visit by Sandburg to elevate the image of Gayeta as a gathering place for writers and artists, describing it in *All's Well* and in a speech to a literary group in Little Rock and reusing the speech as a column in *All's Well*, sharing that he and the Little Rock audience "talked quite freely" of "Carl Sandburg and of [Cabell's] 'Jurgen,' of [Theodore] Dreiser and Anderson."[27] He asked Sandburg to help promote Gayeta and *All's Well*, and Sandburg promised he would "do it right one of these days." He made a start by mentioning the journal to John C. Farrar, the new editor of the *Bookman*. Farrar described their conversation in his July 1921 "Gossip Shop" column: Finger "was William Marion Reedy's best friend," he wrote. He "lives on a ranch and edits 'All's Well.'" Since the *Bookman* gossip column usually focused on writers in New York, this was a special bit of publicity for Finger.[28]

Sheehan returned to Gayeta on a Sunday afternoon, bringing three friends from the English and classics departments at the university for the first of many visits by the local intelligentsia.[29] Twenty years younger than Finger, Sheehan was an interesting fellow, not least because his brother Perley Poore Sheehan was a screenwriter and coauthor of the novella *We Are French!* (1914), a stirring call to patriots and freedom lovers that was made into a film, *The Bugler of Algiers*, in 1916.[30] At Miami University in Ohio, Murray was in the men's glee club and starred in at least two productions of *The Quest of the Quezarre*, a comic farce that featured men in drag. At one performance the cast was heckled, and someone threw a rock that hit him on the shoulder. While he was in graduate school at Harvard University, his poem "Fate" appeared in the *Harvard Monthly*: "Why strive against the hand that drives us? Fate / Is strong to shape the end she first conceived. . . . Think you the oak

could ever be but oak . . . ? . . . She makes you what you are, in joy and pain."
Another of his poems, "Boulevard St. Michael," appeared the same year in
Bruno's Weekly, a short-lived periodical that idolized Oscar Wilde: "Sin, sin,
and be merry. Let who will / Say Bacchus is an evil god, I swear / I'd rather
run my fingers through his hair / Just once, and die, than live insensible, /
Forever!"[31] Not long after meeting him, Finger published Sheehan's poem
"The Wind" in *All's Well*: "Strike hard and test my strength, oh wind, /
Buffet my chest, so I may know / My flesh is firm and my heart is true."[32]

Attuned to Finger's idea of a communal art colony on the Fayetteville
hillside, Sheehan became an entrepreneurial collaborator like Ferdinand
Haberkorn, Finger's music school partner in Texas, although probably not
Finger's lover, considering that he likely had met Maddox by this time.
Sheehan often spent evenings with the entire family, taking turns with
Finger reading aloud. Helen later described the ritual of nightly readings
that dominated family life. "Every evening, it didn't matter whether you had
to study or not, we gathered around the fireplace and listened to readings."
Finger "wanted to be the dominant one, see. Everyone looked at him. [He
read] Dickens and [Thackeray], the good old classics."[33] Late in 1921, Finger
and Sheehan began building a house for Sheehan uphill from Gayeta Lodge.
A stone cabin with two rooms and large windows, it had a view of anyone
walking up the hill from the main house, yet the trees that surrounded it gave
it "utmost privacy." At first they called it "Ebro Hermitage," but by spring
they settled on the name "Hut Canassa" after Finger's story "Canassa," in
which two men circled each other "like fighting cocks." Sheehan sent releases
to the Little Rock newspapers to announce his new residence, describing
decorations in the house as "colored art prints" that threw the "roughly plas-
tered walls . . . into gay relief." One newspaper related he had "settled himself
in comfortable bachelor fashion at 'Hut Canassa'"; another reported the cottage "is one of the most attractive small bachelor bungalows" in Fayetteville.
This was the beginning of making Gayeta a "mecca" for writers, Sheehan
said. He and Finger promoted Gayeta as a working farm as well as a destination for writers and artists, with Sheehan buying hogs and grape plants and
announcing that he and Hubert, now nineteen, were business partners.[34]

More locals began visiting Gayeta for its art colony atmosphere. Julius
Herman Field was a photographer who moved to Fayetteville with his wife
and son after shooting illustrations for William Lighton's 1910 article "An
Arkansas Farm."[35] The managing editor of the *Fayetteville Democrat*, Lessie
Stringfellow Read, disagreed with Finger "on everything under the sun and

quarrel[ed] outrageously but [they enjoyed] each other immensely."[36] The cosmopolitan couple Herbert Sprague and Floy Mahan Sprague lived near Gayeta, in a house that they called Ozarcadia, when they were not working as Chautauqua entertainers on the road in the US or Europe.[37] The entomologist William J. Baerg, tall with thick, dark hair and steady gray eyes, was thirty-six and unmarried and sometimes socialized with the Sheehan set.[38] He took photographs around the farm with various combinations of family members, Nellie gazing at the camera in one scene but smiling in none. One photograph captured how thoroughly Finger adopted Sheehan and Baerg into the family. Finger sat at a wide desk in the library of the main house, appearing to read aloud from a notepad or manuscript. Nellie leaned forward with hands clasped. Sheehan sat on the floor in front of the desk, his back to Nellie, in a shirt with one sleeve ripped and hanging from his shoulder, perhaps a joking reference to his injury onstage in *The Quest of the Quezarre*. Hubert, Kitty, and Charles Jr. are in the picture, but Helen and Herbert are not; perhaps they had gone to bed. Baerg is bent at the waist behind Nellie, gazing enrapt at Finger with one elbow propped on the edge of the desk, holding a shutter release cable out of view.[39]

Finger worked Sheehan into his next published short story, "The Tooth," a pseudo-autobiographical effort with university men named Sheehan and Hancock (for one of Sheehan's friends at the university) who visit Gayeta. The anonymous narrator begins with a fictitious intertextual note that the magazine *Current Opinion* published his home address along with the story "The Lizard God." This brought a mysterious man named H. H. Leaf to his house. Leaf asked, regarding "The Lizard God," "Any foundation? Or is it just mere lies and fantastic work?" The narrator recounts that he told Leaf "the only part which was fanciful . . . was the character of the museum curator. 'Otherwise,' said I, 'the tale is true as I heard it.'" Leaf proceeds to tell of encountering a huge lizard in South America. Another visitor, W. H. Gibson, arrives as Leaf tells his story. This character's name appears to be an homage to the writer and naturalist W. H. Hudson, but Finger based him on Baerg.[40] Resuming his story, Leaf produces a huge tooth and claims it came from one of the long-necked creatures. "Leaf stayed that night with me," Finger's Finger-like narrator concludes, "and, after the children had gone to bed, we sat up long talking about women and adventure. He left early the following morning and walked to town, a dusty, sturdy, lonely looking figure." The *Double Dealer* published this experiment in literary cross-self-promotion in June 1921.[41]

The visit by Sheehan and the professors also provided material for "A Very Satisfactory God," another story in the form of a conversation. Like "The Lizard God" and "The Tooth," it played with notions of gullibility and religion. Several men sit beneath a tree on a starry night, sipping beer and chatting. One, named Nelson, tells a story of being in an exotic location and encountering an African American named George who came from "some Arkansas town," where he worked as "a head waiter or something of that kind." George "got into some trouble in New Orleans [and] shipped to South America under the impression that he was en route for Liberia." He and a destitute American dentist conspired for George to pose as a weird man–animal combination, disguising him with horns and tusks. "The experiment was a winner and when George was . . . put on exhibit at half a dollar a head, they grew rich," but fearing exposure, they fled and became separated. Some natives came upon George and, seeing his horns and tusks, assumed he was a deity. He played along, becoming "a highly satisfactory god." Nelson concludes that the native society was "all the better men because there are no puritanical prohibitions." Another man comments, "much of what passes for mythology and religious belief . . . is a kind of mosaic. Missionary tales are passed round and distorted. There are explorers and runaways too and the tales they tell . . . become misty so that much of what we hear . . . is a mere echo of our own beliefs."[42]

Once again, Finger had incorporated vivid and amusing scenes in a bizarre South American setting and a version of the horned satyr Pan. The story, as the Conrad scholar Peter Lancelot Mallios noted, was an allusion to *Heart of Darkness*. It was also a transparent retelling of the play *The Emperor Jones* by Eugene O'Neill that premiered a few months earlier, in which an African American Pullman porter poses as a man–animal god, itself a retelling of *Heart of Darkness*, thus "passed round and distorted." The *Double Dealer* published a review of the play in the same issue as "A Very Satisfactory God."[43]

Sheehan remained in Fayetteville during the winter break in 1921, talking with Finger by the fireplace in the main house since the cottage was not finished. A celebrity anthologist, Edward J. O'Brien, had included "The Lizard God" in his annual collection of the "best short stories." O'Brien usually compiled about twenty stories plus a list of others that he gave from one to three stars. This recognition was a valuable boost for fiction writers and little magazines, and he tended to bestow his favor on experimental writers and those living outside New York. He first recognized Finger in 1920 by including "Ebro" and "Jack Random" in the honor roll, repeating Finger's exaggerated story that he once spent "a year upon an uninhabited island" accompanied only by 'Sartor Resartus.'" He included Finger again in 1922 with "The Shame of Gold" and in 1924 for "Adventures of Andrew Lang." Some critics belittled the ranking of works of literature, but O'Brien's recognition of Finger held up over time. "The Lizard God" and "The Shame of Gold" appeared in another "best" list in 2000.[44]

Sheehan also had contributed material for a new anthology, one of writings by Harvard men who died in the war. He and Edward Seguin Couch had been on the periphery of the Harvard Aesthetes, a group of young men who gathered in the *Harvard Monthly* office to drink punch or gin and recite their poems to each other.[45] Couch wrote wartime letters to Sheehan that implied sympathy for Greek love, a deep fear that Couch would die without having fully lived, and a hint at the lengths to which a closeted military man might go to avoid recognition. Although Couch wrote to a different friend in a more hopeful tone, vowing "We must live, you and I, and we shall fight stupidity together—in Italy—far from America, never to return." However, he entered the Fort Leavenworth hospital, possibly suffering from influenza, and died of a massive overdose of morphine. His father attributed his death to a mistake by a hospital orderly, but it seems possible that, seeing the morphine within reach, Couch committed suicide. Another of those Harvard Aesthetes, John Wheelwright, later wrote an entire sonnet sequence, *Mirrors of Venus*, in the tradition of Tennyson's "In Memoriam," lamenting Couch's death: "Ned. Ned. / Why after twenty years do I think you killed yourself?"[46]

Sheehan lived in the stone cottage at Gayeta for several years. Even after losing his university job in 1924, he remained for a while, working on a novel. However, Finger eventually evicted him and thereafter disparaged him as he had Haberkorn in Texas.[47] Sheehan used his book, which E. P. Dutton and Company published in 1927, to lampoon Fayetteville, the university, and the Finger family, transforming Gayeta into the small farm of the backward, rural Durnan family. In a fabulist twist, the Durnans' old mare gives birth to a centaur that was fathered by Pan. The centaur, which the family names Dick, is able to speak ancient Greek but, for lack of literate companions, soon suffers mental deterioration. Sheehan found jobs teaching at military schools for boys in Florida and Fort Smith, Arkansas, and then a permanent niche as a tutor for teenaged boys living at the Siamese embassy in Washington, DC. He died in 1963 in Rome.[48]

WORKING IN HIS small office with Margaret Germann—who had rejoined the household as a live-in secretary and maid—typing his manuscripts at an adjacent desk, Finger completed five stories in 1922 that established him as a new literary voice. "Eric," its title a gesture to his and Nellie's youngest child, appeared in an anthology that he published under his own imprint, Golden Horseman Press. Catering to the growing interest in the Ozarks, "Eric" emphasized rural poverty and illiteracy and had a passing reference to racial segregation, but its theme was the struggle to make oneself a writer and even more fundamentally to live according to one's *self.* The character of Eric feels a "crazy" urge to write and has written a story about "a feller who'd understand, and who'd be with me 'warming the winter of my loneliness.' That's the line I liked best, that 'warming the winter of my loneliness.' It's fine, I think." He asks the story's narrator, "Is there any hope? Will I be here always, my work unfinished, myself undone?"—this plaintive question similar to Finger's declaration in "Some Mischievous Thing" that Jack London "went out with his best work undone!"[49]

"Shame of Gold," built upon a passenger's story on a train, appeared in March in the *Century,* possibly after W. H. Hudson encouraged Finger to submit something to *Century* editor Glenn Frank, who was looking for new and unknown writers; around the same time, Frank was negotiating to publish three chapters of Hudson's forthcoming book.[50] "The Jade Piece" appeared in the *Double Dealer* in April. Its setting is a South American Arcadia of "sentient" flowers and "man-beasts," twists on Pan the half-man, half-goat.[51] Next, Frank published "My Friend Julio" in the *Century* in July. A narrator named Carlos tells of becoming embroiled in the Chilean civil war and his friendship with Julio, who was "gay and debonair and all in white, with a bright scarlet sash about his hips and a red rose at his coat lapel," the color scarlet a symbol of homosexuality. Carlos reminisces about walking in a garden and kissing a woman. Finger's juxtaposition of a heterosexual kiss with a Whitman reference (the narrator wears clothes like Walt Whitman's) was the kind of misdirection that the historian Matt Cook calls the "play of visibility and invisibility, and recognition and misrecognition."[52]

Mencken published "My Spottgeist" in October, its title the same obscure German word for a mocking spirit that Finger used in "Some Mischievous

Thing."[53] The story involves a conventional heterosexual love affair, as Mencken had urged in 1919, and the narrator is a business executive representing Finger. He learns his secretary is going to be married and tries to dissuade her, declaring with a crude metaphor that "married life's hell . . . as soon as the first burst is over." Wanting to spend a day together, the two slip out of town on separate trains. Finger's characters "met at noon in Portsdown Park and . . . climbed to the hilltop," rather like the gay men in the novel *Imre* (1906) by Edward Prime-Stevenson (who used the pseudonym Xavier Mayne). They confess their love while in a park outside a city, a symbolic Arcadian garden. The scene also is reminiscent of Finger's stroll on Hampstead Heath with C. J. Peer. Next, Klansmen accost the philandering executive, and he flees down an alley and escapes by jumping on another train. Similarly, the short story "Hands" (1919) by Sherwood Anderson involved a man who is confronted over a sexual transgression—in Anderson's story the contact is with a boy—and beaten and run out of town. Some details in "Spottgeist" resemble the lives of Herbert Bigelow and George Maddox. Portsdown Park could be the location where the Cincinnati commuter train met a short branch line and Bigelow was beaten by Klan members, and Maddox had commanded the occupation of Lexington, Kentucky, during a Klan threat.[54] These stories made clear to thoughtful readers that Finger was blending reportage and fiction. As in "Ebro," which appeared in *Reedy's Mirror* with the subtitle "A Really Realistic Story," he was signaling that his readers were free to guess which parts of his stories were true and which were imaginary.

Needing to support his family, the farm operation, and *All's Well*, Finger juggled these literary endeavors with more prosaic freelance work, the most significant for the publishers Emanuel and Marcet Haldeman-Julius in Girard, Kansas. Emanuel Julius and Marcet Haldeman (they combined and hyphenated their surnames after marriage) published a weekly socialist newspaper, the *Appeal to Reason*, which Finger read as early as 1897.[55] The son of an immigrant Jewish bookbinder in New York, Emanuel had launched a series of pocket-sized booklets on a wide range of popular and academic topics in 1919. Eventually known as Little Blue Books, many contained highly condensed versions of literary classics, sometimes with introductions that the Haldeman-Juliuses commissioned from writers such as Finger. Like the British series J. M. Dent's Everyman's Library, of which Finger owned many volumes, Emanuel's series took advantage of works in the public domain. He had published 239 titles by 1922 and planned 50 more.[56] Emanuel and Carl Sandburg had worked together, and a few months after Sandburg's stop in Fayetteville, Finger and the Haldeman-Juliuses began visiting each other.[57]

Finger, it seems, was starstruck. "It was the jolliest of little suppers that three of us had last week," he reported in *All's Well* after a trip to the couple's home, "in the bright little dining room that looks out on the children's garden." Marcet invited Finger to play her piano, and the couple's daughters performed an impromptu dance. Like his vision for Gayeta, the Haldeman-Julius place was a working farm as well as a gathering place for artists and intellectuals. Like Finger, Emanuel was self-educated and collected books, and he and Marcet were freethinkers on the subject of marriage. Unlike Nellie, however, Marcet had an income from a family-owned bank that supported the property, a large house, and several farm workers, and she was a sophisticated, educated woman. A niece of the social reformer Jane Addams, she attended Bryn Mawr College and worked as an actress before returning to Girard to help run the bank. Marcet collaborated with her husband in writing fiction; their novel *Dust*, a provocative story of a married couple on a Kansas farm, was popular and received some critical acclaim.[58]

Emanuel showed Finger some of the rare books in his library, and Finger told him about some that he owned. The men shared an interest in Oscar Wilde and the translations by Sir Richard Burton. In fact, Emanuel made *The Ballad of Reading Gaol* and *The Rubaiyat of Omar Khayyam* the first two booklets in his series, calling Wilde's work *Ballad of Reading Jail* for the benefit of unsophisticated readers. He invited Finger to write Little Blue Books and accepted at least three by April 1922. He also promoted Finger and *All's Well* in the *Appeal* and paid him to write freelance articles for this and another periodical that he launched, *Life and Letters*. One of the early booklets by Finger, *Lost Civilizations*, quickly became a bestseller. Eager to publish more such "high-brow stuff" because his market, "common people," seemed to "hunger" for it, Emanuel made visits to Gayeta in June 1922 and March 1923.

The first trip may have been an impromptu getaway; around the same time, Marcet told a friend her husband had slipped "away to the Ozarks for a few days" to finish drafting one of the short stories they wrote together. On the second visit, when Finger had a new manuscript, "Oscar Wilde in Outline," ready for him, Emanuel brought John Gunn, an editor and frequent writer of Little Blue Books. Gunn wrote a detailed account for an issue of *Life and Letters* devoted to Finger, calling Sheehan part of "the Finger ménage" who occupied "bachelor quarters" and came down the hill to add "his gay presence" at the "evening fireside" and family read-aloud sessions.[59]

On Finger's second visit to Girard, in the summer of 1922, he found the Haldeman-Juliuses sitting on the lawn with Upton Sinclair, who was a contributor to the *Appeal* and the booklet series.[60] In a report in *All's Well* that the *Appeal* and *Bookman* both reproduced, Finger was fulsome with praise for his new friends: "E. H.-J." was "one far higher than his fellows"; Mrs. Haldeman-Julius was "the soul of generous hospitality."[61] Finger liked working with Emanuel, who paid him reasonably well in spite of his sloppy manuscripts, and wrote at least thirty-seven Little Blue Books between 1922 and 1925. His projects fell into three broad categories: writers and adventurers, the arts and humanities, and gay or possibly gay literary figures, including a second number about Oscar Wilde. (Sheehan wrote six booklets during the same period, gathering material for some of them on a trip to Europe in 1922.) Emanuel thought Finger was a phony but liked him anyway. "If a man's to be a stuffed shirt," he thought, "then let him put in plenty of stuffing and do a good job."[62] The Haldeman-Juliuses were crucial and generous sponsors at a critical time in Finger's emergence as a writer with serious ambition, so his eventual betrayal of them revealed much about the compromises he made to continue supporting his family.

[7]

CAMERADOS!

IN A DEVELOPMENT that profoundly changed the course of Finger's writing career, Carl Sandburg delivered on his promise to help by recommending Finger to a new editor in New York. May Massee had just become the first head of children's books at the publishing firm Doubleday, Page, and Company. As a children's librarian for twenty years and editor of the American Library Association's newsletter *Booklist*, she had been a passionate, persuasive advocate for excellent children's literature, becoming one of the publishing world's most influential critics. Doubleday, Page recruited her in 1922 to create the second children's books department in the US. Massee wanted to find new authors and illustrators who would create beautiful books to expose children to cultures around the world as a means of promoting lasting peace. She was friends with Sandburg and his wife and helped Sandburg submit stories to children's magazines, so she asked him for advice.[1] He recommended Finger and lent her his copy of Finger's Little Blue Book *Lost Civilizations* as a sample of his work.

She wrote to Finger on December 19, 1922, drafting the letter in pencil on two sheets of plain notepaper, crossing out a few words as she changed her mind about phrasing. She agreed with Sandburg that Finger could write "a book of folk lore and legends of South America that would compare with W. H. Hudson's work." Was this a project he would consider? Finger responded immediately, scrawling his answer in ink across two sheets of *All's Well* notepaper. "My dear May Massee . . . it was so good to get that letter . . . and mention of that golden heart, Carl Sandburg, made it seem as though we were face to face." Yes, he replied, "let me write a book on South American folk lore and legends . . . I'm willing and anxious to roll up my sleeves and go to work any moment."[2] From then until September 1923, he worked steadily on the project for Massee as well as another book project, more magazine pieces, *All's Well*, and the constant farm work. Then, taking a short break, he met George Maddox for a clandestine road trip.

"We left St. Louis," where Maddox was stationed at Jefferson Barracks, Finger told his *All's Well* readers, "my companion and I," glossing over Maddox's identity as he always would. They spent two nights in a "shabby hotel" in Missouri, and in case anyone found this strange, Finger explained that a car breakdown forced them to stop. In an amusing deception that Finger delighted in sharing, the two men signed the hotel register as Charles Dickens and William M. Thackeray. For Maddox, who received the Distinguished Service Medal in 1922 and accepted a voluntary reduction in rank to major, evidently as part of a force reduction or reorganization, discretion was vitally important—his closest friends rarely mentioned him in writing except by the nicknames "Major" or "Sep."[3] When he began his career, the army and navy tended to overlook homosexuality in officers who did not attract attention, but after the war that changed. Gay officers were reasonably safe from dishonorable discharge or prosecution only if they maintained the appearance of being straight.[4]

Alone in their hotel room, C. J. and Major probably enjoyed a few drinks and a smoke as they chatted about books and writers. Maddox loved good whiskey and good cigars—a friend observed that he "prides himself on being a good judge of cigars"—and one could easily find a bottle in Gasconade County even though Prohibition was in effect.[5] Finger relished talking about literature "with congenial souls."[6] He had published a poem by Charles Erskine Scott (C. E. S.) Wood, "My Comrade," in the most recent issue of *All's Well*. "Do you not sense from sky and air," the poem asked, "that you and I were always one?"[7] He liked the emotion in Wood's work. *The Blind Bow-Boy*, a confection of innuendo by the almost-openly gay writer Carl Van Vechten, was out. Finger thought Van Vechten was "always amusing and interesting with his odd people and strange places and moving events."[8] Maddox cared about the progress of Finger's career, so Finger no doubt told him that his first original book was in press at R. M. McBride and Company in New York.[9] *Highwaymen: A Book of Gallant Rogues* was a set of stories about daring or heroic figures, some historic, some fictional, with details from Finger's cross-country treks in England and his adventures in Tierra del Fuego. The publisher had commissioned a Detroit artist, Paul Honoré, to illustrate the book.[10] Finger also had sold two more magazine pieces to the *Century*, one a caustic view of the Ozarks that Glenn Frank commissioned shortly after the *Nation* published its own article about Arkansas. The other was a short story, "Where the Foam Flies," which took its title from the poem "Down on the Shore" by the late Irish poet William Allingham. Its hero is a horse thief who saves an officer and crew during a shipwreck; the scene of rowing a boat for miles across a choppy sea was probably drawn from Finger's memory of rowing from and back to Elizabeth Island to help the desperately ill MacLean family. Honoré was going to illustrate this story too.[11] Finger and Maddox's getaway was soon over, but they carried on their conversation, in person when possible and in letters, for the next seventeen years, until a few weeks before Finger's death.[12] This friendship, although they hid it behind a curtain of nicknames and cryptic references, inspired a desire even greater than Finger's lifelong ache for a circle of simpatico friends, turning his dreams of comradeship into hope for a new life with Maddox and ultimately breaking his heart.

He went to New York, the epicenter of publishing, literature, and the arts,[13] the next month to help an old friend from his railroad days. Henry Haigh, the president of the CG&P Railroad, had a son, Andrew Comstock Haigh, who was to have his New York musical debut on October 24. This was an opportunity for Finger to draw a circle of important figures in publishing around him. He urged *All's Well* readers in New York to attend the young pianist's concert, mailed tickets to contacts in the city, and attended the concert himself, probably while staying with his sister and brother-in-law, the Bergmans. Maxwell Aley, formerly the fiction editor for the *Century* and now the fiction editor for the *Woman's Home Companion*, evidently attended with his wife.[14] So did Aley's successor at the *Century*, Carl Van Doren, who was a professor of literature at Columbia University,[15] and Leslie Nelson Jennings, a contributor to *All's Well* whose poem "Stranger" Van Doren had just published on the page preceding Finger's story "Where the Foam Flies."[16] Guy Holt, Finger's editor at R. M. McBride, brought another McBride author, Robert Nathan, with him.[17] Massee was there. She was a charming woman who looked one straight in the eye, comfortable mingling with writers, publishers, and booksellers as well as librarians.[18] Finger's frequent correspondents Michael Monahan and Bolton Hall showed up.[19]

Robert Bergman brought the set designer Robert Edmond Jones with him. While Finger's sister Alice had taken classes in the law school at New York University and become a secretary to Judge Learned Hand of the US District Court (using the name "Helen Bergman" professionally), Berg had become a well-known and influential theatrical set painter. He had a studio at 142 West 39th Street, where he supervised a staff that mixed colors and painted scenic backdrops according to sketches by set designers, sometimes sloshing water on the finished works to create the "Bergman bath" effect. Jones worked in a small room on the fourth floor of Bergman's studio, and Norman Bel Geddes, Lee Simonson, and other designers frequently dropped in. Bel Geddes later observed Bergman's shop was "to designers and painters of New York what the Algonquin was to the writers."[20]

Theodore Dreiser not only attended the recital, even though he was deep into writing *An American Tragedy* and did not like to be interrupted, he received Finger at his apartment near Washington Square in Greenwich Village. Dreiser was grateful for Finger's help two years earlier in promoting his eccentric friend John M. Maxwell. A former newspaper editor, Maxwell had written a book arguing that Sir Robert Cecil or George Somers wrote the plays attributed to William Shakespeare. Finger published two articles by Maxwell in *All's Well* and a lengthy, favorable piece about Maxwell's manuscript that attracted attention in the *Indianapolis Star*. This support had cost Finger some credibility: Mencken goaded him—"Lately, poisoned by the bad water of the region, Mr. Finger has been giving space to an Indiana genius, sponsored by Dreiser, who has amassed proofs that Shakespeare was neither Bacon nor the Stratford butcher's son." A Shakespeare scholar at Columbia University, Brander Matthews, declined to contribute articles to *All's Well*, writing cuttingly to Finger, "I cannot . . . gather with the freaks and cranks who are burdening you with their outpourings."[21] Thus, Dreiser was in Finger's debt. He even paid a visit to Gayeta the next summer, after he began corresponding with a college student in Fayetteville, nineteen-year-old Esther McCoy.[22]

And then there was the illustrator Paul Honoré. Eighteen years younger than Finger, tall with thick and wavy dark hair, "deep-chested,"[23] Honoré seemed to fill any room he entered and was quite comfortable at a classical music performance. In fact, his father-in-law, Francis York, was president of the Detroit Conservatory of Music and had helped judge a competition the year before in which Andrew Haigh received two first prizes.[24] Thanks to a twinkly-eyed charm and York's connections, Honoré was very popular with the wealthy set in Detroit.[25] He was a productive painter, printmaker, and muralist with a London past, having studied there as an apprentice to the great Belgian-British artist Frank Brangwyn.[26] Finger thought Honoré was "an active, imaginative fellow with a quick eye" who looked "more like a sturdy lake-sailor than an artist," "red cheeked and healthy, direct and uncompromising."[27]

He took Honoré with him to meet the publisher Mitchell Kennerley, a close friend of Reedy's who had agreed in January to publish an anthology of Finger's serious short fiction from *Reedy's Mirror*, the *Century*, the *Double Dealer*, and the *Smart Set*. Publication of *In Lawless Lands* had been delayed, and Kennerley was known to back out of financial arrangements with writers—he once caused Reedy intense embarrassment by borrowing $30,000 from a book collector in St. Louis after Reedy introduced the two— so Finger was anxious about the project.[28] The publisher showed him and Honoré the galleys and book jacket and promised the book would be ready in a week. "Life will be desolatingly [*sic*] empty to me until this book appears," Finger wrote after he returned to Gayeta. "My heart's much set upon it."[29]

McBride released *Highwaymen* in December, the same month that Finger finished the manuscript for Massee. He was very pleased with Honoré's illustrations, although if he saw the review of *Highwaymen* in the *Detroit Free Press*, it must have stung. Honoré's woodblocks, the newspaper said, "will undoubtedly be the raison d'etre for many purchases of the book." More pleasantly, *Highwaymen* received immediate support from the *Brooklyn Daily Eagle*, which listed the book in its Christmas recommendations.[30] Kennerley finally released *In Lawless Lands* in March 1924; it was one of only four books that he published that year. Soon, newly frustrated by Kennerley's failure to advertise the book, Finger disseminated publicity material himself using Margaret Germann's byline, emphasizing his wanderlust. A reviewer in Rochester, New York, compared Finger to Conrad and recommended *In Lawless Lands* as "grave and gay."[31]

FINGER'S NEXT TRIP to New York was with Maddox in April 1924, and it filled him with joy and the hope that they would someday share a life of adventure and literary fellowship with no need for secrecy. Maddox had been reassigned from Jefferson Barracks to Fort Jay, the army's Eastern Branch Disciplinary Barracks on Governors Island in New York Harbor, and invited Finger to accompany him on his drive across the country. They carefully planned their trip to disguise its romantic nature, Finger presenting it to *All's Well* readers, and probably to Nellie and the children, as a spontaneous idea and identifying Maddox only as "my friend, a man *erect* and brown, clear eyed and *active*, a fellow of gentlemanly good sense [emphasis added]."[32] He was learning to hide not only the nature of his relationship with Maddox but its very existence, once writing of him as "one who has become a friend—one of those who grow to be a part of the woof and web of a man's life. He is an army officer and his name does not matter" and, in a witty layer cake of queer allusions, as "the man who plays Amis to my Amiel." Edward Carpenter had excerpted William Morris's translation of a French legend of devoted friends, Amis and *Amile*, in *Ioläus*. Finger's misspelling of "Amile" seems to have been not a typing error but a reference—what Hurley might call "a conscious, if slanted, repackaging of intertextuality"—to the Swiss diarist Henri-Fréderic Amiel (1821–1881), who suffered from unfulfilled homosexual longings. He had read a 1922 translation of Amiel around the time he made the Missouri road trip with Maddox. This little joke was additionally daring because another new book, *The Doctor Looks at Literature* (1923), mentioned Amiel's ambivalent sexuality.[33]

Maddox drove to Gayeta to pick up Finger, meeting the family, Murray Sheehan, and Bill Baerg. On the way to New York, he and Finger stopped to see Dreiser's friend Maxwell in Indianapolis; Claude Meeker, Finger's friend from railroad days in Columbus, Ohio; and Meredith Janvier, a rare book dealer and friend of Mencken's in Baltimore.[34] At Fort Jay Finger stayed in guest quarters, working on a series of historical articles during the day and reading drafts aloud to Maddox and other "army officers, theatrical people and literary folk" at night. In such a tizzy over this whole experience that he called the base by the wrong name, "Fort Sill," Finger wrote in *All's Well* that he "got into red-ripe relations with men of many activities, relations personal to the core with reflective men, men of large interests and men in authority."

One of those men was Maddox's friend Henry McAuley Bankhead, whom close friends called Jack. Bankhead was the third son in a powerful political and coal-mining dynasty in Alabama. His father was US Senator John Hollis Bankhead Sr., and his brothers had followed their father into politics: John Jr. in the Alabama legislature and William Brockman Bankhead in the US House of Representatives. Henry enjoyed some early fame in Alabama as the captain of the university football team, but after joining the army, he rarely returned. As Maddox observed, "Henry Bankhead left Jasper [Alabama] for the Spanish American War . . . and has scarcely been back there since."[35] Their friendship began in the Philippines, where their postings under General Charles Bailey overlapped. Once Bailey received command of the 81st Division in France, he had Bankhead and Maddox assigned to his unit.[36] Bankhead's final military appointment was at Fort Jay as education and recreation officer. He retired as a lieutenant colonel in 1922 and moved with his wife, Alice Stickney Bankhead, and their adult children to an apartment in New York.[37] Finger had not met someone in this stratum of transatlantic society before. No matter the topic, the Bankheads could go one better. Finger was born in London? Bankhead had attended more than one royal event, and his niece Tallulah was a wildly popular (and risqué) actress in London. When Alice traveled with her late adopted father, US Consul-General John G. Long, she met Lord Frederick Roberts, the commander-in-chief of the British Forces, and Lord Horatio Kitchener, England's secretary of state for war.[38]

While he was at Fort Jay, Finger also saw Carl and Irita Van Doren. He had something deeply personal in common with Carl, whose father had been president of a small interurban railroad that went bankrupt in Illinois. "People put money into [the railroad] because he asked them to," Van Doren recalled. "Thoughts of these people [robbed] him of much sleep."[39] Van Doren perceived Finger quite clearly, saluting him in a private note as "an honest man" yet observing "the line between fiction and fact" was one "Mr. Finger does not take too seriously." He recognized that Finger's stories took place on "those margins of life which are outside the established order" and "what interests him above all things is courage, the insolence with which a robber, a *lover*, or a traveler *challenges the customs which would tie him down* [emphasis added]."[40]

Van Doren's mentor at the University of Illinois, Stuart P. Sherman, had just become head of the book review section for the *New York Herald Tribune* and hired Irita as an assistant editor. She was warm and friendly and flattered reviewers with the idea that they were experts on their favorite topics. She invited Finger to write reviews, and he saluted her in *All's Well* as "one of the most delightful women in the world, charming even in a dusty office walled with books, a woman thoughtful, cultured and intellectual."[41] Irita and her new colleagues became crucial supporters of Finger, publishing nearly two hundred of his reviews, an average of twelve each year, of nonfiction and fiction about exploration, pirates, and colorful criminals.[42] The reviews were an important source of freelance income—at times Gayeta's bread and butter—and an important medium for communicating through sly jokes with book-loving queer friends around the country. For example, Finger remarked in one that he had an "encyclopaedic . . . knowledge of queer folk who did strange things" and "a minute familiarity with strong-minded gentlemen who were determined to march out of step." Calamity Jane, he observed, was "one of those queer characters" who exhibited "a gay wantonness."[43]

During this visit Finger also attended a party at the Hotel Brevoort, probably at the Van Dorens' invitation and probably with Maddox. The gathering was an informal get-together with the novelist May Sinclair, who had just arrived to represent England at the second annual international meeting of the PEN Club. Finger met Sinclair, Edna Ferber—whose novel *So Big* recently appeared along with Finger's *Highwaymen* on a newspaper's list of favorite new books—and Mary Austin, an essayist who knew Finger's *All's Well* contributor George Sterling and the late Jack London. Someone invited Finger to say a few words about his current projects. He reveled in the Brevoort gathering for months.[44]

Finger and Maddox saw the editor Michael Monahan who "was in fine feather, talking from the bottom of his heart what he felt and believed about literature." Monahan wrote to Finger afterward, addressing him as "my dear Berserk," a variation of the Icelandic word *berserker* for Norse warrior, and recalling how Finger smoked "vigorously[,] now and then turning upon me the glance of those great eyes which seem at times to reflect the strange landscapes they have seen." Finger reproduced this note in *All's Well*, and two months later, Carl Van Doren repeated the joke, entitling his review of Finger's new books "Baresark in Arkansas." His sister-in-law Dorothy Graffe Van Doren also reviewed *Highwaymen* favorably in a literary and political journal, the *Forum*.[45]

One evening in New York, Finger and Maddox noodled around on piano and guitar, possibly at the Bankheads' apartment. Another night, they strolled to the Cloisters on Washington Avenue for a concert. They went to East Orange, New Jersey, to meet Wilbur Macey Stone, apparently taking Bankhead along. Stone had been one of Reedy's correspondents. Five years older than Finger and married with two adult children, he was a bibliophile and a collector and designer of bookplates with a fondness for images of Pan.[46]

Finger's view of life changed during this leisurely interlude with Maddox. In a transparent paean to the pleasures of encountering other gay men on the road, he wrote of "the brawny young men in the repair shops dressed in easy costumes, their attitudes and curved limbs and significant smiles." Having mingled in New York with friends and new acquaintances who did not look askance at his relationship with Maddox, Finger rejoiced. "Camerados!" he exclaimed in *All's Well*—as Whitman did in "So Long!"—"The city is greatest that hampers none, permitting all." He used the image of stepping along a cliff as an analogy for entering a homosexual relationship—"Brave, his skirting of precipices, the leaping down dangerous declines"— seeming to reflect Bayard Taylor's *Joseph and His Friend*, in which Joseph considers killing himself by leaping from a cliff. Alluding to Whitman's poem "One's-Self I Sing," Finger proclaimed, "I sing the automobile and its joys . . . I sing the song of strength and speed! O the swift and powerful machine, full of perils, full of joys [and] the loud crack of an exploding tire and the fierce joy of it." In a final orgasmic exclamation, he wrote of Maddox and to him: "O the joy of the man at the wheel! The loud tooting of horns! . . . The fresh speeding faster than ever[;] the strong, terrible game! . . . The splendid collision, the splinterings, roarings, flames, shattered machinery, accusations, fierce threatenings, weightier battles in courts of law. I sing the automobile and its joys!"[47]

Within three months of this trip, Carl Van Doren published Finger's short story "Adventures of Andrew Lang" in the *Century*.[48] The story's title was a tribute to a Scottish writer who edited an edition of *Arabian Nights* and was an important supporter of R. L. Stevenson. Finger owned copies of Lang's *How to Fail in Literature: A Lecture* and *Books and Bookmen*. Naming his story's villain Andrew Lang was a coy reference to human duality, which was one of Stevenson's themes, and perhaps a wink to readers who thought the real Lang was gay. "Adventures" is set in Punta Arenas. Lang provokes a knife fight between two gauchos drinking at a boliche—Finger, of course, had managed just such a grogshop—and both men are mortally wounded. The death scene contains an element of an acclaimed but controversial work by Stevenson, whose style Finger had recently recommended. One man's "shirt suddenly became bright red, a rapidly spreading stain that fell in a broad streak over his thigh and down his leg." This image of blood "rapidly spreading" resembles one in Stevenson's story "The Beach of Falesá" that the literary scholar Oliver S. Buckton likens to "an orgasmic moment" in which one man punches another so that "blood spread upon his face like wine upon a napkin" and then stabs him so that his victim's blood "came over [the attacker's] hands . . . hot as tea." Finger's story was impressive enough that Edward O'Brien included it in his next anthology.[49]

DOUBLEDAY, PAGE RELEASED the project for Massee, *Tales from Silver Lands*, in October 1924 to immediate praise. Sherman's review editor for children's literature, Anne Carroll Moore, devoted her entire weekly page in the *Herald Tribune* to *it*, comparing Finger to W. H. Hudson and praising the illustrations by Honoré. The centerpiece of the page was a lengthy review by a Chicago critic, one of Sandburg's friends, who humorously called Finger "a self-effacing troubadour, never diverting the interest of the reader from his story to himself."[50] Finger was hugely pleased by the attention that Honoré brought to his work and dedicated the October issue of *All's Well* to him.[51] McBride released Finger's third book of stories, *Bushrangers*, also with illustrations by Honoré, in time for holiday sales. This book's title evoked the Jack Harkaway series Finger enjoyed as a child in London. It included "Adventures of Andrew Lang," and Carl Van Doren obligingly promoted the book in the *Century*. The *Bookman* compared Finger to Stevenson: "We like his tales about as well as anything we have seen since the golden days of 'Treasure Island.'" Again, Honoré's work was an essential part of Finger's success. The *St. Louis Post-Dispatch* ran a large image of one of his illustrations with a caption noting it was "from 'Bushrangers,' the text by Charles J. Finger, the illustrations from woodblock prints by Paul Honoré."[52]

Finger left Gayeta in December 1924 to see Honoré and editors and writers in Detroit and Chicago. He and Honoré were collaborating on a lucrative, freelance series for the *Dearborn Independent*, a weekly general interest magazine owned by the car manufacturer Henry Ford. Ford used the *Independent* to promote his cars and his nostalgic views of society and culture. Because his editors focused on wholesome fiction and nonfiction by English and American authors, Finger was an appealing potential contributor, but his association with Honoré, one of Detroit's best-known artists, had helped him win the assignment.[53] Finger met with the *Independent* editors and visited Honoré at his studio, a salon of sorts where artists, writers, and other guests dropped by late each afternoon to sit before a large fireplace and talk over coffee. An apprentice later said watching Honoré "sketch and execute a mural . . . was like living with the impressionists on the Left Bank of Paris."[54] Honoré showed Finger his plans for some murals, and they talked about the artist Brangwyn, whose muscular men and use of chiaroscuro were obvious influences.[55] "We get along very well, Honoré and I," Finger thought.

In Chicago Finger visited the office of the *Chicago Daily News* to call on Harry Hansen, the critic who reviewed *Silver Lands* for the *Herald Tribune*. A friend of Sandburg's, Hansen listened respectfully to Finger's opining. Finger may have suggested that Hansen take a turn with Little Blue Books; the next year, Hansen wrote a pamphlet about Sandburg for the series. He later linked Finger to Sherwood Anderson, Willa Cather, Ring Lardner, and others in a new generation of short-story writers, praising his fiction for its "dramatic intensity."[56]

While he was in Chicago, Finger had dinner with Sandburg—now a film reviewer for the *Daily News*—perhaps at Schlogl's, a restaurant near the newspaper office where Sandburg and Hansen often ate. Sandburg took seriously the responsibility of supporting his family and had continued to work for the *News* following the success of his early books, spending three days a week seeing and reviewing new movies and devoting the rest of his time to the massive biography of Abraham Lincoln that he was writing. Finger wrote that they talked for two hours, "discussing things with tremendous zest." Perhaps Sandburg shared with Finger his conclusion that Lincoln had a "lavender" nature because of his long friendship with another man, someone else with "a streak of lavender," before either man married.[57] The obligations of marriage were on Finger's mind—reviewing a memoir the month before, he commented that the author had "a certain moral insensibility" because he left "his wife in greatest poverty." He was struck that Sandburg was "rare as a modern in that he did not get divorced when he won fame."[58] His wife, Lilian Steichen Sandburg (whom he called Paula), the sister of the painter and photographer Edward Steichen and a committed leftist, was dedicated to creating a home where Carl could make writing the focus of his life. She read his manuscripts and gave him helpful advice; their marriage was a passionate romance.[59] In this, as in so many things, Nellie Finger compared poorly. She was not collaborative like Lilian Sandburg or a professional partner like Helen Hallock, the woman Maddox was about to marry.

Sketch of Charles J. Peer by Charles J. Finger
(Special Collections, University of Arkansas Libraries, Fayetteville).

The Old Woolpack Inn (1908), lithograph from a sketch made in 1889 by Henry Somerfield (Courtesy of the New Art Gallery, Walsall, England).

Charles J. Finger (left) and others on a small boat in the Strait of Magellan (Special Collections, University of Arkansas Libraries, Fayetteville).

Charles J. Finger, possibly on an ornithological expedition on Tierra del Fuego, c. 1893 (Special Collections, University of Arkansas Libraries, Fayetteville).

Interior of Arc Light Saloon by M. C. Ragsdale
(Courtesy of Fort Concho [Texas] National Historic Landmark).

Eleanor Barbara Ferguson
(Special Collections,
University of Arkansas
Libraries).

Ferdinand Haberkorn, George Ferguson, and Charles J. Finger in San Angelo,
c. 1901 (Special Collections, University of Arkansas Libraries, Fayetteville).

Herbert S. Bigelow
(Ohio History Connection).

Robert Hobart Davis
(Special Collections,
University of Arkansas
Libraries, Fayetteville).

Portrait of Charles J. Finger by Robert Hobart Davis, c. 1922
(Manuscripts and Archives Division, New York Public Library).

Portrait of George W. Maddox by Robert Hobart Davis (Manuscripts and Archives Division, New York Public Library).

Charles J. Finger reading to family and friends in the Gayeta library with Nellie Finger and William J. Baerg on the right and Murray Sheehan with torn sleeve. Photograph by William J. Baerg, 1924 (Special Collections, University of Arkansas Libraries, Fayetteville).

May Massee
(Courtesy of Special
Collections and Archives,
Emporia [Kansas] State
University).

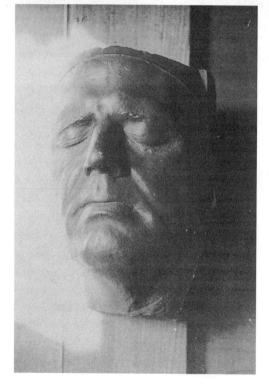

Photograph of death mask
of Jack London (Special
Collections, University
of Arkansas Libraries,
Fayetteville).

(*Above*) Paul Honoré with an art
student in Detroit, 1937 (Courtesy
of the *Detroit News*).

(*Right*) Portrait of Helen Finger
by Robert Hobart Davis, c. 1936
(Special Collections, University of
Arkansas Libraries, Fayetteville).

[8]

PERFECT BONHOMIE

MADDOX GOT MARRIED in January 1925, just before a new commanding officer arrived at Fort Jay. Speculation had spread in the fall that Maj. Gen. Charles Pelot Summerall was to become commander of the Second Corps Area of the army and be stationed at Fort Jay. Maddox worked for Summerall in Kentucky, carrying out his orders during the occupation of Lexington in 1920, and knew that Summerall took an extremely close interest in the romantic lives of his officers, wanting them to meet "nice girls." Summerall also tended to engage in feuds with senior officers and was unforgiving of what he called "neurosis."[1] Maddox's friend Henry Bankhead probably thought it was a good idea for him to acquire a wife before Summerall arrived. Bankhead's own marriage had been a strategic alliance; when he married Alice Stickney, whom his family had known for years, in a small private ceremony in 1903, she was in a delicate situation—without any means of support following the sudden death of her adoptive father but anticipating a sizable bequest once his estate was settled, and possibly with a newborn child.[2] The general's appointment became official in December, and George Maddox and Helen Luana Caldwell Coyle Hallock were married in New York three days before Summerall formally took command at Fort Jay.[3]

As with so much about Maddox's personal life, how he met Hallock is a mystery, but it could have been when he accompanied Summerall to Chicago in 1920. Summerall went there twice that year, and both trips involved social events where Hallock could have been a guest.[4] Perhaps she and Maddox began a friendly correspondence. Her principal skill, learned from her mother, Martha Beach Caldwell Warden Wright of Battle Creek, Michigan, was to locate prospective husbands by entertaining wealthy acquaintances and military officers.[5] She knew the protocol and was adept in the kind of social situations Summerall enjoyed.[6] Her first husband was a navy man, Irwin Dunn Coyle. Their daughter, Ann Coyle, was born in Shanghai in 1913, and Helen sent her to live with Martha in Battle Creek. Helen returned to Battle Creek in 1916 and, with her mother and sister, opened a restaurant that catered to military officers at Camp Custer.[7]

Next, Helen got a job with the American Red Cross Motor Corps helping to care for influenza patients at Camp Custer.[8] When her mother took a job at the Battle Creek Country Club, Helen became an assistant hostess.[9] After meeting a Chicago banker named Neil C. Hallock, Helen won a divorce from Coyle, giving custody of Ann to Martha, and married Hallock the following day. She returned to court twice to fight her ex-husband over child support payments; their conflict was a topic in newspapers around the country. The Michigan Supreme Court ultimately approved a shared custody arrangement that gave Helen responsibility for Ann ten months out of each year. She and Neil separated in October 1924, the same month that rumors spread of Summerall's appointment to Fort Jay, and were divorced within three months.[10]

Knowing the risks for gay men in the military, having himself married a woman in distress, with no choice in the matter, Finger understood Maddox's decision to marry. He sent a copy of *Highwaymen* to Helen, inscribing it with an epigram about the cruelty of laws: "What thousands, Law, thy handiwork deplore / Thou hangest many, but thou starvest more."[11] For her part Helen helped Maddox and Finger pull off their next rendezvous by accompanying her husband to Louisville in May to meet his good friends William Nettleton Cox and Josephine Cox. Finger joined them there. To justify leaving the farm during the busy spring season for the second year in a row, he had prevailed upon Claude Meeker and his daughter Marjorie Meeker Wing to line up two speeches in Columbus, Ohio. Again he characterized a trip with Maddox as a spontaneous idea and cast himself as a dutiful husband, father, and farmer who only temporarily left his post. For his inner circle of understanding readers, Finger added, "I find myself in a mood of delight. . . . If he had called on me to sail once more those leaping seas and to round those lean promontories where once I sailed, I would go." At Churchill Downs on May 16, he sat with the Maddoxes in the Coxes' private box. (Two years earlier, Maddox and Bankhead had attended the Derby with the Coxes.) The party moved on to the Coxes' imposing mansion and continued for several days, with the Coxes taking their guests to other parties. Then, as Helen proceeded to Arizona to visit her mother, Maddox and Finger

departed for Columbus and New York. "The two of us," Finger related in
All's Well the next month, "talking of world riddles, of books, of vanished
days and days to come, all of it that real pleasure which men who understand
one another may have when there is perfect bonhomie."[12]

As they drove, they brainstormed a story that became *The Spreading Stain:
A Tale for Boys and Men with Boys' Hearts*, Finger's first book-length fictional
work and the most fully realized product of his long romantic and creative
partnership with Maddox. The title repeated the vivid line in "Adventures
of Andrew Lang" and was such a compelling image for Finger that he also
used a variation of it in a letter in August, referring to arguably pornographic
scenes in works by Robert Burns as "sap rising in him so forcibly as to over-
flow and stain the bark."[13] The subtitle resembled the dedication "to all the
big and little boys who read" in *King Solomon's Mines* (1885) by H. Rider
Haggard, whose hypermasculine heroes and homosocial adventures were an
early influence on Finger. Haggard and the real Andrew Lang collaborated
on *The World's Desire* (1890), a fantasy novel based on Odysseus; now Finger
and Maddox were collaborating on *The Spreading Stain*.[14] The story they
concocted involved a blight, somehow created by an herbicide, that destroys
forests and fields, causing famine and mass migrations. The protagonist and
narrator is a youth named Joseph Graham, his first name the same as Finger's
middle name, his surname like the Socialist hero in Victorian London, R. B.
Cunninghame Graham. References to Finger's and Maddox's experiences
run through Joseph's story. The mansions that Finger saw in Louisville
inspired a setting where a survivor plays a grand piano. The military occupation of Lexington informed a martial law scene. A minor character, "Mr.
Honoré," lives in Detroit and performs some chemical analysis, fittingly
since the real Honoré was developing an experimental stucco material for
murals for Dow Chemical Company.[15]

"Mr. Maddox" is a leading, almost godlike, figure in the story. "You felt
he'd stand by you if you played the game square," Joseph says. "You felt strong
because you knew that he was strong." With a man like Mr. Maddox, a boy
who felt "hunger for art and music" could go on "enchanted wanderings,"
reflecting the Haggard–Lang version of Odysseus, in which the hero is "the
Wanderer." Like Eric in Finger's eponymous short story, who longed for "a
feller who'd understand," Joseph "knew [Mr. Maddox] would understand
your mistakes." The narrator mentions a teacher, Mr. Massey, a nod to May
Massee. In a twist at the end that reflects Ambrose Bierce's "Occurrence at
Owl Creek," a story Finger said "clung to me," Joseph reveals that he used

Daniel Defoe's book *Journal of the Plague Year* as a model for this story because Defoe could "write in a style to make you believe that fiction was fact." The story has been a high school writing assignment, an experiment in narration, and, one could surmise, Finger's response to a challenge by Maddox. "Here's that boys' story we planned on that memorable ride," he wrote in a copy for Maddox after *Stain* was published.[16]

Honoré met Finger and Maddox in Columbus, probably to celebrate because the *Dearborn Independent* had finally begun publishing "Romantic Rascals," a series of illustrated historical adventure stories on which he collaborated with Finger. Finger gave his speeches to the Ohio State University Faculty Club and the Kit-Kat Club, a literary club named for an eighteenth-century gentleman's club in London. One of his talks was a diatribe against modernist literature that he developed for the Dearborn editors. His speech duties completed, the three went on to New York. As they crossed the Cumberland Mountains, "the sky grew overcast," Finger related later, so they stopped "to buy heavy woolen shirts." He paid for a shirt for himself and one for "the Major," who, as he described this incident further in a second column in *All's Well*, "came forth a big, well-shapen man in comfortable gray." Finger "took the first thing that offered and that it did not fit me I failed to realize until too late." The entirely boring subject of buying shirts led to his real point, that "at night I had to be skinned out of it."[17]

Once they reached New York, Honoré apparently returned to Detroit, but Finger lingered, seeing editors and friends and staying in guest quarters at the fort again or in the apartment the Maddoxes had taken on Charlton Street in Greenwich Village. A few weeks earlier, a critic for the *Nation* had singled out "Adventures of Andrew Lang" as one of the best in O'Brien's new anthology. Now Finger went with Carl and Irita Van Doren to the office of the *Nation*, where they had lunch with the editor, Oswald Garrison Villard, and several associate editors and writers. It was the kind of gathering Finger liked, "one of tolerance, openness, consideration." The *Nation* staff was a family, not just in Villard's sense of a congenial group but literally—Carl's brother, the poet Mark Van Doren, and Mark's wife, Dorothy Graffe, were two of the editors. Along with the two Van Doren couples, several of the city's boldly leftist thinkers were at lunch that day: Freda Kirchwey, an advocate for birth control for women who was so unconvinced that monogamy was feasible, despite being married, that she sponsored a forum on the question; Hugo Gellert, a young illustrator for an exciting new culture magazine called the *New Yorker*; and Joseph Wood Krutch, an editorial writer who was soon to go to his home state of Tennessee to cover the Scopes trial.[18]

The highlight of Finger's New York stay was an evening he and Maddox spent with Robert Hobart Davis and several of Davis's friends. The fiction editor for the Munsey group of magazines, later a columnist for the *New York Sun*, Davis was a friend of a great many fiction writers and poets of the day, a kind, fun-loving man who often took aspiring writers to lunch at the grill in the Fifth Avenue Hotel, advising them on plots and details much as Reedy did for Finger. He particularly sought stories that were "queer, outré, unusual, bizarre, exotic, [or] misfit" and worked closely with O. Henry, Edgar Rice Burroughs, and Joseph Conrad. He had published stories by Murray Sheehan's brother Perley in *All-Story* and collaborated with him on *We Are French!*[19] Also a prolific amateur photographer, Davis made many portraits of figures in the literary world, often photographing them in his office at 280 Broadway.

He had a large circle of friends, most of them other men who were writers and unmarried or, like Davis, married with supportive wives. For example, his friend Oscar Odd McIntyre ("Odd" was his actual middle name) was a popular syndicated columnist with a fondness for bright-colored silk pajama sets, a wife named Maybelle, and a close companion—Texan William Clifford Hogg. As another of McIntyre's friends put it, the couple and Hogg had a "mutual understanding." McIntyre and Hogg often joined Davis and his friend Irvin S. Cobb, a writer, for breakfasts that lasted until dark. Columnist Herbert Corey commented that Davis and Cobb were "chatty boys to have around."[20]

Finger wrote vaguely that he first met Davis at "the house of a friend." This could have been William Griffith, the editor of *Current Opinion*, who was another friend of the late O. Henry.[21] However, considering that Finger discreetly avoided naming their mutual friend, that person probably was George, who could have met Davis after returning to the US from France in 1919. Davis photographed Finger and Maddox, and Finger had proudly published one of his portraits in the October–November 1922 issue of *All's Well*. Davis included two pictures of Finger, along with portraits of Mencken, Dreiser, and D. H. Lawrence, in a spread in the *Bookman* in 1929 and used one in a 1932 book, *Man Makes His Own Mask*.[22]

The dinner party was like a glittering, grown-up version of the book club at the Poly, a perfect realization of the salon life Finger was trying to create at Gayeta. "It was one of those happy-go-lucky, man-conducted functions," Finger wrote, "with the guests doing the cooking and the preparing and the table-setting, all in high good-humor." Davis cooked steaks, and it was "a joy to watch him at the stove." Griffith was at the party. *Current Opinion* had just ceased publication, absorbed by the *Literary Digest*, and Griffith seemed "a little cynical [but] ninety per cent optimist." Ernest Boyd, an Irish critic, writer, and translator who served in the British consular service, apparently was another guest; Finger called him a "conversationalist, full of delicate tact, who seems to have read everything and remembered what he read." Davis's friends Cobb and Stuart Olivier, a wealthy Baltimore executive and playwright, also were present, so this probably was a gathering of the New Face Club, an informal, secretive group that Maddox, Davis, Cobb, and Olivier invented during an earlier gathering at Maddox's apartment. Its jokey mission was to throw an annual, intimate fete in honor of a "congenial male who had served to lift the intellectual standards and advance . . . human resources." Maddox provided the meeting place, Davis the meal, Cobb the cigars and tobacco, and Olivier the drinks. A few weeks after this dinner party, Davis wrote to Finger to praise his "sublime power" as a writer, casually mentioning that he had seen Maddox since the dinner.[23] The ties of friendship and romance between Finger, Maddox, Davis, and other men in their circle—connections that Maddox in particular was careful to disguise—became the most important relationships of Finger's life.

From New York Finger went to Detroit for dinner with Honoré and two executives with the *Dearborn Independent*, managing editor Benjamin R. Donaldson and business manager Fred Black. They were expanding the magazine from sixteen to thirty-two pages, so there would be much more opportunity for the writer–artist team of Finger and Honoré. Back at Gayeta Finger began work on a series of articles about Magellan for the *Independent* and sent an early draft of the first to Maddox, who replied quickly, endorsing Finger's interpretation that Magellan was "not the first to see the straits, and certainly not the first world circumnavigator."[24] Then, on June 15, 1925, Finger received the news that he had been chosen as the next recipient of the Newbery Medal for *Tales from Silver Lands*. The honor, he confided in *All's Well*, "was breath taking, and I had to walk awhile to get used to it."[25]

[9]

SHARED SECRETS

FINGER'S RECEIPT OF THE Newbery Medal was part of a wide and rapid expansion of the field of children's literature that took place thanks largely to the leadership of two women, his editor May Massee at Doubleday, Page and Anne Carroll Moore, one of the assistant editors of the *New York Herald Tribune* book reviews. As the chief librarian for children at the New York Public Library, Moore helped persuade the ALA and the American Booksellers Association to cosponsor Children's Book Week in 1919. In 1922, the same year that Massee joined Doubleday, Page, the ALA launched the annual Newbery Medal award, naming it for an early British author and printer, John Newbery, and designating it for an American citizen or resident whose book, written for children fourteen years old or younger, was published in the previous year.[1]

Massee knew what librarians and teachers looked for in children's literature and had given Finger advice that his book reflects.[2] He used simple rhymes—"They sing and they play / For half of the day"—and other predictable elements—"There is the day after that and the next day and the next day"—so adults could entice children to recite the unfolding tales with them. He used his time in South America to establish himself as a credible storyteller and his role as a father as evidence he was a trustworthy writer for children. For example, in "Rairu and the Star Maiden," the narrator and his "friend Pedro of Brazil . . . were gold digging on the upper Santa Maria [when] there came without warning a fierce blizzard." "The Tale That Cost a Dollar" was the story "my daughters, Julia and Helen," liked the best.[3] Doubleday sent galleys of the book, with Paul Honoré's illustrations, to Moore soon after Stuart Sherman and Irita Van Doren took over book reviews at the *Herald Tribune*.[4] Moore was struck by traces of the late English writer W. H. Hudson, whom she deeply admired, in Finger's tales.[5] In the package of articles about *Silver Lands* that she ran in the *Herald Tribune* on October 26, she wrote that Finger's stories for children were transformed by "light, sun, wind and tropical rain."[6]

The ALA had chosen the first three Newbery winners on the basis of write-in votes from children's librarians around the country, but for the 1925 award, it established a committee-led selection process, and one of the committee members was a librarian who reported to Moore.[7] The committee considered three books: *Silver Lands*, *The Dream Coach* by Anne Parrish (Macmillan), and Anne Moore's own *Nicholas: A Manhattan Christmas Story* (Putnam).[8] Choosing Moore's book as the winner would have been unseemly; thus, Finger's good fortune was in part a consequence of diplomacy in the publishing world. The prize was a boost for Doubleday, Page as well as Finger, and the publishing house quickly invited him to write an introduction for the first volume in a planned collection of Joseph Conrad's works.[9]

Doubleday, Page also paid for Finger to go to Seattle in July 1925 for the Newbery Medal ceremony at the annual meeting of the ALA. Leaving Nellie at Gayeta as usual, he made the trip by train and checked into the brand-new Olympic Hotel. So many librarians crowded into Anderson Hall at the University of Washington for the Newbery presentation that the ceremony had to be moved outside. Finger thanked Massee and Carl Sandburg for their help, made some of his usual remarks about modernist literature and writing for children, and spun a fictional story about being "cast upon an uninhabited island." A librarian from Wisconsin found him captivating, admiring "his gray hair and bronzed face [that] show his years of outdoors and of adventuring which keep him young." "It was a wonderfully exciting affair," Finger thought.[10] Bob Davis, Stuart Olivier, and Henry Bankhead gathered at the Maddoxes' apartment in New York on the night of the awards ceremony to toast Finger's new success. As Maddox relayed in a telegram to Finger: "Bob Stuart and Jack with us last night. All send warm greetings and big handshake of congratulations." Finger embedded a message to Maddox in his next "Free Fantasia" column, mentioning a ballad he heard on the Seattle trip and adding, "If it does not please my friend Major Maddox I am no judge."[11]

––––––––

AFTER ACCEPTING THE AWARD, Finger went to San Francisco to meet George Sterling, an *All's Well* contributor and friend of Bill Reedy and Mencken, who was Finger's closest link to Jack London—the man he called his literary "blood brother." Sterling was an Easterner who considered the priesthood before migrating to San Francisco, where he clerked in an uncle's real estate office and was married until his wife killed herself in 1913. He had repeatedly urged Finger to move to San Francisco too, telling him, "You could do so much better, all ways, in California." He had promoted *All's Well* to James Cabell and contributed poems that were too long for Mencken's magazines to the journal. Finger had published at least twelve of Sterling's poems and dedicated the January 1925 issue to him.[12] He found the tall, beak-nosed poet in his home at the Bohemian Club, an exclusive residential hotel popular with artists.[13] Fifty-five years old and frequently depressed, Sterling had been hospitalized twice in recent months. He drank heavily most of the time but usually put on what an acquaintance called "the mask of play" when friends came to visit.[14]

Sterling was surprised at how old Finger appeared, telling Mencken, "Finger was with me for a day—an enjoyable chap. He's two years younger than I and looks ten older. Has had much responsibility, I suppose."[15] He took Finger to meet his friend Rosaliene Travis, a songwriter who had set several of Sterling's poems to music. She lived on Russian Hill in a large house with a wall of windows overlooking Golden Gate Bridge. London's daughter Joan, who gave occasional public lectures about her father and wanted a career as a writer, also was visiting.[16] Sterling apparently became annoyed at how much Travis drank. "Damn her!" Finger said Sterling exclaimed. "I took Mencken there for a pleasant evening and it was the same thing. Drunk! The rational thing to do 'd be to drown her in the bay."

They left Travis around midnight for Flowering Wall, another house on Russian Hill and the home of the poet C. E. S. Wood and his lover, Sara Bard Field. A venerated progressive, Wood was on the advisory board of the *Public* when Finger wrote book reviews for it. Finger already had a connection with Wood and Field; Reedy had dined with them a few nights before he died, and later Field contributed an account of that evening to *All's Well*. The couple was friendly and welcoming despite the late hour, and Finger and Sterling stayed for about two hours. Sterling posed, "his eyes bright and shining, his sensitive hand resting on the edge of the table," to read aloud a humorous poem that Mencken published three months later.[17] Wood and Field probably wondered why Finger was in San Francisco when the biggest story on Earth, the Scopes trial in Tennessee, was unfolding a few hundred miles from his home; their close friend Clarence Darrow was representing the high school biology teacher John Scopes and Mencken was covering the trial for the Baltimore *Evening Sun*. It was the sort of American absurdity that Wood reveled in mocking. He wrote a skit in which a delegation of apes calls on God to complain that humans are insulting their species by implying they are related. Finger unfortunately had little to offer on the subject. "I accept the philosophy of evolution [but] we are not at the apex of human knowledge," he observed slightly incoherently in the next issue of *All's Well*. Despite Finger's astonishing failure to see the importance of the Scopes trial, Wood stayed in contact with him, sending him a poem that he wrote by hand on hotel stationery in New York.[18]

Leaving Flowering Wall, Finger and Sterling resumed their meander through the San Francisco night as Sterling reminisced about his own first guide to the city's nightlife—Jack London. They had enjoyed talking about socialism and drinking to excess and even tried hashish together. London and his wife, Charmian, often had picnics with George and Carrie Sterling and other bohemian friends. Sterling became London's editor, encouraging a rhythmic, rhyming, expressive voice. He posed in the nude for London to photograph. London called him "the Greek," and Sterling called London "Wolf," the same endearment that Charmian used for him. Sterling inspired the character of Ross Brissenden in London's autobiographical novel *Martin Eden*. London evoked their parties in *The Valley of the Moon*. He even wrote an erotic poem, unpublished during his life, about Sterling as a god-like man who "ran his finger underneath the edge" of a flower bud and "unfolded it." Sterling was London's "great Man-Comrade," who loved "the flesh, as he should the spirit," a fact that enraged Charmian. When Sterling and his wife built a lodge at Carmel as a gathering place for their artist friends, he hoped the Londons would build a house nearby and was deeply disappointed when London instead established Beauty Ranch near Charmian's family. "I am afraid that the dream was too bright to last—our being near each other," London wrote to Sterling. "It's not through any fault of yours, nor through any fault of mine. The world and people just happen to be so made." "To any man who ever failed to keep the love of another man," London's biographer James L. Haley observed, "no more gentle reproof could have been possible." Nonetheless, Sterling was at Charmian's side in 1916 when she entombed London's ashes. Finger came to believe London committed suicide, perhaps because of his conversation with Sterling.[19]

Before Finger left San Francisco, Sterling presented him with a "great treasure," a death mask of London. He also gave Finger a photograph that

London may have taken of Sterling holding a rifle and some birds. Finger kept the mask and whatever secrets Sterling told him during their ramble but hinted to his readers, "Sterling's reminiscences are his own and some day he must tell his own story, for he has notable things to say." He pointedly described Sterling as "masculine-minded" but added a veiled reference to the poet's bisexuality: Sterling was "an ice-hidden spring that would burst forth under the warmth of perfect understanding."[20] The image of liquid bursting forth was transparently suggestive, while Finger and some of his friends seem to have used the phrase *perfect understanding* to represent a shared consciousness or shared secrets: The character of Eric poignantly wished for "a feller who'd understand, and who'd be with me 'warming the winter of my loneliness.'" In the "fullness of life," Finger observed, men "forge links of fellowship" and "get a closer and finer understanding of one another." Reviewing Finger's book *Ozark Fantasia*, Stuart Olivier invited readers to "come . . . to know" Finger "more intimately and more understandingly." Describing a reunion of Bob Davis and a long-lost friend, Odd McIntyre wrote, "They . . . smiled in perfect understanding."[21]

Sterling entered a hospital again within a week of seeing Finger off and died of suicide the next year, a few days before the tenth anniversary of London's death. It was during a visit by Mencken that he had mentioned to Finger in a letter. Sterling was expected that day at a luncheon in Mencken's honor but did not appear, instead drafting a poem on the back of a menu and noting "Send this to Mencken" before swallowing cyanide. "It's justifiable," Finger wrote later. "If you don't like life, then open the door. The key is in your hand." Sterling was "my friend, and I loved him," he wrote, quoting one of Sterling's poems: "Desires and Adorations, / Winged Persuasions, and veiled Destinies, / Splendors and Glooms and glimmering Incarnations / of hopes and fears and twilight fantasies."[22]

———

FINGER AND HONORÉ received many letters and invitations because of the Newbery Medal, including a commission by The Century Company for a series of stories, to be illustrated by Honoré, that it would publish in its magazine for children, *St. Nicholas*, and reissue in an anthology. Busy with work for Henry Ford's magazine and a speaking tour in Texas, Finger accepted this deal but declined other book projects. "As I told the Major," he wrote to Ben Donaldson at the *Independent*, "it won't do to change one's habits."[23] Missing Maddox, he wrote to Wilbur Stone in November, "Friendship is the greatest reality in the world, and he is my dearest friend."[24]

By this time Nellie was *de facto* mother to Maddox's stepdaughter, Ann Coyle. Helen Maddox evidently had continued to find the day-to-day care of her daughter a challenge. Perhaps in return for Helen's complicity in his relationship with Maddox and probably in exchange for a boarding fee, Finger had persuaded Nellie to let Ann live with them at Gayeta "like a sister" to thirteen-year-old Helen Finger.[25] When he described the family Christmas of 1925 in detail for the readers of *All's Well*, he mentioned her with his own youngest children as "Helen and Ann and Herbert." Nellie appeared almost as support staff in his rhapsody about the holiday. In lieu of spending Christmas with Ann, the Maddoxes sent a radio that became the central source of entertainment, news, and relaxation for the family. Finger thanked Maddox in *All's Well* without naming him. "Then the radio! That came the last thing on Christmas eve, a present from that companion of mine with whom I've taken enchanted wanderings. . . . May the giver of gifts give all men such [a] one."[26] Jesus, Finger had mused in a letter to Donaldson, was "large minded" enough that even with a man who was different than him, "there would be perfect understanding."[27]

The cross-fertilization of Finger's and Honoré's careers continued. Fred Black, the *Independent*'s business manager, invited them to a dinner party with the chief editor, William J. Cameron, and Carl Sandburg at the Dearborn Country Club in April 1926. Sandburg had performed folk songs earlier in the day at a Jewish temple in Detroit, but the men probably did not talk about that since Ford and the *Independent* were notorious for anti-Semitic articles and faced a lawsuit by a Jew whom the magazine had libeled. Perhaps the group stuck to the topic of Sandburg's two-volume *Abraham Lincoln: The Prairie Years*, which Carl Van Doren had called "magnificently satisfying." Wishing he could recreate the convivial evening at the luxurious, Tudor-style club with Maddox, Finger wrote, "If I wanted to enjoy a social evening in which there would be no unpleasant friction and grittiness, but real good fellowship, I would [invite] Cameron, Donaldson and Black, and Major Maddox," Honoré, Wilbur Macy Stone, and a few other men who would steer "past differences with a delicate tact, none of them without a healthy and sane sense of proportion." On the same trip, Finger saw a mural that Honoré had painted. In a typical wink to the inner circle of *All's Well* readers, he mentioned the depiction of "young rowers stripped to the waist, their rippling muscles, their glistening skins, their wind-blown hair." He also went with Sandburg to "a gambling joint" in Detroit to collect folk songs for a book Sandburg was preparing.[28]

Finger saw Honoré and Sandburg again the next month at the annual convention of the American Booksellers Association in St. Louis, where he was an invited speaker.[29] Meeting Opie Read, an elderly writer whose *Opie Read in the Ozarks* (1905) was a set of sketches of Ozark residents,[30] Finger and Honoré brainstormed going on a trek in the mountains for an illustrated article like the one Finger sold to the *Century* in 1923.[31] Public panel discussions and live radio interviews were emerging as popular promotional events in publishing, and Finger took part in one of each at the convention.[32] On a panel with Sandburg and Stuart Sherman, he joked, "It is said that there are 99 books for every inhabitant of the United States. In my State there are 99 inhabitants for every book," and after telling several stories concluded, "That's all."[33] Finger, Honoré, and Sandburg joined Sherman and the adventure and travel writer Richard Halliburton—whose first book, *The Royal Road to Romance*, was just out—for a live radio conversation at midnight. Finger was immediately jealous of Halliburton, who was young and handsome, with a degree from Princeton University, and, to the observant, gay. Although Halliburton was lonely and depressed at the time, tired of posing as a straight man, Finger felt no sympathy for him and thought he showed "immeasurable conceit."[34]

Back in Michigan in August, Finger went with Honoré to the Dearborn Country Club for another dinner, this time meeting Henry Ford.[35] They must have sold the Dearborn group on the idea of a feature about the Ozarks since Honoré came to Arkansas for the expedition the same month, bringing his son York with him to spend a few days at Gayeta. Paul signed Nellie's guest book "Paul Honoré of the Ancient Order of Rascals," adding a sketch of a pirate wearing a bandanna and giant hoop earring, but Finger wanted him to leave more of a mark at Gayeta. At his own home, Honoré sometimes invited guests to carve messages on the oak beams in his living room. In the main house at Gayeta, he painted scenes on three of the interior doors, one of a white-haired man at a writing desk with a view of sailboats and a vast blue sky. Finger wrote two articles about their jaunt into the Ozarks that the *Independent* published in November, articles Helen Finger believed were embellished to the point of being fictitious.[36]

There was a spare bed for young York because Ann Coyle was away, spending the summer with her mother. When Helen Maddox had come to Gayeta to pick her up, she had dinner with Finger and Nellie and a crowd of their local friends at the Green Tree Inn in Fayetteville. The inn belonged to Laura Lighton, the widow of the writer William Lighton; she bought the colonial-style house to operate as a restaurant after he died. It had a dining room large enough to seat fifty customers and a smaller one for private parties. For the most part, Lighton ran the restaurant herself, building on experience entertaining guests at her former farm, Happy Hollow, and a job at the university Campus Club. She offered luncheons and teas six days a week and dinners and special parties by appointment. Bill Baerg had a dinner party for twelve, including the Finger family and Murray Sheehan, on Thanksgiving Day the first year.[37] The inn was the kind of business enterprise that interested Helen Maddox.

George became seriously ill that summer, and Helen sent a letter or telegram to Gayeta that threw Finger into despair. "There he was, my friend, broken by sickness, so I was full of strange fancies," he told his *All's Well* readers, emotion making his writing more florid than usual. He dedicated the issue "to my friend Helen C. Maddox" but found it difficult to work until she reported on Maddox's recovery in a "reassuring letter."[38] Ann returned to Gayeta in the fall, and Finger and Maddox planned a rendezvous in November at Long Beach, Mississippi, where Maddox went to spend time with his sister and brother-in-law. Finger would join him there after the speeches in Texas. "I met my friend's sister," Finger wrote later, disguising Maddox's identity as usual.[39]

Elizabeth Maddox Cox, two years older than George, was dean of home economics at Gulf Park College, and her husband, Richard G. "Dick" Cox, was the school's founding president. On a broad property shaded with live oaks, pecans, and magnolias, just across US Highway 90 from the Gulf of Mexico, Gulf Park by the Sea was a residential high school and two-year collegiate program. A trolley track ran parallel to the highway, linking the school with the towns of Gulfport and Biloxi. A three-story, Spanish mission–style dormitory and a two-story classroom building dominated the campus.[40] Getting acquainted, the Coxes and Finger chatted about the poet Vachel Lindsay, who was one of the early visitors to Gayeta. Cox and Lindsay had been friends in college, and when Lindsay became ill in 1923, he came to Gulf Park to convalesce, teaching a poetry class to earn his keep and sometimes perching with his pupils in a giant live oak on the campus. However, he left Gulf Park before fulfilling his teaching contract, and Cox disavowed him as a friend.[41]

Finger no doubt entertained Maddox and the Coxes with his encounter, a day or so earlier, with a literary celebrity. On the way from Texas to Mississippi, he stopped in New Orleans to visit John Peebles McClure, one of the editors of the *Double Dealer*, the literary magazine that published three of Finger's stories, and book editor at the New Orleans *Times-Picayune*. McClure's house was on the narrow street known as Orleans Alley (and later as Pirate's Alley) across from Saint Louis Cathedral.[42] When Finger rang the bell, no one responded, so he shouted "John McClure!" and McClure's wife, Grace Binford Smith, came to the balcony and threw a key down to him. He let himself in and climbed the stairs to their second-floor apartment. The three chatted before McClure took Finger to Ye Olde Book Shop on Royal Street, which he and Grace owned, and to lunch, perhaps at Tom Anderson's tavern on Rampart Street, where McClure, William Faulkner, and other writers in the French Quarter often went for sandwiches and Cuban beer. They talked about Sherwood Anderson, who had lived in New Orleans until May, and Mencken, whom McClure took to Tom Anderson's a month earlier when he came to town hoping to help revive the *Double Dealer*. It did not appear that anything could save the little magazine.[43]

Being with Maddox in Mississippi inspired Finger to write a passage packed with sensory impressions. "An air of peace pervade[d] the entire countryside," he wrote in a travel piece for the *Independent*. The gulf was "a sweep of pale blue, here alive with flashing white sea gulls, there ... hardly to be distinguished from horizon haze." Some lines presaged the most homoerotic passage of the memoir he later wrote: "Sometimes, quite close to shore, so close that you may hear the voices of the men and the creaking of blocks, you see a fishing schooner beautiful with bellying sail of brown or white, though the wind is hardly strong enough to ripple the water."[44] Finger's account of this visit was vivid yet vague, meandering in sequence and location like one of the wide, slow rivers on the coastal plain, unclear about when he was with the Coxes and when he was alone with his unnamed friend. He wrote that he slipped away one day, implying that he did so alone— "My kindly hosts ... did not realize that penchant which I have for the rough and raw, so I had to slip off quietly to dock land"—but he used the pronoun "we" elsewhere. At Biloxi he and Maddox climbed steep stairs to the top of a tower, probably the Biloxi Lighthouse, and "heard the murmur of the sea." Lighthouses could represent, as the scholar Holly Furneaux puts it, "interstitial spaces of imaginative possibility"; Finger had made the narrator of "Some Mischievous Thing" a lightkeeper. Looking at tall ships in the harbor and the shimmering, winking waves, Finger "was ablaze with a desire that things which had been, might be again," he wrote, his phrases colorfully suggestive. "And while my companion talked, in me was a memory of tropic nights, and of scented winds, and of the lullaby of lapping waters, and the strange green fires of the sea, and a morning sun that leapt out of the ocean at the end of a lane of flowing gold."[45]

Maddox returned to duty in New York in late November, and Bob Davis reported to Finger, "Maddox and I get together occasionally. Some of our conversation is about you."[46] Helen Maddox came back to Gayeta in December alone to spend Christmas with Ann. "Nothing lacking but Sep's presence," she wrote in Nellie's guest book, "to make this my most wonderful Christmas."[47] Finger had written a Christmas story for the *Independent*, "The Affair at the Inn," in which a steward for a tax collector tells of finding Mary and Joseph a place to rest in a stable. (The author of the first book to win the Newbery Medal used a similar device.) The climax of Finger's story comes when the steward awakes the next morning, remembering "visions" of "a great star," and feels a "secret hope [for] a world with good will between man and man." Finger told Donaldson the story demonstrated that "all men hunger for companionship" and called him "one of my two real Dearborn friends[,] the other Fred Black—and may they always go forward in true *understanding*, counting me as the third in a trio [emphasis added]."[48] Finger used *understanding* so often in letters to Donaldson that it seems Donaldson understood his attraction to men.

Finger's New Year's greeting in *All's Well* was another message of hope and a secret message to Maddox, seemingly hinting at a shared goal: "It is still yours to be a warrior-lord, never-despairing[.] Here's to endurance, and discipline, and a goal! With all my heart, A Happy New Year!"[49] He managed to endure being apart from Maddox only until February before going to New York, purportedly to deliver the manuscript for *The Spreading Stain* to Doubleday, Page. Finger was excited about the book and thought it was "the most engaging thing I've ever done." He stayed with the Maddoxes at their apartment, enjoying their "pleasant, book-lined room[,] a place where neither anxiety nor trouble could enter." "The three of us"—he, George, and Helen—were "all-sufficient," their conversation "easy and natural." William Griffith, who now worked for the publishing house William H. Wise and Company, joined them one night. Delighted, Finger felt their "sociability" had a "quality . . . like sunshine touching a crystal fountain." On a side trip to Quebec City, presumably with Maddox since he never identified his companion, Finger stayed at the Château Frontenac, an enormous hotel that loomed over the St. Lawrence River. He was struck by the view that stretched from one edge of his peripheral vision to the other, like the Strait of Magellan when he viewed it from that high and splendid ridge on Tierra del Fuego.

Going on to Detroit, he had dinner with Donaldson. He was reworking a biography of David Livingstone, a project for Doubleday, Page, into a three-part series for the *Independent* and suggested the Dearborn group publish *The Spreading Stain* in serial form too, but Cameron did not really like serials. Finger even pitched a series about figures in the New Testament, but Donaldson doubted he had time to do a credible research job.[50] Donaldson probably was distracted; Henry Ford had been sued by the Anti-Defamation League, and the trial was about to start.

[10]

BETRAYAL

WITH NELLIE plus five children, two in college and others approaching college, and Margaret Germann—who worked for the Fingers until her cottage at Gayeta burned in 1936—all depending on him, Finger never earned enough money. The family ate mutton and potatoes produced on the farm, Helen Finger later recalled, and Finger "sometimes . . . had enough money [but] sometimes . . . was just about flat broke, especially when it came time to pay the taxes."[1] Maintaining Gayeta as a working sheep farm and a destination for Finger's literary friends was a constant round of work. He corresponded continuously with his editors, organizations inviting him to speak, and contributors and readers of *All's Well*. As fast as he drafted new books and articles, Germann retyped the manuscripts and filled the occasional order for copies of Finger's books or the review copies he received free from publishers and sold as used. For Nellie food preparation was an endless chore. The oldest children, Hubert and Kitty, were students at the University of Arkansas; Hub also tended the new lambs, and Kitty was Nellie's right hand. Charles Jr. was more interested in chess than chickens, and more interested in women than chess, but under pressure from Finger, he kept enormous flocks of poultry that he and his father sold under the name Ozark Barred Rock Farm. The youngest children, Helen, Herb, and Ann Coyle, were at school.

To help him make a little money from work he had already done, several of his friends conspired to publish and promote an anthology that Finger called *Ozark Fantasia*. The collection included the articles that he wrote about the trek with Paul Honoré and others from *Reedy's Mirror*, *All's Well*, the *Century*, and the *Herald Tribune*. Few of the pieces had much bearing on the Ozarks. A section called "A Brace of Friends" resembled one of Theodore Dreiser's books, *Twelve Men* (1919), which Finger owned and

Dreiser considered his most popular book. The only person whose full name Finger did not provide—among Bob Davis and Stuart Olivier of the New Face Club, the editors Stuart P. Sherman and Carl Van Doren, and other literati—was "Major Maddox."[2] Finger hoped Honoré would provide illustrations, but that did not happen. Charles Morrow Wilson, a local aspiring novelist who had recently graduated from the University of Arkansas and occupied the stone cottage, assembled the manuscript for the typesetter.[3] (Wilson used the cottage as the setting for his first novel, *Acres of Sky*, a story of a mountain man rather like the protagonist of the hugely popular 1912 novel *The Harvester* by Gene Stratton-Porter, who was "bronzed and Pan-like [with] a languorous grace." That book met lukewarm reviews.)[4] Fielding P. Sizer, a lawyer and arts patron in Monett, Missouri, paid for printing *Ozark Fantasia* and reviewed it in the newspaper that Olivier owned, the *Springfield Leader*. Olivier also published his own review, characterizing Finger as a "hidden" lord of Arcadia. "This mighty warrior of high romance . . . has sought and found it in all the lands and all the seas and those other lands—that—never—were of the spirit." Another of Finger's correspondents, a syndicated columnist in New York, Charles B. Driscoll, praised the book (and later kindly plugged *Acres of Sky*), and the *Nation* gave *Ozark Fantasia* a brief notice.[5]

The collection received little other attention, undoubtedly because it was one of six books by Finger to come out in 1927, creating Finger fatigue among the country's book reviewers. There had been *Tales Worth Telling*, the anthology of stories from *St. Nicholas*, which May Lamberton Becker praised in the *Saturday Review* and the *Nation* gave the briefest possible notice.[6] The first major review of *Romantic Rascals* apparently was in February 1928, too late for Christmas sales. The other three 1927 books were from Doubleday, Page: *The Spreading Stain*, *Frontier Ballads*, and *David Livingstone*. The publisher promoted *Stain* in a quarter-page advertisement in the November issue of *Boys' Life*, but the book was a clunky story—the narrator's language too mature and his perspective too well informed for him to be a believable boy hero.[7] Finger padded the song collection *Frontier Ballads* with an introduction, a lengthy "discursive note," and three stories. The actual music in the book was arranged by David Guion, Finger's little piano student in San Angelo, who was now a piano teacher himself and beginning to compose music inspired by his early life in west Texas.[8] Ever generous, Carl Sandburg plugged *Frontier Ballads* in his own new book, *The American Songbag*, and wrote a humorous critique of it for the *Saturday Review*.[9] The

New York Times was positive, giving the book and a sample of Honoré's illustrations more than half of a page in the Book Review, but there were few other notices.[10] *David Livingstone* received no serious reviews until late in 1928, when the *Saturday Review* offered modest praise.[11] Doubleday, Page had pushed, or permitted, Finger to write too much—one reviewer related later that "some critics" believed Finger was guilty of "over-production."[12]

Hustling in the years 1925 to 1927 to maintain the *Dearborn Independent* and the *New York Herald Tribune* as steady freelance employers, gambling on one risky book project after another, Finger fell into a pattern of disloyal scheming. To cultivate Henry Ford and Ford's staff at the *Independent* and Stuart Sherman, the book editor at the *Herald Tribune*, who abhorred modernist literature, Finger refashioned himself as a standard-bearer for decency on an "anti-sex-faddix [*sic*] psychoanalyst campaign." There were hints that what he *really* opposed was bigotry against gays and lesbians—the character of Ebro implied that puritanical Christians were to blame for "unsatisfied sex-hunger[,] smutty talk and worse"; describing a friendly debate about modernist literature with Edgar Lee Masters, he briefly praised the salacious, closeted dramatist Harry Hervey, calling his work "cultured and intelligent."[13] Nonetheless, Finger was hypocritically attacking the same kind of sexual material he once praised in the work of James Branch Cabell. He called *Fantazius Mallare* (1922), a controversial novel by Sandburg's Jewish friend Ben Hecht—whom Donaldson detested—"filth" and told a reporter "the trouble with Ben Hecht and Sherwood Anderson"—another of Sandburg's friends in the Chicago literary world—"is that they roil up their own self-consciousness, shovel out a lump and call it beauty. What they've actually got is a gummy, grimy mess that is neither art nor life. Hothouse stuff."[14]

Worse than this pontificating, Finger turned against Mencken—who had encouraged Finger to write serious fiction, published three of his short stories, allowed Finger to engage him in humorous jousting in the pages of *All's Well*, and given several of his books positive notices—because Mencken was a proponent of modernist literature and thus Sherman's philosophical opponent.[15] At the same time that Sherman and his assistant editors began assigning book reviews to Finger, Finger began attacking Mencken. He first tried to sell an article on the Sherman–Mencken dispute to the *Independent*, and Donaldson, who found modernist literature highly distasteful, invited Finger to write about the feud, even promising to "step up" the usual fee, but the magazine did not publish Finger's article "Battle of the Bookmen" because the chief editor, William Cameron, did not want to give Mencken the publicity.[16] Finger alluded to the Sherman–Mencken dispute in *All's Well* the same month that Sherman's assistant editor Anne Moore plugged *Tales from Silver Lands* in the *Herald Tribune*. Referring to Masters, who had visited Gayeta, Finger wrote, "Masters is a dyed-in-the-wool Menckenite[,] four-square opposed to Stuart P. Sherman" and called his newest book "harsh" and "repellent." For balance he noted that he had a copy of Masters' *Mitch Miller* in his library, "tucked between Mencken's Prejudices and Masefield's Enslaved." By March Finger apparently thought he went too far with his between-the-lines criticism of Mencken and mentioned that he and his family read "a good deal" of Mencken's work on winter nights around the big fireplace at Gayeta.[17] At the same time, however, he asked Donaldson to "please, please, please tell Mr. Cameron to see the blinking, malign, reptilian character of so much of this ultra-modern stuff."

Finger frequently used Donaldson as a back channel for impressing Cameron. Referring to an autobiography by Frank Harris, the British editor and friend of Oscar Wilde whom Finger courted in 1919, he fumed for Cameron's benefit: "Like Joyce in Ulysses he uses words and terms that have been hitherto restricted to the walls of privies . . . If the Independent does not take up this ultra-modern madness, who will?" However, when Cameron thought Finger should write articles criticizing modernist art, a subject on which Finger knew almost nothing, he tried to finesse the problem by quoting Honoré, who said modernist artists were "experimenters[, not] frauds or fanatics." Finger and Donaldson dropped the idea of comparing Sherman and Mencken after Sherman died unexpectedly in the summer of 1926, but Finger continued his attacks on Mencken. Ironically, Mencken and George Sterling agreed in an exchange of letters that Finger was "hopeless" for always praising writers. "He writes only rhapsodies," Mencken commented.[18]

Worse than the hypocritical diatribes against modernist writers in general, worse than his betrayal of Mencken, Finger engaged in anti-Semitism to sell more work to Ford. He may have been oblivious to the *Independent*'s anti-Semitism when he courted the magazine, considering that he gave Emanuel Haldeman-Julius as one of his professional references, but Cameron was a self-anointed Presbyterian preacher with a fixation on Jews, who published constant anti-Semitic articles that received widespread and high-placed scorn.[19] The anti-Semitism that Finger adopted after Cameron and Donaldson began buying his work was a clear reverse in moral direction. Before then he sporadically, strategically criticized anti-Semitism: In 1920 he noted in *Reedy's Mirror* that his employer, Henry R. Fishel, was a Jew and "a success because he has made others successful. He invests in men and in brains of men." In 1921 he called anti-Semitic propagandists "wretched" and accused them of stirring "stupid minds" to "hatred." In 1922 he directly challenged anti-Semitism in a Little Blue Book for Haldeman-Julius, observing that ideas such as "Jews [are] very much given to cheat" were "idle and pernicious clap trap." In 1924, in another booklet for Haldeman-Julius, he quoted Mark Twain on Jews as "a marvelous race." However, that was the last year that Haldeman-Julius bought work from Finger.[20] By then Finger was placing anti-Semitic comments in *All's Well*. In October 1924, the same month that he pitched a Sherman vs. Mencken piece to Donaldson, he wrote that in the railroad business, "fat fortunes were made by shrewd Jewish traders." In April 1925 he called Fishel's partner, Joseph D. Marks, "a young Jew" who bought railroads "for the syndicate of Jews" and referred to a scientist at the University of Arkansas as a "Russian Jew."

The Anti-Defamation League and B'nai B'rith sued the *Independent* in 1925 for libeling a lawyer, Aaron Sapiro, but Finger kept up his low-key alignment with the Dearborn group's anti-Semitism, calling the publishing house Simon and Schuster "a Jewish firm" in a letter to Donaldson in December and complaining because the company offered to become his exclusive publisher, "which would have caused me to sever connections with all other publishers." Of Gilbert Frankau, an English novelist he met at the booksellers' convention in St. Louis, Finger told Donaldson, "I had no idea that Frankau was a Jew, but I was sure there was something wrong about him. He is a bounder and a conceited ass, and, I dare say, a good deal of a fraud." The following year, Finger made a public record of his disdain for Frankau, calling him "a very pushful [*sic*] young Jew" in a revised piece about the convention that he included in *Ozark Fantasia*.[21]

At Donaldson's urging Finger even began attacking Haldeman-Julius, who was his friend and had been a source of significant income. "One or two correspondents have called my attention," Finger wrote in December 1924 in *All's Well*, "to a kind of debate that the enterprising and energetic Haldeman-Julius has been carrying on . . . to decide whether Jesus is greater than Heine, or Spinoza. One good friend made the suggestion that I take part in it" but "that I have no desire to do," he said, trying to stand tall in the middle as he did about the Scopes trial. "I carry no tag religious or political, but . . . if a man's religion is a source of sweet consolation to him . . . no man should step out of his way to strike a blow at the thing held sacred." Still, Haldeman-Julius was "all at sea" for comparing Jesus, Heine, and Spinoza because,

Finger explained in a strikingly asinine analogy, "the work of Jesus was in the field of feeling," while the others were "in the field of thought." Besides, there really were three kinds of men: "men of thought, men of action, and men of feeling . . . It is idle to argue about which is the greatest." Hoping this would satisfy the Dearborn editors, he wrote to Donaldson, "You said 'Take a shot at Julius[.]' I did." Unfortunately, Donaldson thought Finger's article was "too well-tempered" and suggested Finger write another to show how Haldeman-Julius "typifies the essential characteristics of his group and shows up so plainly that peculiar twist of mind that leads so many of his kind into the sort of thing which he is doing." Finger tried to redirect Donaldson, commenting, "We can't waste precious time and life in controversy." Two days later, he responded again, trying to avoid explicit anti-Semitism by proposing they criticize Haldeman-Julius for promoting "sex-stuff" and for being an atheist.[22]

The Sapiro suit went to trial in March 1927. To settle it, Ford conceded in July that the *Independent*'s articles about Jews were false, published a retraction of the articles about Sapiro, blamed Cameron and the editorial staff, and agreed to stop publishing the *Independent* by the end of the year. This development was a major news story.[23] Finger had received at least $5,000 in payments from the *Independent* between April 1924 and September 1927.[24] He wrote sympathetically and repeatedly to Donaldson, hoping Ford would launch another periodical, still trying to curry favor with Cameron. He hinted that he was going to sue a "Yiddish publisher" who had plagiarized his 1923 book *Highwaymen*. Donaldson confided, "W. J. C. still feels keenly the sting of the 'retraction' and in a sense feels that he has been made a martyr" but hinted that Cameron, who was an alcoholic, deserved some of the blame.[25]

Over the next few years, it seems, Finger tried to make amends for his attacks on Mencken and his complicity in Ford's anti-Semitism. He reached out to Oswald Garrison Villard at the *Nation*, who had criticized Ford as a threat to freedom of the press. In his hurry he mistakenly addressed the letter to "Oscar Garrison Villard" and suggested cryptically that "some of us must translate the ideals religious and ethical into very practical matters." Villard replied promptly and courteously and published a profile of Finger by Charles Wilson (Finger's "closest circle of friends" included "army officers, outlaws, [and] editors," Wilson wrote), but the *Nation* never became a significant source of income for Finger.[26] He made his way into Mencken's new magazine, *American Mercury*, in 1929 with an article that ridiculed Ford.

When a new ally who was Jewish stepped forward in 1932 to underwrite *All's Well*, Finger issued another veiled *mea culpa*, blaming Ford for manipulating "working men" into debt and comparing Ford's "foolish anti-Jewish propaganda," in a notably verbose and unclear aside, to Reedy's being for "all that which brimmed the channel of life." He criticized "prejudice-mongers" in 1933, calling them "enemies of the human race," and mentioned "when I managed the affairs of Fishel and Marks in Cleveland I joined as heartily as I could in the festival of Yom Kippur."[27]

Just as the *Independent* work ended, a new editor took over for the Century Company and made clear he was not interested in Finger's work.[28] Fortunately, the book section editors at the *New York Herald Tribune* still wanted him to write reviews. Beginning in April 1928, he also received a few review assignments from the *Saturday Review*, but as Finger scrambled to maintain his freelance income, prospects for any of the children taking over Nellie's support seemed poorer than ever.[29] Hubert moved to Akron, Ohio, after his graduation from the University of Arkansas in August 1928. Kitty had been attending the University of Arkansas, and Finger envisioned her remaining at Gayeta after graduation, perhaps contributing to the household by working as a librarian, but she had a suitor at the university who wanted to find work in Akron, like Hubert. Objecting to their relationship, Finger pressured Kitty into transferring to Knox College in Galesburg, Illinois.[30] She did so and then grudgingly returned to Gayeta, but Finger confided to Donaldson that she was "rather rebellious." To placate her, he planned to take her and Helen to the Great Lakes region, driving with acquaintances from Oklahoma City, after he finished another book project.[31]

The new book was *Heroes from Hakluyt*, a discussion of the writings of a seventeenth-century English explorer, Richard Hakluyt. The Scottish writer R. B. Cunninghame Graham contributed a short preface, indicating he had never met Finger. "We do not know what kind of horse the other likes; or if the other fellow admires dark or fair women [or] drinks whiskey or vermouth," but they had in common that they were "wanderers." Finger told someone, probably Kitty, he would dedicate *Heroes* to Nellie and did so, but not by name, simply calling her "first mate on that voyage during which we steered the family ship through perilous seas"—perhaps because Nellie, like Maddox, did not want him to refer to her by name. He expanded the dedication with a veiled message to Maddox and other "glorious fellows who write letters to me, and who plan meetings and contemplate long cross-country drives during which we can think aloud as real boys do." The final line hinted at a future move: "How, then, shall I stake out a claim in so glad and glorious a world of fellowship?"[32]

The Henry Holt Company, a new publisher for Finger, published *Heroes* in two editions that Honoré designed and illustrated, one for the book trade and a handsome limited edition of 320 copies, signed by Finger and Honoré, which Holt marketed to wealthy book collectors.[33] The deluxe edition was printed on rag laid paper, bound in green fabric, with plates printed in red, green, and gold from woodcuts by Honoré, half-page and quarter-page illustrations printed in black, and endpapers, printed in green on cream, with Honoré's picture of a sea god holding a trident and a two-masted schooner sailing with a giant moon in the background. Honoré signed his name in the upper left corner of the last of the full-page illustrations, a scene of a man kneeling, with a sword at his side, before a large stained-glass window. Holt released *Heroes* in November 1928, and, thanks to Honoré's involvement, the book was more of a hit than any of Finger's six 1927 releases. Four major periodicals, the *Saturday Review*, *New York Herald Tribune*, *New York Sun*, and *Detroit Free Press*, obliged with positive reviews in time for Christmas sales, with much of the attention on the illustrations. Around this time Honoré was elected to the National Society of Mural Painters and was the guest of honor at an exhibit observing Children's Book Week at the New York Public Library.[34] *St. Nicholas* published its last Finger–Honoré story, "Barthema the Bold," in November. Doubleday, Page promoted the Finger–Honoré collaboration in a collection of profiles, *Authors and Others* (1928), calling it "a partnership of two robust adventurers who had seen much of the colour and glamour of life,"[35] but *Heroes* and "Barthema" were the last projects Finger did with Honoré.

[11]

AN AUTOBIOGRAPHICAL ROMANCE

DOUBLEDAY, PAGE DECLINED to publish the Magellan series as a book, so Finger revised the material as a juvenile novel with a working title and protagonist borrowed from Kipling's *Captains Courageous*. In "Comrades Courageous," young Dick Osberne becomes a captain in Magellan's fleet and sees the world, finding a special friendship with a handsome Patagonian native. Finger entered the manuscript in a contest with a $2,000 prize, which Longmans, Green, a venerable London publishing house, sponsored to attract strong manuscript submissions and boost sales.[1] One of the judges was May Becker, an Anglophile and the columnist for the *Saturday Review* who called *Tales Worth Telling* "brilliant." She thought Finger's book was the best entry, and her opinion prevailed.[2]

He used the money for a two-month idyll in the summer of 1929 with Kitty and Helen, his first and last return to England since emigrating to the US. While Nellie, Charles Jr., and Herbert remained at Gayeta and Ann Coyle spent the summer with the Maddoxes,[3] Finger and his daughters spent three weeks in London, seeing scenes and friends from his childhood. He managed to meet Cunninghame Graham, who joined him for a meal and a drink. A prolific writer, Cunninghame Graham sifted and reworked his early experiences in South America and the American Southwest for a book each year, more or less. Finger had reviewed two in the *New York Herald Tribune*—the headline for the double review dubbed the Scotsman "the golden horseman."[4] "My heart rose up," Finger wrote about this long-awaited encounter. "There he was, a knight still." They had a "merry" conversation about W. H. Hudson, Joseph Conrad, and William Morris, probably touching on the great Trafalgar Square rally on November 13, 1887. To protest a government ban on public meetings, Cunninghame Graham had called for every liberal to meet him at the massive plaza between the National

Gallery and the River Thames, and thousands marched into the square. Police blocked the marchers, arresting dozens and injuring hundreds, three fatally—the event became known as "Bloody Sunday."[5] Finger may have been at the rally (Edward Carpenter admitted he went "as a sightseer"), but he wrote nothing of it in his journal, and when the young men in the Mutual Improvement Society met a few nights later, they apparently did not even discuss the event, although the French Society talked about it until nine o'clock.[6] Nonetheless, this conversation with Cunninghame Graham apparently emboldened Finger to make much of the rally in the memoir he was writing.

Leaving London, the Fingers joined Benjamin B. Blakeney and his bookish wife, Evelyn Whittaker Blakeney—the Oklahoma friends who accompanied them to the Great Lakes a year earlier—to rent a house at Henley-on-Thames. From there they took day trips to Cambridge, Oxford, and Rye, passing through the hops country that twenty-one-year-old Finger had explored on a ramble.[7] One day, the New York columnist Charles Driscoll, on his own tour of England and Europe, joined them. A bibliophile and the executive editor of McNaught Syndicate, Driscoll had been one of Finger's friendly correspondents since their long-distance introduction by a mutual friend, probably Philip Cornick.[8] Driscoll had promoted *Ozark Fantasia* and boasted, "I have a standing invitation from Mr. Finger to go out to his place in Arkansas [to] dwell in his stone house, eat his mutton, and indulge in a conversation." The Finger-Blakeney-Driscoll party went in two cars to the village of Chalfont St. Giles, where John Milton wrote "Paradise Lost," and to the village of Stoke Poges, where Thomas Gray wrote "Elegy Written in a Country Churchyard" in memory of his youthful love, Richard West. "Seldom have I enjoyed travel so much as with this good companion," Driscoll later recalled. The day he spent exploring the English countryside with Finger was a memory for his "Golden Book."[9] The word *golden* was gaining significance for Finger. In 1930, referring to Ferdinand Haberkorn, he spoke coyly of having known "a golden knave . . . who could sing and play the violin"; in 1931 he mentioned a "Greek spirit that searches for golden realms."[10]

———

LONGMANS, GREEN changed the title of Finger's novel to *Courageous Companions* and commissioned James Daugherty to illustrate it. Daugherty was a popular book illustrator and modernist painter who studied under

Frank Brangwyn in London, like Paul Honoré. His drawings showed semi-nude, sinewy young men aboard ships or crouched and peering down at the Strait of Magellan from a rocky precipice.[11] Promotion and release of the book in the fall of 1929, soon after the Fingers returned from England, renewed Finger's celebrity and seemed to promise that his second decade as a writer would be even brighter than the first.[12] The new Junior Literary Guild, an offshoot of one of two major books-by-mail marketing programs in the US, with Carl Van Doren as editor-in-chief, made *Courageous* its September selection for boys ages twelve to sixteen.[13] May Becker plugged the book twice in the *Saturday Review*.[14] The *Chicago Tribune* devoted a generous part of its Saturday books page to the book and Finger's idea that boys wanted literary heroes who were "gay, strong, undefeated."[15] A reviewer for the *New York Herald Tribune* found it "a well turned tale" although, as a fan "accustomed to Paul Honoré's decorations," he thought Daugherty's illustrations were inferior. (Daugherty went on to illustrate at least eleven books for May Massee.)[16]

Marketing of *Courageous* reached a crescendo with a reception for Finger at the Savoy Plaza, a towering new palace at Fifth Avenue and 58th Street made even more dazzling by the fact that Winston Churchill was a guest on his own book tour.[17] Publishers' receptions in New York were a crucial part of book marketing—Harry Hansen at the *Chicago Daily News* called them the "flourishing author's tea racket." Some reviewers, critics, and columnists attended teas as often as possible to take advantage of gossip and the "large silver trays laden with choice canapés and sandwiches," barely paying attention to the author of the day. The columnist Richard Massock joked, "Book reviewers count that week practically lost in which there isn't a single [tea]." Massock probably attended the tea for Finger since he mentioned him in a column a few months later, relating the amusing story that when "Herbert Brenon, the movie director, first came over from England," he "borrowed $25 from . . . Finger." Driscoll came. Henry Clarence Pitz, a young illustrator in Philadelphia with whom Finger corresponded, showed up. Despite seeing friends and being the center of attention, Finger did not enjoy the reception very much. He struck one columnist as an "uneasy guest of honor," and Driscoll acknowledged that "Mr. Finger doesn't look anything like a New York literary fellow" but promised "his conversation is about the best you'll find anywhere, and his book is a wow."[18]

On the way home from New York, Finger passed through Louisville for a brief rendezvous with the Maddoxes at the Coxes' home. Maddox had just retired, with the rank of lieutenant colonel, and he and Helen were driving west to buy a cattle ranch near her mother and stepfather in Arizona. The stock market collapse began while they were in Louisville, but initial news reports stressed that prices were quickly stabilizing. Maddox went "on, free as the air," Finger wrote, "quite unaffected . . . about money lost in the stock market crash" to buy "a piece of land he thought well of in the Arizona mountains," a new home he planned to call "Goldendays Ranch."[19]

———————

THE ATTENTION TO *Courageous* made finishing his memoir Finger's logical next project. Even before he received the Newbery Medal, at least two publishers—R. M. McBride and the Stratford Company, a small publishing house with ties to Emanuel Haldeman-Julius—approached him about an autobiography. However, Finger had struggled to imagine *how* to tell his life story. He worried about committing "indecent self-exposure" and deplored Sherwood Anderson's memoir *A Story Teller's Story* (1922), telling Ben Donaldson, "Anderson says nothing of his leaving his wife destitute . . . with five children." (Anderson actually only had three children. Did Finger's mistake in the letter to Donaldson reflect inaccurate information he heard somewhere, such as from John McClure in New Orleans, or was it a subconscious acknowledgement of the longing and reluctance Finger felt about leaving his own wife and five children?)[20] Bob Davis urged Finger to tell his story as fiction, but John Cowper Powys, an English writer, thought he should make the book a memoir.[21]

As Finger worried over this in 1926, he heard from his old friend in Patagonia, Ernest Schumacher. "Dear Friend!" Schumacher wrote, "assuming that you are the man whom I first met some thirty years ago in Aleck McKenzies' shanty at Fish river in faraway Patagonia[,] I am writing these lines to you to prove that old acquaintance should not be forgotten."[22] Schumacher's letter was a reminder that there were men here and there who knew Finger's life as a family man was not the whole story.

Perhaps, Finger thought, he did not have to choose between truth and fiction. There was a long tradition of combining fact and fiction in memoirs and travel stories, including Dickens's "Autobiographical Fragment," Melville's *Typee*, and Conrad's continual retelling of seemingly autobiographical tales. Jack London wrote several autobiographical novels, including *Martin Eden*. Thinking of his book as fact *and* fantasy, as "truthful as I *can* make it [emphasis added],"[23] Finger enjoyed the writing more. He later hinted, in a sly comment in a book review, that he crossed and recrossed the line between fact and fiction: Though the book he was reviewing might be a hoax, it was "far more convincing than many an author has been in his own autobiography."[24]

The memoir, *Seven Horizons*, became Finger's most ambitious attempt to merge a story of his alter ago, a world traveler and adventurer rather than a humble ranch hand and small-town newspaperman, with layers of literary allusions and queer references. For example, a story of going to Brighton as a child and chatting with an elderly man at a pier suggested Hilaire Belloc's story "The Little Old Man" in Finger's well-used copy of *On Everything*, in which the narrator encounters an "old man ... looking out to sea" who comments on "the short, sweet grass of the Downs." In Finger's version the man says "a lad whose name is Carpenter" sat at the same pier with him. Finger realized later, he wrote, that the boy was Edward Carpenter, who did in fact spend time as a child and adult walking on the Downs above Brighton.[25] Thus, Finger transformed a walking trip to Brighton with Henry Somerfield in 1889 into an homage to Belloc and Carpenter—the effect not in the style of this passage, for it lacked any, but in the assemblage of clues for readers familiar with those other writers. He embellished his part in the great rally at Trafalgar Square. Before meeting Cunninghame Graham in London, he only claimed to have seen the Scotsman in the square on an unspecified day. Shortly after meeting Cunninghame Graham, perhaps realizing the Scotsman would not dispute any claims Finger made about his participation, Finger wrote that he saw the police arrest Cunninghame Graham and was himself knocked unconscious. He repeated this claim in a vague, verbose passage of the memoir, adding the detail that he marched arm in arm with the Episcopal priest and socialist Stewart Headlam. Finger "went down from a cudgel blow wondering at the sudden darkness of the day," and then he and Headlam escaped in a taxi. None of the details of this incident are clear in *Horizons*, and Headlam had died so was not available to dispute them.[26]

Finger included four unconsummated heterosexual romances in the book. His most intriguing female love object is Maude Fotheringay, the wealthy young wife of a wool broker. Her first name rhymed with that of Finger's generous friend Claude Meeker in Ohio, who had been the American consul in the wool center of Bradford, England, and her surname contained the word "gay." Finger falls in love with Maude, but she guesses his true nature and encourages him to strike out on his own, giving him some money to help him on his way and urging him to "be a knight with a shield for the lonely who yearn for fellowship." Perhaps this story was actually about Dan Cauthorn, the American woolgrower who encouraged young Finger to leave England.[27] None of the *Horizons* stories about women were as vivid or suggestive as his accounts of friendships with men in Patagonia. There, Finger wrote, "men were not afraid of the pleasures of life [and] the sap ran freely" in "the . . . perfection of manly intimacy." He changed during "those years of free wandering," becoming "something that has since made me entirely separate from life about me. For years afterwards I hungered for a companionship that I could not find."[28]

He gave that hunger its most intense and explicit expression in a story reflecting the stopover in Las Palmas on Grand Canary Island in 1890, a tale that practically overflowed with signals to the knowing readers of the time and, he may have hoped, would clearly reveal to future readers that he was, as he hinted as early as 1902, a man lover. Sitting in a wine shop in Las Palmas, Finger meets "a tall and straight-limbed young man with brown skin and white teeth and a pleasant smile." The stranger is a sailor, an archetypal gay man.[29] Their encounter reflects Whitman's scene in the poem "A Glimpse" and the Victorian fascination with North Africa as a destination for clandestine gay encounters, as well as the poem "Rough Weather Friends" by Joseph Kitir, which Carpenter quoted in *Ioläus*—"At a tap-room table . . . We two bartered kiss for kiss"—as well as Jack London's fictional autobiography *John Barleycorn* (1913), which depicted a homosocial world of saloons where men congregated to tell stories that expanded from truth to romance and adventure.[30] When the sailor invites Finger to charter a trip on his boat, the wine shop proprietor tells Finger that sailing with the handsome stranger "would be a wonderful romance," his comment a double entendre suggesting a trip with the sailor would be a romantic, or sexual, experience *and* a hint that this story was not true—in a literary sense, *romance* connoted adventure stories and stories that were not true. Most transparently, this story was an homage to *Romance*, Joseph Conrad and Ford Madox Ford's collaborative novel in which a seductive Spanish nobleman invites a conventional young hero to sail away with him.[31]

In reality Finger and his friends departed Las Palmas aboard the SS *Gulf of Akaba* after one night, but in *Seven Horizons*, he accepts the sailor's invitation. He calls the sailboat *Ferdinand* for his friend Haberkorn, and the adventure reflects his experiences with Schumacher. Ships at sea, as in Conrad's story "The Secret Sharer," were liminal places where men could form relationships, and once Finger joins the stranger on the boat, the story becomes more homoerotic. The boat "rose and fell on the gentle swell and looked like a sensitive living thing." They sailed about the Canary Islands, stopping at Tenerife, where Finger "climbed the mountain to look down at Punta Rasca where Magellan had anchored, and found . . . myself . . . at a precipitous place." Finger linked the scene of mountain and island to the danger of gay liaisons: "I found myself highly desirous of taking the new way, fearing to creep sideways back along the path I had come," he wrote. This passage reflected Carpenter's poem "The Peak of Terror" (1873), in which a man falls from a mountainside to his death just after he reaches the "golden summit" with his lover. An American writer, Gertrude Atherton, used the same situation of a narrow ledge and a gay lover who falls to his death in "The Striding Place" (1896).[32] Finger first used the image of creeping along the edge of a cliff in his rapturous account of the 1924 road trip with Maddox and referred to diving "in deep waters off the Canaries" the following month.[33] In the memoir, after he found his footing and "the terrified half of me fled," he and the sailor "crossed to Africa from Fuerteventura" and "the little craft flew over the sunlit waters," the image of men sailing rapidly over open water like the nineteenth-century idea of men "cruising" or seducing each other.[34]

As Finger knew from an article pasted inside his copy of Symonds' *Walt Whitman: A Study*, Whitman was never satisfied with anything he wrote about sailing ships. "The ship at sea has always eluded me," Whitman said. "I could never put down on paper any words about them that entirely pleased me." Perhaps Finger wanted to write something truly evocative about sailing, for the next lines of his memoir are the most homoerotic of his work. "For me it was perfect fullness of life to be at the tiller and feel the ship answer every little movement, to see the foam streaming past, to hear the music of rushing water, to feel the boat rise on a wave . . . The curve of the sail, the green-white wake, the curl of the waves, the rhythm of the motion, the gulls and curlews that played about us." The detail of birds resembled Oscar Wilde's poem "Impressions," in which "a sailor boy clambers" aboard a boat "in careless joy with laughing face" as "overhead the curlews cry." "The fish that leaped and raced [and] the light noise that was the song of the ship" filled Finger "with a joy that is not to be written about," echoing Wilde's line, "the love that dare not speak its name."

"We ran all night," Finger went on, "for the sheer pleasure of it." Life aboard a boat was free from societal pressures, but life on land was a different matter. Finger's nameless brown-skinned man eventually admits that he has a wife and children back in Las Palmas. They part, and Finger concluded this story with the rueful admission that "the adventure cost me almost all my money."[35]

He described meeting another handsome stranger on Tierra del Fuego, a man with "the body of an athlete, deep-chested and sinewy and strong-looking," a beautiful body "with the sunset touching it, shining dull bronze." Like the handsome and athletic Kalua in Carpenter's memoir *From Adam's Peak to Elephanta* (1892), who was "remarkably well-made and active and powerful," Finger's friend could "in swimming and running [outdo] me with ease."[36] He gives the man part of a biscuit—an amusing reminder of Finger's pretense that he originally thought *galleta* meant "biscuit"—and they eat together. After the man steals Finger's gun, Finger uses a comically obvious phallic image: "Hanging by a thong round his waist was my revolver." Finger reads aloud to the man from *Sartor Resartus* by Thomas Carlyle and even nicknames him Thomas Carlyle because he is so adept at repeating lines—a plausible detail as the Yahgan people on Tierra del Fuego were known as good mimics.[37] No evidence survives to show that Finger actually had a Yahgan friend, but he did know a Cape Verdean ranch hand who was "very quick at picking up bits of information" and learned to play Finger's accordion. However, Finger's reference to *Sartor Resartus*, a work that combines fact and fiction, satire and history, was a signal that this anecdote was fictitious.[38]

Most of the stories in *Seven Horizons* are about his experiences in England and Patagonia; about twenty pages deal with his years in Texas. In a book of 457 pages, Finger barely mentioned his marriage, referred briefly to Christopher Ferguson, and wrote nothing specifically about Nellie. Reversing the order of events, he wrote without elaboration that six months after starting to work for a railroad, "I married." He declared at the end of *Seven Horizons*, with obvious self-pity, that the final horizon was the duty to support his children, this seemingly tepid goal a hint that he sacrificed bolder dreams to care for his family.[39]

Finger completed the manuscript in the last months of 1929. Its first-person narration, length, excessive detail, and lack of a dramatic arc doomed *Seven Horizons* as a novel, and Finger's editor at Doubleday, Page, Harry E. Maule, who also handled the Livingstone book, decided to promote it as a memoir by the adventuresome English author. After reviewing the galleys and index, Finger was gripped by second thoughts. Perhaps, he wrote to Maule, "the title page should carry some explanatory sub-title ... to indicate that it is ... an autobiographical romance ... rather than an autobiography."

He confessed, "I invented names for some of my characters. At times I threw the picture somewhat out of focus." Maule used the letter as an introduction but did not add a subtitle.[40]

Doubleday, Page promoted the book heavily, comparing Finger to Jack London by calling him "A Modern Sea Wolf."[41] A columnist in the *Herald Tribune* called the book "a gallant story of highly spiced adventure." The *Philadelphia Record* called it "as strange and colorful an Odyssey as one will find in contemporary letters" and compared Finger to James Huneker.[42] The *Herald Tribune*'s official review was by Harvey Fergusson, a journalist with his own new book about an art colony in Taos, New Mexico, in which he used fictitious names to disguise the "goings-on . . . among the art boys and girls," as a reviewer put it. "I like this book and the man revealed in it," Fergusson wrote, but "I am bound to say that from a literary viewpoint it leaves much to be desired." Finger "has no clear perception of what is relevant to the theme . . . The result is sometimes confusion and sometimes dullness."[43]

The *Saturday Review* placed a short, unsigned review on the front page, hinting at the reviewer's familiarity with Finger. "The capacity for friendship which early brought him into *intimacy with men* . . . remained with Mr. Finger through the years [emphasis added]." Harry Hansen and Richard Massock gave the book brief mentions. Donald Davidson, the book editor for the *Tennessean*, published a somewhat critical review, while Odd McIntyre called *Horizons* "a swell book."[44] Then in mid-May came one of the highlights of Finger's professional life. With a large portrait of Finger and an illustration of mid-Victorian London, the *New York Times* devoted the entirety of page 3 of its Book Review to *Seven Horizons*. Rose C. Feld, a staff writer, called the book "the expression of a deep, rich personality who has lived rebelliously, adventurously and well." His writing was an "art so subtle that it seems no art at all," with language "reminiscent in parts of Swift and Addison, of Defoe and Thackeray[,] like drinking a spiritual beaker of good brown ale."[45]

As the reviews accumulated, Finger still worried that his combination of truth and fantasy would backfire. "Many people will fail to see how . . . mixing fact and fiction and [calling] the resultant book . . . biography can make for culture," he wrote. (A few years later, he admitted he was "guilty of all sorts of crimes" involving fabrications in his work.)[46] Indeed, a reviewer for the *Bookman* found the book "baffling" in not being "an autobiography, in the accepted sense of the term." The *Nation* published a belated, brief, negative review of the memoir in September, finding Finger's final horizon "limited" and "commonplace" and the book "very curious," with "vivid vistas" that were "flattened out now and then under the heavy weight of platitudes." The *New Republic* also published a brief, negative review.[47]

Some members of the Finger family failed to appreciate the omissions and fabrications. The complete absence of Arnold Fox from the story of his early life in London and the Patagonian period enraged Arnold and Phillipina's daughter Mildred. Confusing Finger's voyages to Chile and the US, the first with Fox and the second with his brother George, she asked one of Finger's friends, "Did Charles Finger . . . mention . . . that two men were with him on his longest voyage—his brother, and a man who became his brother-in-law? I suspect not."[48] Helen resented his entire omission of Nellie. "It's so unfair," she told her sons later. "He said, 'I married.' I mean, her bearing five kids and that's all the credit he gives her. And then he said, 'Mrs. F gathered up her lamp and went back and cooked dinner.' And it was an old iron cookstove that you fed wood."[49] Perhaps to smooth things over with Helen, who had entered Gulf Park College with Ann Coyle and one of Ann's cousins, Finger made a quick trip in mid-April 1930 to visit her and took her and a classmate sailing.[50]

Despite the mixed reviews, publication of *Seven Horizons* created a new wave of attention and speaking invitations, including one from the Rowfant Club in Cleveland. For Finger the gathering at an exclusive men's club was a fantasy come true, with a candlelit dinner in a paneled room among men who were "the sort to seek a life fine and free" and after-dinner conversation in the library with Finger as the center of attention. Even though one of the members, the literary editor for the Cleveland *Plain Dealer*, pointed out typographical errors and other problems in *Seven Horizons*, Finger enjoyed the evening, calling it "a gay comedy."[51]

[12]

GOLDEN DAYS

FINGER TOOK HIS DAUGHTER Helen on two lengthy driving trips in the
US in 1930 and 1931, in part to launch her as an illustrator. The first trip
was with an old friend from London, Charles A. Newman, whom Finger
knew in 1884 when he was an apprentice teacher at the parish school where
Newman's father was the schoolmaster.[1] Finger, Helen, and Newman made
a four-week cross-country driving trip while she was on summer break from
college, seeing parts of Texas, Mexico, New Mexico, Arizona, and Colorado
before turning east for New Orleans and the Gulf Coast, camping many
nights and occasionally getting a hotel room for Helen. The highlight of the
trip was a stop at Maddox's new cattle ranch in Arizona. Finger, Newman,
and Maddox plunged into conversation with "that large understanding and
keen discernment which makes for the proper entertainment of friends."[2]
They read aloud from Robert Burns's cantata "The Jolly Beggar," a declaration of the rights of men to love and fellowship—perhaps from the 1914
edition published by Thomas Bird Mosher, a small, beautiful book printed
on handmade paper that included an introduction by William Reedy and
commentary by Andrew Lang and R. L. Stevenson. (A close friend of Reedy,
Mosher had published works by Oscar Wilde and Walt Whitman.)[3]

One can imagine that after enjoying a few of the drinks Maddox liked to
serve, Finger and Maddox gave a dramatic performance of a poem George
had written, in collaboration with their mutual friend Stuart Olivier, that
reveals the fun-loving nature of Finger's most secretive friend.[4] It was a par-
ody of Bob Davis's well-known poem "I Am the Printing Press" (1911) and a
rhapsody on alcohol and Greek love. The title was "An Ode to the Majujah,"
a humorous reference to Majiouge, the Arabic name for a legendary giant.[5]
Alluding to Tennyson's poem "Ulysses," the poem's speaker declares, "I
gave the blood and fire to the veins of Ulysses and the high courage for his

great questing of the Happy Isles." Finger-like, Maddox and Olivier worked their literary friends into the piece: "I have lured Cobbs and Davises . . . and Fingers and Maddoxes to the heights and have shown them the grandeur that was Greece and the glory that was of a French vineyard." The poem is a declaration of independence and tolerance: "I am yet the Captain of my Soul. I am tolerant of all save Intolerance." It ends "I am the King of Kings. I am King Alcohol."[6] Davis liked the poem and envied Maddox for moving to Arizona and stepping "out of the maelstrom of life onto a broad highway that will lead you to ultimate happiness," something Davis felt he would never have the "nerve to do." "Dear Sep," he told Maddox, "Whitman's philosophy was the only philosophy."[7]

The landscape at Maddox's ranch reminded Finger of Tierra del Fuego. The sun rising over the Arizona plain gradually lightened the terrain of muted browns, greens, and grays, slowly bringing the strong limbs of the acacia trees into relief. The scarlet throats of hummingbirds, darting from flower to flower, flashed like a gaucho's satin-lined cape. After the sun set at the far rim of the vast, sweeping, quiet night, the stars seemed to flicker like a lover winking from across a room, a country, the years. It was a place of "health and activity and freedom," Finger told the readers of *All's Well*. "A man could drift to eternity, in such conditions."[8] Apparently leaving Helen and Newman at the ranch, he and Maddox made a trip to Mexico, driving south on Highway 82 through mountains and wide valleys, past meadows and tree-lined streams. In the border city of Nogales, Americans were free to enjoy drinks without risking arrest, and men ambled along narrow, dusty streets, in and out of bars, billiard halls, and small hotels that had second-story iron balconies. In a saloon where "a sort of cool twilight" made patrons hard to recognize, Finger "needed no invitation to accept the amber colored glass of lager beer." "How fine" it was "to be away from people" who were "timid and anxious and despondent and ill-natured and complicated!" He felt he was at a turning point. At Goldendays with Maddox, he "dwelt in shining realms[,]a world engrossing and beautiful, [of] golden prospects. . . . The rugged mountains, the cacti and the queer snake cactus fences" (cactus hedges), "the sun-flooded valleys, the dark water of the mountain stream glimmering in the shade, the far haze-hung mountains: all these stay fast in the memory." There on the border, they did not have to draw "a curtain between us and happiness."[9]

Back at Gayeta Finger felt "renewed strength, and finer courage" to "meet dark days as shadows through which we must pass,"[10] like Tennyson's Ulysses who believed—despite being burdened with "an aged wife"—it was "not too late to seek a newer world," to "sail beyond the sunset" and find "the Happy Isles."[11] He went to New York in September 1930 to pitch a travel book with Helen's sketches to the publishing house William M. Morrow and Company, which accepted his proposal.[12] While he was there, he went to Yonkers to visit Charles Driscoll. Driscoll was planning a trip with his good friend Jacob Omansky, the business manager for the *Philadelphia Record*, whom Driscoll met when they both worked for the *Cleveland Press* in 1924.[13] He had introduced Finger and Omansky by letter, and Finger had sent Omansky a copy of *Seven Horizons*, provocatively inscribing it "to Jacob Omansky who, I understand, has mingled generously with men[, b]y his friend Charles Finger."[14]

He called the travel book *Adventure under Sapphire Skies* and promoted it as a guide for tourists, but the book was a typical, meandering Finger narrative with little practical information, some of the detours actually veiled references to mirthful times with friends.[15] Morrow accepted a few simple drawings by Helen for the book and released *Adventure* in the spring of 1931. A reviewer for the *New York Herald Tribune* noted the book's lack of useful detail but praised it as "a charming companion for the stay-at-home."[16] At a time when fewer Americans could afford driving vacations, this was a selling point, and other reviews of *Adventure* were positive, if usually brief.[17] As the good reviews accumulated, Morrow placed a large display advertisement for *Adventure* in the *Saturday Review*, where it appeared directly below an advertisement for *The Caliph of Bagdad*, which Bob Davis had written with a coauthor. In Mencken's *American Mercury*, positive reviews of *Adventure* and *Caliph of Bagdad* appeared in the same issue.[18] Helen's drawings received little attention, but Finger was determined to launch her as an illustrator and worked with her in 1931 on a collection of folktales about Paul Bunyan that he had privately printed. A principal strength of *A Paul Bunyan Geography* was the two-page map that Helen drew. Driscoll called it "most charming," and the *New York Times* noted, in a sidebar to a full-length review of James Stevens's *The Saginaw Paul Bunyan*, that Finger's text was "amusing," the printing beautiful, and Helen's map "delightful."[19]

Helen completed the two-year program at Gulf Park that May and planned to enter the Kansas City Art Institute in September.[20] With libraries around the country buying *Adventure*, Morrow commissioned a second travel book, and Helen and Finger ventured forth again, this time with Charles Jr. and Henry Pitz, the illustrator from Philadelphia who came to the Longmans, Green reception. Pitz was an excellent, prolific drawer and painter who worked for *St. Nicholas* and *Boy's Life* and had illustrated several books.[21] Leaving Nellie at Gayeta as usual, the four went to Colorado, Utah, Arizona, California, Washington, Vancouver, Montana, and the Dakotas. At Santa Barbara, California, they visited the studio of the artist John Edward Borein, who kindly gave Helen a pen-and-ink drawing. They visited Nellie's father and sister May in San Francisco.[22] In Oakland Finger saw Ernest Schumacher for the first time since they parted in Patagonia. The two old friends talked about how they coped now with the tedium and responsibility of everyday life. Schumacher built model ships that he sailed on the bay with his son. He showed Finger a model of a schooner that "was like a jewel," Finger marveled, "built plank on plank though the tiny planks were not more than a third of an inch wide." The old friends wished they could buy a sloop to "sail among the Aleutians [and] enjoy the sight of great crested breakers and far headlands, [to] recapture old moods of delight when we sailed into strange ports at twilight to see some tall lighthouse shining like an evening star."[23]

Finger enjoyed "Grecian companionship" with Pitz on this trip, but "there were times" when he wished "for the presence of a certain friend."[24] He may have seen Maddox in Seattle, where George's brother lived; later, he fantasized about departing Seattle to leave behind the responsibilities of life on land.[25] He concluded the new travel book, which he called *Footloose in the West*, this way: "The tour was at an end. But was there ever a congenial crowd that separated without regret? Was there ever a gay company that did not prolong its farewells[?]" He went on, "Life is sweet when each new day beckons to adventure, and when one flees, with good companions . . . and we need not everlastingly occupy ourselves with ends and aims. . . . Here's to those who know the breezy hill-top," he concluded in a crescendo of veiled exhortation. "Above all, here's to those who know the greatest thing in life—true companionship!"[26]

Morrow published *Footloose* in March 1932. Positive reviews appeared in major newspapers and the *Saturday Review*. Most promisingly, the *New York Times* said, "the pen-and-ink sketches by Helen Finger add to the charm and color of the book."[27] Helen was becoming the "artist in bloom" that Finger "wanted her to be," giving him hope that she could take over as the primary breadwinner at Gayeta.[28] Before she came home that summer, he expanded a small stone playhouse on the hillside below the lodge into a studio for her. Helen thought it was a "dear little studio," and she and her friend Arista Arnold, a classmate at Gulf Park and Kansas City who spent part of the

summer at Gayeta, worked on drawings and paintings there, her father drop-
ping in at the end of the day to see their progress.[29]

"Far from happy in his marriage," Maddox came to Gayeta repeatedly.[30]
The situation at Goldendays had become untenable. As Davis put it, Maddox
had retired from the army to "live the life you wish to live [and] read the
books you had no time heretofore to read," but Helen Maddox and her
mother, the consummate party planners, envisioned Goldendays as a busy
resort for middle-class residents of Tucson and Douglas who could afford
a day trip to the mountains and wealthy East Coasters who could stay for a
month or longer. Entrepreneurial landowners in Arizona were converting
cattle and sheep ranches, even small suburban properties, to dude ranches
that attracted paying visitors for a day, a month, or the summer with restaurant meals, like Laura Lighton's Green Tree Inn in Fayetteville, and weekend
parties with horseback riding and polo. This sort of dude ranch was a logical
culmination of Martha's years of experience in the hospitality business. She
and Helen began using the main house for buffet meals and bridge parties
and adding guest cottages and buying ponies for paying guests to ride.[31] They
even changed the name of the ranch to Hacienda de Los Encinos, for the
evergreen oaks in the Sonoita Valley, and rented it to another couple to run.
Helen began going by Mrs. H. C. Maddox, so it seemed George was no longer a crucial part of her lifestyle or identity.

Finger thought Maddox should divorce her. He and George spent their
days at the stone cottage, the retreat that Finger called his "forest office,"
where he had a sofa and comfortable chairs and kept books and maps and a
globe.[32] One day, Finger roasted a beef joint in the cottage fireplace and wrote
a letter to Wilbur Stone while Maddox sat "at the green baize table by the
long window" reading old issues of *Reedy's Mirror*. They walked down to the
main house for suppers that Nellie prepared and listened to records or read
aloud before the big fireplace in the evenings—Finger from something by
Hamlin Garland and Maddox from Andrew Lang's translations of Homer's
Iliad and *Odyssey*. "These were 'golden days,'" Finger told Stone.[33] Elizabeth
Cox joined them for the holidays, while Helen Maddox and Ann went to
the Wrights' home in Douglas.[34] As Helen and Martha gave more parties at
the ranch in the early months of 1931, Maddox continued traveling between
Sonoita and Gayeta.[35] He evidently went to Long Beach in February, taking
Finger with him.[36] In April he helped Finger entertain a few local friends
at Gayeta. By the end of 1931, Maddox worked out an arrangement to sell
Goldendays to his in-laws so that Helen and her mother could continue

operating it as a dude ranch. Confiding to Stone, "I'm always glad to see him," Finger looked forward to Maddox's next visit to Gayeta.[37]

"Gayeta must be kept running," Finger told his son Hubert in a letter, in spite of the high costs of Helen's art school tuition and the financial drain of *All's Well*.[38] The little magazine was more expensive than ever—he had begun having it printed as a saddle-stitched booklet with a blue paper cover and cover art by Pitz depicting a giant in a broad-brimmed hat, holding a lasso and waving a cape, with a sailing ship and mountains in the background—so Finger worked out an agreement for Driscoll's friend Omansky to become a half-owner and take over its production and printing costs, with Finger to mail copy to Philadelphia. They announced this arrangement in April 1932: "Our publishing of All's Well for Charley Finger is giving him an opportunity to do the best work of his extraordinary career," Omansky declared optimistically, calling on subscribers to help them double the subscription list from five hundred to a thousand names.[39]

"If Major Maddox is in your vicinage give him a hand-clasp for me," William Griffith wrote to Finger in December 1932.[40] Maddox did visit that month and helped host a large dinner party in the main house, a Gayetan version of the New Face dinners that he and the rest of their New York friends held each year. The guests were university professors, Charles Jr., and Emil Finger, who had moved with his family to Farmington, Arkansas. In a lengthy account of this occasion, Finger referred to Maddox as his "counterpoise." "There were twelve of us, and the conversation, desultory (as table talk should be), but lively, kept up well until cigars were lit and the table cleared." Here Finger alluded to *Dr. Johnson's Table Talk*, an anthology of excerpts from Boswell's biography that became the model for a type of memoir focusing on impromptu comments made around a dining table. His reference to clearing the table was the only hint that Nellie helped host the party.[41]

Maddox evidently spent Christmas elsewhere, perhaps in Tucson. He had become acquainted with Conrad Richter, a writer who lived next door to the house that the Maddoxes maintained. Encouraged by Richter, he was writing poetry and had at least two poems accepted by the *Atlantic Monthly*, although he apparently used a pseudonym, protective as ever of his anonymity.[42] Despite Maddox's absence, the holiday at Gayeta was a particular pleasure for Finger, with a tree twinkling with candles, Helen's friend Arista again a houseguest, a little wine on Christmas Eve, and the hustle and bustle of Emil and Amelia and their children arriving. They played charades and musical chairs after dinner and sang "Auld Lang Syne" at midnight.[43] As he wrote his usual New Year's greeting for *All's Well*, Finger recalled the harbor in Seattle and repeated his longing for a new adventure with a few companions, magnanimously hinting that one could be Omansky. He wanted to escape "nonsense about money" and live "golden hours" of games and talk and music and "friendly silence." From Seattle they could sail away, "knowing that strange delight that comes with the farewell to land, and the sight of far-flung, haze-hung mountains." Employing the eroticism of the sailboat on open water that he introduced in *Seven Horizons*, Finger imagined "the delight of the music of waters; and the delight of flying sea-birds sharp etched on blue and gone in a flash." His rhapsody went on: "There would be tropic nights, after the tropic sunset all copper and gold and crimson glory, with legions of stars." The suggestive image of the precipice came to him again: Mountains would be "rough ramparts from which unleashed lightnings [*sic*] might leap." Reaching the Chilean archipelago, he and his unnamed friends would be "free and unrestrained and liberal." "O, come, let us go, bold hearts!" he exclaimed.[44]

[**13**]

HIS GAYETAN DREAM

RATHER THAN MORE "golden hours," the mid-1930s brought a series of crises and setbacks including the defection of Finger's youngest child, cancer, loss of his virtual literary society—the readership of *All's Well*—and the reconciliation of George and Helen Maddox. It began with the disappearance of seventeen-year-old Herbert Eric. As the children knew, Finger wanted them all to remain at Gayeta to help and support Nellie—Hubert to work as a contractor, Kitty as a librarian, Charles Jr. raising chickens, Helen as a freelance illustrator, and Herb running the farm. Now Charles Jr. planned to be an archaeologist, and Hub and Kitty both were in Akron. Kitty had married her suitor, Felix Helbling, over Finger's objection, and he had seethed about her departure. Helen later believed that he sent her to the remote women's college in Mississippi to prevent her from going the way of her older sister.[1] Herb, the youngest child, had no interest in farming and left home without warning in February 1933 to seek a shipboard job. Nellie was "crushed," and Finger, in Helen's words, "felt very sorry for himself."[2] How could he hope to ever leave Nellie if none of the children took over as breadwinners?

Two months later, he learned that he had skin cancer. "It took a little stiffening to receive that news," he confided to Hub. Treatment involved temporarily strapping one or more small platinum tubes containing radium salts to the affected area of his head. "I walked about the clinic with $8000 worth of radium for ten hours" and "saw my savings vanish." It was a devastating expense without a guarantee of success, and Finger waited weeks to learn if the treatment stopped the spread of the cancer. Once the physician told him the radiation worked, Finger could joke. He had thought if he must die, he might take "some political upstart with me into the dark—say some European tyrant who is harrying Jews, and Catholics, and Socialists in

Central Europe!" This was a gesture to Jacob Omansky, who was Jewish by birth if not by practice.[3]

Money was a serious problem. Finger's production of new books and his critical reputation were declining, royalties were unreliable, and despite eliminating the expensive covers, *All's Well* cost $800 more than it earned from subscriptions in 1932, forcing Finger and Omansky to convert the semi-monthly magazine to a quarterly journal. Finger floated the idea of a book on the history of the fur trade in North America but had no takers.[4] On a quick visit to Gayeta in July 1933, Omansky offered to recommend one of Finger's book ideas to his friend John R. Fraser, the vice president of the Philadelphia publishing house John C. Winston Company, but nothing came of that for several years.[5] Finger compiled a collection of his essays on writers for E. P. Dutton, but the publishing house released the book too late for Christmas sales in 1933. The title, *After the Great Companions: A Free Fantasia on a Lifetime of Reading*, alluded to the lines "Allons! After the great companions!" in Walt Whitman's "Song of the Open Road."[6] Reviews were mixed, and the negative ones were brutal. Edward M. Kingsbury, who received a Pulitzer Prize for editorial writing and almost never signed his book reviews, wrote a signed review in the *New York Times* that mocked Finger as one who "never . . . had to wear a college harness." The *Los Angeles Times* called the book "astoundingly bad." Finger wrote bravely to Wilbur Stone that publishers were making offers, but Dutton did not publish any more of his books, and Finger sold almost nothing else until 1935, when D. Appleton-Century brought out a collaboration by Finger and Henry Pitz, *The Distant Prize: A Book about Rovers, Rangers and Rascals.*[7]

Finger had revived his professional association with the Century Company after it merged with D. Appleton, Bob Davis's publisher, in 1933, writing an introduction for a new edition of *Beowulf* that Pitz illustrated.[8] *The Distant Prize* was a series of loosely told stories of explorers and other figures in history, including some material Finger reworked from *Seven Horizons*. Among the positive reviews, the *New York Times* gave it a full column, praising Finger's "fictionesque narration."[9] D. Appleton-Century published one other book by Finger, *Valiant Vagabonds* (1936). It was another treatment of his experiences in Patagonia—its title a Dickensian gay innuendo—with references to the schooner *Rippling Wave* and Schumacher, "a companion of mine in the Magellan country [when] we were young and beautiful."[10] Again Finger used the image of flying birds seen from the deck of a ship; again he evoked Whitman in a veiled plea to Maddox to take to the road with him:

"What is a vagabond but a wanderer? And who, reading Whitman's 'Song of the Open Road' would not wish to be one, if he had the courage!" The *New York Times* and *Los Angeles Times* gave *Vagabonds* brief, positive reviews.[11]

Finger and Pitz worked together on two other projects in 1935, *A Dog at His Heel* for John C. Winston, where Omansky put in a word two years earlier, and *Our Navy: An Outline History for Young People*—a book destined for elementary school libraries—for Houghton Mifflin. *A Dog* was the story of friends in Australia who transport sheep to Patagonia with their dog Jock. Helen Ferris, Carl Van Doren's successor as editor-in-chief of the Junior Literary Guild, had reviewed the first draft and suggested revisions that Finger gladly made.[12] Pitz also was the illustrator for Finger's first book for Henry Holt since 1928, *When Guns Thundered at Tripoli* (1937), but there was no guarantee that book would earn Finger much money. *Kirkus Reviews*, a fairly new book review magazine based in New York and targeted to booksellers, pigeonholed Finger as a staple for schools and libraries and said he was hard to read.[13]

Finger continued selling book reviews during this period, principally to the *New York Herald Tribune*. After William Rose Benét of the *Saturday Review* visited Gayeta while on a lecture tour in April 1936,[14] Benét's colleague Christopher Morley commissioned three reviews from Finger for the *Review*, the first since 1930. One was of a biography of James Radburne, one of the gauchos Finger knew in South America. Morley, who regarded Finger with affection, devoted a full page in August to his memories. "When I was young and beautiful," Finger wrote, "I rode with Jimmy . . . and knew him as a good companion." He declared the biography "to be authentic." He also reviewed *Early Americana and Other Stories* by Maddox's friend Conrad Richter, proclaiming it "a book of beauty and of power" and awkwardly adding that Richter "realizes the eternal permanence of human emotions."[15]

To introduce Helen to the publishing world, Finger worked with her on a small book that he probably sent out as Christmas gifts in 1933. *The Magic Tower* (1933) is about four children who live at a place that resembles Gayeta. The tower is a perch in a tree where Ann looks into a magic globe and sees the kind of scene that Finger used vividly and repeatedly to represent his dream of sailing away with Maddox: "a sunlit sea[,] many flying gulls, [and] a splendid ship, gay with white and shining paint." The Kings Arms Press, a new small imprint of a publishing house in Pennsylvania, printed the fable as an octavo with illustrations by Helen, and Finger inscribed a copy "To GWM: Christmas 1933, this Gayetan dream."[16] Finger also found Helen some freelance work for Bellows-Reeve Company, which published a sub-scription anthology series, *Journeys through Bookland*, for children. He had made a new friend in the company's Scottish vice president for sales, James Keddie, who contracted with Finger to write material for a series of read-ing guides for parents and occasionally bought drawings from Helen. Finger proposed that Bellows-Reeve pay him and Helen to produce an illustrated weekly for children. Keddie's boss rejected that idea, but after Finger's illness, Keddie put him on the Bellows-Reeve payroll as an editor for a retainer of $20 per month. Keddie also became friendly with Omansky and Pitz. When Bellows-Reeve published Keddie's memoir, *Shady Corner*, Finger wrote a foreword, and Pitz designed the jacket.[17]

After Helen left the Kansas City Art Institute in 1934 and returned to Gayeta, she and Finger began making trips to meet prospective publishers and strengthen relationships with professional artists and potential spon-sors.[18] One of their first trips was to Massachusetts to see Keddie, who took them to the small resort town of Rockport. Surrounded on three sides by the Atlantic, with shifting water and clouds providing endlessly changing scenes for landscape painters, the town was one of the country's best-known art colonies. One could wander up and down quiet lanes, in and out of art-ists' workshops, and into the Blacksmith Shop for coffee.[19] It was "a queer artists' colony," Finger observed in *All's Well*, modifying this comment, for readers who might not appreciate his meaning, with the explanation that "men and women went about in inartistic garments." Helen told him, "I know . . . what's at the back of your mind. You'd like to live here—part of the time at least." She was right, Finger told his *All's Well* circle—he did want to live near water in the company of artistic friends. They went on to New York, visiting the Museum of Modern Art and staying at the Algonquin Hotel, probably thanks to Omansky. They saw Omansky, Pitz, Charles Driscoll, and Philip Cornick, but this pleasant interlude came to an abrupt end when Nellie contacted them with the news that a storm had blown the roof off the house. The damage was disastrous, Finger shared in *All's Well*.[20]

Back at home Helen revived the reputation of Gayeta as an art colony, rather than an unsuccessful farm, by drawing a "cartograph" of the farm and Gayeta Lodge for the family to use as a Christmas card. It was a humorous map depicting the farm as a legendary stopping place for writers and artists: "Here Carl Sandburg meditated," "Here Herbert Sprague played 'Rip Van Winkle,'" here was "the studio where Helen and Associates slap paint." She placed the Maddoxes, George with a cigar and suitcases and Helen holding the leash of a small dog, in the lower left corner with the caption "The Major and Helen M. Decide to Settle in Arkansas for the Winter." The Maddoxes had reached an accord, leaving Tucson to begin a nomadic life of summers camping on lakes north of Ottawa—in near constant communion with Henry Bankhead, who was posted at the American Legation as commercial attaché—and winters in the South with Bob Davis a frequent companion. They actually stayed at Gayeta only about a week in December 1935, leaving in time to meet Davis at Long Beach for Christmas and "a tour amongst the bayou folk." Maddox wrote to Richter that while he was at the Fingers', he reviewed the final draft of *Dog at His Heel*, "going over the brute, stroking him from nose to tail, smoothing out his rough coat," and mentioned that he thought Davis's new memoir was a "knockout."[21]

The next summer, Finger and Helen drove to Iowa to visit Jay G. Sigmund, one of his long-distance friends through *All's Well*. Sigmund was a successful regionalist writer who, as an insurance executive, could support various artistic enterprises. He was an important patron of the rising regionalist painter Grant Wood. Wood was staying in a rented cottage near Sigmund's summer home in Waubeck,[22] and Sigmund took the Fingers to meet him. Wood was working on, or may have recently completed, *Death on Ridge Road*, a painting inspired by an automobile accident involving Sigmund and Sigmund's wife. His most famous painting was *American Gothic* (1930), a disturbing portrait of a farmer and his daughter standing before a small farmhouse, but some of the rather openly gay artist's paintings were highly suggestive scenes of nude men. Those paintings were ambiguous and provocative, the sheen of the sun-kissed skin reflecting the male gaze, a rejection of cosmopolitanism and urbanism, yet arguably a form of modernism—the expression of a man who, like Finger, drew creative energy from a sense of displacement.[23] Finger was intrigued by Wood's recent marriage to a slightly older woman, Sara Sherman Maxon, who cared for Wood's ailing mother. Quite unlike Nellie Finger, Maxon regarded her marriage as a friendship in support of her husband's art.[24]

Finger's account of meeting Wood was in one of his last columns in *All's Well*, because he and Omansky suspended publication in late 1935. Finger had understood that without sufficient paying subscribers, Omansky could not support the little magazine forever. "There are probably not," Finger admitted, "more than a thousand people who are interested in the sort of thing for which . . . *All's Well* stands." He was losing that circle of understanding readers that had been his consolation during the last fifteen years of domestic life at Gayeta, the secret club he created after many years of drifting and isolation. He felt the loss keenly.[25]

Reviews in 1936 of *A Dog* were positive, although Anne Thaxter Eaton, one of two children's book reviewers for the *New York Times*, was less enthusiastic and waited until June 1937 to notice the book, calling it "a disappointment" despite Pitz's illustrations because "the story rambles along without [a] clear-cut dramatic sequence."[26] However, Eaton's counterpart at the *New York Times*, Ellen Lewis Buell, endorsed *Our Navy* for children and adults, and Houghton Mifflin advertised the book in the *Los Angeles Times*.[27] Even better, Finger and Helen received commissions from two juvenile magazines in 1936. *Story Parade* was a project of two women in New York, Barbara Nolen and Lockie Parker, with the Association for Arts in Childhood as sponsor. The Arkansas poet John Gould Fletcher, whom Finger had known since 1927, and his wife, Charlie May Simon, may have recommended them to the editors. The Fingers had become friends with Fletcher, and Charlie May's former husband, Howard Simon, was the art director for *Story Parade*.[28] Nolen and Parker invited Finger to serve on the magazine's editorial board, and Simon invited Helen to illustrate a story.[29] Around the same time, *Scholastic* published Finger's story "The Hero of Mexican Folklore," with illustrations by Helen, in its May issue.[30] For the first time, it seemed possible that Helen could earn a living as an illustrator, freeing Finger to leave Gayeta. The prospect was exhilarating. "I'm not through yet," Finger told an interviewer. "I have not chosen my home."[31] Then, in June, an editor in Los Angeles, Helen L. Hoke of the Julia Ellsworth Ford Foundation, reached out to the Fingers, inviting Helen to illustrate *Bela the Juggler* by Jeanette C. Shirk, which the foundation planned to publish, and predicting that she could become a famous illustrator of children's books. Gratitude outweighing his ethics, Finger committed a remarkable act of nepotism by reviewing several Ford Foundation books, including *Bela*, for the *Herald Tribune* without acknowledging that Helen was his daughter.[32]

He and Helen made a fast trip to the Northeast in June 1937, stopping in Washington, DC, for the ethnomusicologists John and Alan Lomax to record Finger singing a few folk songs at the Library of Congress and seeing Pitz in Philadelphia.[33] They spent just one day in New York, probably to see Nolen, who wanted to talk face to face about how they could collaborate more closely, and Hoke, who had left Los Angeles to oversee juvenile publications for Henry Holt and Company and was preparing to release *When Guns Thundered*.[34] Hoke had commissioned Helen to illustrate a book for Holt,

Chimney-sweep Tower by Rita Kissin (1937), which had the potential to be a bigger revenue stream for Gayeta. *Kirkus* called it "delightful," and the *Los Angeles Times* predicted it would be popular with children.[35]

———————

THE MADDOXES RETURNED to Gayeta in November 1936, arriving in a travel trailer with Davis. They stayed just one night, with all three sleeping in the trailer, but the Fingers made the most of their visit, cooking over camp-fires and inviting friends and local journalists to meet their guests. Finger entertained by playing the piano and reading aloud from a collection of Irish legends.[36] The Maddox–Davis party continued west to visit Richter and his wife, Harvena, in Albuquerque and spend Christmas with Helen's mother and stepfather in La Jolla, California.[37] The following week, Davis's newspaper, the *New York Sun*, gave *Vagabonds* a lengthy, positive review, probably thanks to Davis; book reviewers frequently praised books as favors for the authors or the authors' friends. The *Sun*'s attention apparently prompted other reviewers to give the book a few words.[38] Davis also promoted Finger in a column packed with classic and new fabrications, calling "the Squire" a "restless soul," "steeped in the world's operas [and trained] for the concert stage." Unlike Finger, Davis sometimes used Maddox's full name in his columns, once calling him "my old bunkie, Major George F. [*sic*] Maddox," but in this column about Gayeta, he gave George and Helen the aliases Stephen and Luana (her middle name).[39] Finger and Maddox saw each other again in Portland, Oregon, in December, as Maddox traveled north to Seattle to see his brother and Finger arrived to spend Christmas with Kitty and her family. (Felix Helbling had gotten a job in Portland. If Nellie accompanied Finger, he made no note of it.) Something about this rendezvous moved him to observe, "romance requires distance." While he was gone, whoever was at Gayeta on his birthday enjoyed the ham that Omansky sent the family.[40]

The Maddoxes paid a third call at Gayeta in October 1937, again pulling their trailer on their annual migration from Canada to the South. They gathered with the Fingers as usual around Nellie's table for a meal and a long, jolly catch-up conversation. They loved the beautiful flowers, the excellent fishing, and the views at their summer home on a little island in Grand Lake in Quebec. Ann spent part of her summer with them, Helen's relatives visited, and Davis sometimes took fishing vacations at their cabin. The Bankheads had an enormous summer home on a four-acre island nearby, where they often entertained Henry's brothers, William Bankhead—who was now speaker of the US House of Representatives—and US Senator John Bankhead, and their wives or other government officials.[41] The Maddoxes had driven through Detroit to see Honoré, who had established the Paul Honoré Fellowship for young artists who studied with him. He and his wife, Kate, were preparing to move to Maryland to establish their own art colony, a place he intended to be "a fraternity of art."[42] Maddox had urged Richter to get to know Honoré.[43] As for the Fingers, there had been a group show on the university campus the week before for Helen and several others in the Gayeta circle.[44] Despite this, Gayeta was a sad place. Nellie's father, their niece Alice May Finger, Jay Sigmund, and Alice Bergman all had recently died.[45]

The Maddoxes apparently suggested Finger take the spring Caribbean cruise that the Coxes were planning for students and friends of Gulf Park College. Hopeful, Finger went so far as to obtain a letter of introduction to an official in Puerto Rico but did not make the trip.[46] Work was still slow, even though the publishing industry was recovering from the worst of the Depression. Aside from *When Guns Thundered*, which was too new to have yielded any royalties, his primary output in 1937 had been twenty reviews for the *Herald Tribune*—by this time the second most popular literary review in the country—and a few other miscellaneous articles. Fortunately, he and Helen had a new project underway for Holt, a story inspired by Kitty's daughter. Kitty had returned to Arkansas with her husband and child and lived nearby. *Bobbie and Jock and the Mailman* (1938) was a charming, if overly long, story of a little girl and her "Uncle T. J." Helen's drawings illustrated each two-page spread. They planned to dedicate this book to the memory of Alice May.[47] Omansky's friend Fraser at John C. Winston also had accepted another book from Finger, *Give a Man a Horse*, and Kitty was going to help Finger review the proofs.

Give a Man was a book-length adventure story for older boys with a sixteen-year-old protagonist named Bob Honore. A firm called Helbling and Company, named for Kitty and her husband, orders a load of corrugated iron to be shipped to Patagonia. There is a ranch boss named Fraser and a ranch hand named Eric for the Fingers' sea-wandering son. All of these references were clear to anyone in the family. Beyond that point, however, Kitty probably did not fully grasp what she read because *Give a Man* was the most devilishly tongue-in-cheek story Finger published, so packed with gay innuendo that his more understanding friends and fans must have howled with laughter as they read it aloud. When Bob reaches Patagonia, he thanks "his lucky stars that he had escaped monotony and could be vivid and active in a glorious world." He becomes friends with a young native man named Dara, and they take out a small motorboat called *Delight*. For this Finger reused his classic homoerotic shipboard episode: "A thousand sights and sounds combined to proclaim the joy of living[:] the sunlit sky and the racing winds; the poising [*sic*] and swooping sea gulls." When the engine dies, Bob and Dara are "swept into the tumult"; they struggle in a storm and later they share blankets. "Bob, stripped of his wet clothes, found a real delight in the rough warmth of the blanket" and before dozing off thought to himself that Dara was an "attractive character." When they make it to shore, Dara builds a fire to cook some fish. "'I didn't think of that,' ejaculated Bob, as the thought rushed to him that there was such an art as making a fire by the rubbing together of sticks." Later they find some gold lying on the ground, and Bob ejaculates again: "What a land!" Eventually, the story ends when one character declares, "Here's good luck to all of you! Here's luck to horses and to men! . . . Above all, here's to friendship!"[48] Finger dedicated *Give a Man* to Fraser, whom he called "executive and man of affairs, who plays the game of life with zest and enjoyment," possibly another sly joke as Fraser later was accused by a New York dress designer of having an affair with the designer's wife.[49]

Maddox may have found this kind of semitransparent ribaldry unseemly or even risky. Circumspect, reserved, self-contained, he was very different from Finger, who was a performer and, one might even say, exhibitionist. A few weeks before he and Helen left Canada that fall, the *Herald Tribune* published a diatribe by J. Edgar Hoover of the Federal Bureau of Investigation in which Hoover worked to incite fear and hatred of homosexuals.[50] Maddox was so careful to maintain the privacy of his circle of personal relationships that he had declined to be in Davis's beautiful album of photographic portraits and hinted at gay relationships in writing only once, in his humorous poem "Ode to the Majujah," when he referred to some of his friends in pairs—Cobb and Davis, Finger and Maddox—whereas Finger incessantly proclaimed the importance of male friendships in his life.[51] What the two shared, fundamentally, was a love of the written word and nearly two decades of shared secrets. Finger still loved Maddox deeply and completely. "No squarer, fairer man exists," he wrote to him in an inscription.[52]

[14]

THE END OF THE TALE

THE CYCLE OF pitching, writing, and promoting books continued. Finger and Helen went back to the Northeast in the fall of 1938, and Charles Driscoll mentioned in a column that Finger came to New York "once a year, to do business with his publishers." "A little group of New York and Boston folk, friends of Finger," sometimes joined him for "dinner at a downtown restaurant."[1] That New York circle included Omansky, who had gotten married "after years of bachelorhood at the Algonquin hotel," Driscoll observed, to a fashion editor who was—like the women George Maddox and Grant Wood married—divorced with a child. They now had an infant daughter.[2] If the Fingers saw Omansky in 1938, it was the last time. He died in December in circumstances that it seems Driscoll quickly rallied to obscure. Reportedly, Omansky was "taking a canter" in Central Park with a friend, twenty-three-year-old John Stevenson.[3] Stevenson's story was that Omansky had a sudden heart attack while in the saddle; the horse slowed to a halt, and Stevenson then lowered Omansky to the ground. Driscoll wrote about Omansky's death twice in his column, emphasizing that Omansky was married with a child. The owner of the *New York Post*, David Stern, reinforced this portrayal of Omansky as a happily married man and reiterated that he was in the saddle, not on the ground, when he died.[4]

Finger's past editor Helen Ferris made *Bobbie and Jock* one of the Junior Literary Guild's selections that year, and the *Saturday Review* gave the book a brief plug, calling it an "unusual adventure of a little girl" with "amusing pictures in black and white by Helen Finger." Libraries around the country purchased copies.[5] Barbara Nolen's organization, the Association for the Arts in Childhood, produced a series of radio broadcasts by authors in March 1939, and Finger performed by reading an excerpt of *Give a Man a Horse*. He did some freelance work for the Federal Writers' Project and struggled to finish a novel for boys, *Cape Horn Snorter*, to satisfy his editor at Houghton Mifflin.[6] As the Maddoxes meandered toward Gayeta in April or May for another catch-up visit, Finger's friends John Gould Fletcher, who had visited a few times, and Carl Van Doren received Pulitzer Prizes, Fletcher for a collection of poems and Van Doren for a biography of Benjamin Franklin.[7] As for the Maddoxes, they anticipated more cross-continent travel, possibly to Mexico with Henry Bankhead, whose wife had died. Paul and Kate Honoré were settling into their new life in the Maryland countryside overlooking the Susquehanna River, where their art colony was taking shape.[8]

Finger and Helen worked that summer on another project for the John C. Winston Company, a set of twelve brief, invented folktales to be called *Golden Tales from Far Away*.[9] These stories hint that Finger had begun thinking about his legacy. In one a storyteller named Charlie pauses to light his pipe and advises the nameless narrator that his story should "be made into a book." In another a boy says "The memory of good deeds die if they are not set down in black and white. Will you write it down?"[10] Finger's oldest friends, Charles Peer and Henry Somerfield, were dead, Peer in 1934 and Somerfield in July 1939. He mused in a letter to Wilbur Stone that he was the last of his circle in London. Wanting nothing as much as to see England again, he wrote rather desperately to Bob Davis, offering to provide an introduction to the lord high chancellor and travel sketches by Helen if he would take them to London. Davis responded kindly that he was about to leave for the Adriatic and Mediterranean, but perhaps when he returned there could be "a Charles-Helen-Robusto dash in whatever direction profit lies."[11]

England declared war against Germany in September 1939. On the radio Edward R. Murrow reported from London each night, sometimes from rooftops as bombs fell around him. His updates were like a tour of Finger's England. "This afternoon," he said, "I spent two hours and gallon of precious gasoline looking at London from Hampstead Heath," where Finger and Peer ambled on that romantic day in 1890, "to St. Paul's," near the coffeehouses and halls where the radicals gave speeches, to "Fleet Street, the home of London's newspapers [and] down the Strand," where Finger saw *The Gondoliers* at the Savoy Theatre, to Trafalgar Square, the site of Cunninghame Graham's stand. On New Year's Eve, Murrow delivered a message rather like Finger's annual greeting but in a sorrowful, chilling context: "The end of 1939 finds . . . one million men are under arms in Britain. . . . Homes have been broken up by evacuation [and] tens of thousands of men and women [are] manning searchlights and antiaircraft guns, fire engines and ambulances. . . . I wish for the stupid a little understanding, and for the understanding a little poetry.... Those words were written by a German, Heinrich Heine."[12] Finger had read Heine, marking this line in the essay "The Liberation": "The deepest truth blooms only out of the deepest love."[13] The Fayetteville newspaper began running a serial story called "Blackout" that took place in London.[14] In March Murrow reported that the British people did not understand the US government's focus on a negotiated peace because "peace negotiated with the present German government . . . would be something in the nature of a supercolossal Munich."[15]

Finger's literary prospects grew cloudier. *Kirkus* dismissed *Golden Tales* as "fairly conventional" without "any particular reason" to exist.[16] He became embroiled in a feud between John Fletcher and a writer named Clyde Brion Davis. Fletcher had wanted to write a book about the Arkansas River for a series that Farrar and Rinehart was developing, but the publishing house gave the project to Davis.[17] When the book was released, Fletcher urged Finger to criticize it in the *New York Herald Tribune*. Finger did so immediately on several grounds, including a poor index, impressionistic content, and implausible dialogue. Davis retaliated in a review for the *Saturday Review* of Vance Randolph's new *Ozark Anthology*. A former writer for Emanuel Haldeman-Julius and a prolific freelancer and self-taught folklorist, Randolph had included a version of Finger's old account of exploring the mountains with Honoré.[18] Davis ridiculed Finger's essay as "average magazine fiction about hillbillies" and provided an excerpt that was Finger's cryptic, bloated writing at its worst: "There are other worlds than ours where sunshine and rain are nonexistent and no flowers grow, but in which we need to dwell. In this thought there is comfort. It came upon me to realize that it is good to be alive." Davis concluded, "that will give you an idea."[19]

Finger became more depressed as Germany advanced upon England and the Lord Privy Seal Clement Attlee told the House of Commons, as Murrow reported, "We are free men fighting for our lives, and in order that we may fight more effectively we must give up our freedom." During the Battle of Dunkirk, Murrow described a man in Regent Street with a sign that read "Watch and Pray." Murrow drove around southern England, "through hop fields [and] between high hedges," the countryside where Finger took a "great tramp" in 1889. Prime Minister Winston Churchill told the House of Commons "We shall go to the end. . . . We shall fight in France, we shall fight on the seas and oceans, we shall fight on the beaches, in the fields, in the streets, in the hills; we shall never surrender."[20] Finger could hardly bear to listen to "war news over the radio. It makes me sick," he wrote to Fletcher.[21] There was deep conflict in the US over whether the country should intervene militarily. Finger's old friend Carl Sandburg thought the US should stay out of the war, while Lilian Sandburg believed only the US could defeat the Axis.[22] When the liberal *Nation* abandoned its opposition to US military intervention, Oswald Villard resigned in protest. Freda Kirchwey, the editor Finger met over lunch in 1925, declared "isolationists and pacifists occupy a dream world" and "a system of highly organized tyranny . . . is attempting to impose itself on the world."[23] Germany bombed London in August 1940, Murrow capturing the sound of air raid sirens and describing the West End's underground shelters.[24]

Finger was not well. When Fletcher and Simon came for a visit in November 1940, his face was deeply lined, his hair thin and white, and his eyes tired. He had to lie down on the sofa to chat with them. The couple took him on a drive, and Finger surprised Fletcher by confessing that recently he had begun praying—he recited the Lord's Prayer in the car. The Fletchers departed on Armistice Day. Bidding them farewell, Finger asked in Spanish, "When shall we meet again?"[25] Five days later, a large bomb hit Shepherd Market in Mayfair, and fires broke out on the streets that were the setting of Finger's earliest memories.[26] Ten days after that, he went to Fort Smith to sign an application for US citizenship. Gazing at the photographer for the picture that was attached to his application, Finger did not smile.[27] War news was relentless. The CBS "European War Broadcast" had been a fifteen-minute report once a day, but in December the network added a second daily update.[28] The Fayetteville newspaper reported that Southampton, where Helen remembered a "forest of chimney-pots," was "engulfed in 'an ocean of flames'"; Bristol was bombed heavily and repeatedly. Hitler's promise, reported on December 10, was to "defeat the entire world."[29]

Then, on December 11 or 12, 1940, Finger received a devastating letter from Maddox. Six weeks after sending Richter the same news, Maddox finally revealed to Finger that he had decided to build a house on Honoré's property in Maryland to use as his home base with Helen. In a letter with Port Deposit—the town near the Honorés' place—in the position for return address, he wrote, "Dear Squire—A birthday remembrance went to you by express today. I brought it out of Canada for you in October, thinking then to put it into your hands at Gayeta." But he had gotten no further south than Honoré's place, "whereby hangs a tale. Paul has been insisting . . . on building us a stone house . . . to serve as a sort of staging post on the route of our seasonal migrations." Maddox had resisted the idea, he wrote, but the proximity to a military commissary, hospital, and dental clinic—and even, he joked, a cemetery—made it attractive. He and Helen would not be on the move "forever[. A]lready I feel (60 this week) the inclination for a more settled existence." They would be near Stuart and Sara Olivier in Baltimore; in fact, the Oliviers had driven over for a visit the day before, and it took them only fifty minutes. Emphasizing the practical aspects of the plan, Maddox went on, "Paul of course is doing all the architectural work and much of the labor and will look after things during our periods of absence. All in all you can see it is a pretty fortunate arrangement for our declining years." Construction was not complete, however, so they were leaving by train the next day for Ottawa to stay in Henry Bankhead's apartment "until the Spring thaw." (Bankhead, Maddox later told Richter, was "alone in a huge apartment [and] begged us to break his solitude.")[30] After this matter-of-fact admission that he had chosen Honoré's place, not Finger's, as a retirement home, Maddox finished, "Oh Lord, there is so much to say and such a wishing for long talks with you." He hoped Finger would visit them at Port Deposit so they could "yet retrieve some of the neglects and losses of separation." His understated closing was "meanwhile my affection as ever, love to all at Gayeta, Merry Christmas and Happy New Year, Major." Thus it became clear that Finger's "Gayetan dream"—of an Arcadian art colony on the mountainside in Arkansas, with Maddox sharing his stone cottage, or a life together on a sun-kissed beach—would never come true. The hope that they would sail over sparkling waters to a distant shore had been a fantasy, concocted over drinks, perhaps—as George put it in "Ode to the Majujah," alcohol was "the great builder of dreams."[31] As the scholar James Gifford observed, writers left "the real world far behind" in their visions of Arcadia: "Such Edens of their imagining ultimately proved insufficient[; their] dreamscapes were finally inadequate." As Jack London told George Sterling, it was a dream "too bright to last."[32]

A NEW GRANDCHILD, Charles Jr.'s daughter Jenell, was born on New Year's Eve, 1940.[33] London was not bombed that evening. The air raid shelters were only half full; hotels were crowded with Londoners singing "Auld Lang Syne"—like the fellows in the Poly Parliament in 1889, with Finger at the piano, and the revelers at Lake Romero Ranch in 1894. Did they sing it at the New Year's Ball in Finger's studio in San Angelo in 1902? The local newspaper didn't mention it, but "three tremendous cheers were given," and Finger placed an advertisement in the paper to express his New Year wish for all of his friends and critics in the town: "May music and kindness disperse the cloudy fumes of care." He did so in Ripley in 1916 too. "Wishing you a Happy New Year," he wrote. After their move to Arkansas, Gayeta was the scene of many happy New Year's Eve celebrations with all the young people who passed through the Fingers' lives. It was "good to be here, in this House of Life," he wrote in a New Year message in *All's Well* in 1926.[34] A story in *Golden Tales* contained a line that might have been an apology to Nellie: "That's the end of the tale, for they were married and troubles came thick and fast, sure enough, but presently misfortune made them wise, though that was when they were both very, very old."[35]

The Fayetteville newspaper carried a news feature on New Year's Day, 1941, about the journalists in London who stayed at the Hotel Savoy, the scene of Oscar Wilde's downfall. "One can still enjoy the dine and dance side of life there," the Associated Press reported, "in the specially bomb-proofed 'river room.'" Finally, on Monday, January 6, 1941, President Roosevelt asked Congress to grant funds for an offense in Europe, but Finger was ill, with Nellie caring for him, and may not have heard this news. He had a heart attack and died the next day.[36] Someone at the house sent word to Elizabeth and Dick Cox, and they responded that they "wired Col Maddox care Col Bankhead." Then came a telegram from Maddox: "Shocked and deeply grieved by your message love and sympathy to all of you."

Hubert and Kitty and Herbert came home, and the family had a memorial service outdoors at Gayeta on January 9.[37] They flew the flag of England at half-staff during the service, and an Episcopal priest officiated. Bill Baerg, the entomologist at the university who took Finger caving, was one of his pallbearers, and Helen read a poem that John Fletcher wrote for the service. Fletcher seems to have captured the duality of Finger's life, that although he was "steadfast" in caring for Nellie, he was "untamed": "Few men have known this steadfast, changeless man; / Broad, deep, untamed, as those unfettered seas / Which beat on Patagonian cliffs, to span / The ages with their storms, their broken memories."[38]

The Associated Press report of Finger's death appeared in newspapers around the country. It was a typical combination of fact and fiction: He was born in Willesden (fact); he came to the US in 1887 (fiction); he "was shipwrecked in Patagonia, where he lived for months with aborigines" (fiction); he married "Miss Nellie B. Ferguson, of Crockett County" (fact). The *New York Times* ran a two-paragraph article: "Word was received here last night of the death yesterday of Charles J. Finger, author and editor, at his home, Gayeta Lodge, Fayetteville, Ark. Finger . . . was best known for his tales of adventurous life in wild regions and for his autobiography, 'Seven Horizons.'"[39] Implicitly recognizing the two lives Finger led, Driscoll mentioned he had children and called him a man who never conformed "to other men's ideas of what he should do."[40] John Tate Appleby, a contemporary of Charles Jr. who performed the dual roles of Jack and Ernest in a Gayeta production of *The Importance of Being Earnest* in 1924, now lived in Washington, working for Murray Sheehan at the Siamese embassy. He wrote a eulogy that ran on the front page of the "Books" section of the *Washington Post*. Finger "loved great literature above all things," Appleby said, and "I love him as a man and as my dearest and oldest friend."[41] In London the editor of *Polytechnic Magazine* expressed "regret at his death but [joy] in the success that met his literary efforts in the States."[42]

The Maddoxes drove from Ottawa to Arkansas, arriving January 20 and recording their visit in Nellie's guest book, Helen writing "once again the great joy of being at Gayeta," George adding "And 'Major' with ever growing admiration and esteem."[43] They returned to their campsite on Honoré's farm in March in time to see Davis. He had driven to Mexico and back with a friend, stopping at the Honorés' place on the way south, spending a night with the Oliviers in Baltimore, and going to Mississippi to see the Coxes, arriving there one or two days after Finger died and no doubt raising a glass to his memory.[44] On the return leg, Davis and his travel partner, Frederick S. Mathias, spent two or three nights at a hotel near the Honoré farm, sharing several meals with the Honorés and Maddoxes, enjoying highballs that Maddox mixed and lamb chops that he grilled and a Mexican dinner that Helen prepared in the trailer kitchen. "The name of Charles J. Finger came up, writer of romantic road-agent stories as well as tales for boys," Mathias wrote in a book about the trip. He summarized their conversation in two sentences: "All three men knew him well. Paul had illustrated most of his books with wood-cuts, 'Sep' had corrected most of his copy while Bob had read everything he wrote with approval." Mathias did not fully identify Maddox.[45]

AFTERWORD

GEORGE AND HELEN MADDOX returned to their cottage on the island in Ottawa for the summer of 1941, entertaining Henry Bankhead and another member of the US Legation in June and Bob Davis in August. With the house at Port Deposit still unfinished, they planned to spend Christmas at Long Beach. Helen had plunged into American Red Cross work again. Maddox was bitter about the progress of the war, telling Conrad Richter, "there is not a brain on either side—only blind fury, burning hate, insatiable greed, lust for blood and all the baser attributes."[1] Davis joined them on the Gulf for Christmas that year and may have stayed into February, as he made a reporting trip to Mississippi with Maddox that month. He died in Montreal in October 1942, probably after visiting the Maddoxes, and George went to New York for the funeral.[2]

Elizabeth and Dick Cox placed a tribute to Davis in the Gulf Park College magazine, mentioning that he celebrated Christmas with them four times in recent years and reprinting a poem from the *New York Sun* that they explained was "unsigned, but evidently written by one who knew him well." Considering the details about fishing in the poem and considering that Maddox previously wrote the humorous tribute to alcohol in the style of Davis's "Ode to the Printing Press," the author of this anonymous rhyming tribute probably was Maddox, still clinging to anonymity but wanting to capture and preserve the intense camaraderie among eternal boys that Finger so often celebrated:

> Wherever there is love of fellowship—
>   No tempered stuff, but rugged, full and free—
> Where firm are handshakes, and the laughter deep,
>   There rests Bob Davis for eternity.
> Wherever vital spirits love to meet
>   Through all the span of time in fullest joy,
> There Bob is present, gusto in his mood,
>   And there, as ever, the eternal boy.[3]

Nellie and Helen had the Maddoxes as guests at least one more time, for Thanksgiving in 1949, when they wrote in the guest book that they were "happy to be at beloved Gayeta again." They may have stopped by in April 1953, when Maddox told Richter he and Helen had driven through the Ozarks, or when he went to the military hospital in Hot Springs, Arkansas, for checkups.[4] They continued their yearly migrations between Honoré's farm in Port Deposit and their cabin near Bankhead's place in Ottawa, spending winter holidays at Long Beach and occasional interludes of trailer camping in Florida or Mexico. Honoré died in 1956 and Bankhead in 1957.[5] The Maddoxes moved to Arizona in the 1960s to be near Helen's daughter, Ann Coyle Maddox, who was a swimming instructor and recreation director for the American Red Cross.[6] During the last decade of their lives, they occupied a trailer home in Nogales, Arizona, the border town that Maddox and Finger visited in 1930. His handwriting growing weaker and his punctuation and capitalization irregular, Maddox wrote often to Richter, who received the Pulitzer Prize for *The Town* (1950) and the National Book Award for *The Waters of Kronos* (1960). Maddox died on March 27, 1971, at the age of ninety, and Helen died the following day. Ann continued living in her parents' trailer and died in 1994.[7]

───────────

AS GAYETA'S ONLY BREADWINNER, Helen Finger raised Scottish terriers and Airedales for sale and continued freelancing.[8] She illustrated two more books for J. B. Lippincott, *Here Comes Mary Ellen* (1940) and *Cabin on Kettle Creek* (1941)—the latter sponsored by the Junior Literary Guild thanks to Helen Ferris—and two others for small publishing houses. She went to Washington, DC, in 1943 for a war job, drawing maps for the Coast and Geodetic Survey, and Nellie advertised for "a middle age[d] reliable couple" to live at Gayeta as caretakers.[9] While Helen was in the capital, the Houston Shipbuilding Corporation conferred the name *Charles J. Finger* on one of the Liberty ships in the US merchant fleet. This tribute was instigated by one of Finger's old friends in Cincinnati, possibly with intervention by the Bankheads; a few months earlier, another Liberty ship was dedicated in memory of William B. Bankhead, the late speaker of the US House of Representatives.[10] When Nellie became ill in February 1944, Helen gave up the Washington job and came home. In June they gave a tea for John Fletcher and Charlie May Simon.[11]

Nellie received royalties from Finger's works. Although *Fighting for Fur*, the book he had in review at Winston when he died, never appeared, several of his friends continued publishing his work for decades. With Henry Pitz as illustrator, Barbara Nolen used two of Finger's stories from the magazine *Story Parade* in a series, "Story Parade Adventure Books": *A Yankee Captain in Patagonia* in 1941 and *High Water in Arkansas* in 1943. She included at least four of his other stories in anthologies for children, and other editors also reprinted his stories in collections for various publishers. Phyllis Fenner, a member of the *Story Parade* advisory board, used Finger stories in at least five collections between 1942 and 1951.[12]

Helen married Robert A. Leflar, a long-ago intern of Murray Sheehan at the university news bureau, in 1946. Leflar was a lawyer who had run unsuccessfully for Congress, worked for the War Relocation Authority in Washington, and was now the dean of the University of Arkansas law school. They lived in town and had two sons, naming the first Robert B Leflar and the second Charles Joseph Finger Leflar.[13]

Nellie cut back farm operations at Gayeta but continued raising pedigreed dogs. She sometimes hosted meetings of women's clubs, entertained old friends who continued to visit and sign her guest book, and carried on the Gayeta Thanksgiving and Christmas traditions. Governor Sid McMath of Arkansas visited Gayeta twice, probably in the company of Bob Leflar.[14] She moved into Helen and Bob's house in town in 1957 and died in 1965. She was buried in Farmington Cemetery near Emil Finger, and her sister Amelia was buried there two years later.[15] At some time the family moved Finger's remains from his grave at Gayeta and reinterred them beside Nellie. The Gayeta property was sold, but later Robert B Leflar bought a two-acre parcel including the house, barn, and Helen's studio. He and his wife, Sarah May Leflar, raised their daughter, Sarah Helen Finger Leflar, there.

NOTES

Archival Collections

William J. Baerg Collection, Special Collections, University of Arkansas Libraries

James Branch Cabell Collection, Albert and Shirley Small Special Collections Library, University of Virginia

Boyd Cornick Family Papers, Special Collections, Texas Tech University Library

Philip H. Cornick Papers, Division of Rare and Manuscript Collections, Cornell University Library

Ida Craddock Papers, Special Collections Research Center, Southern Illinois University

Robert Hobart Davis Papers, Manuscripts and Archives Division, New York Public Library

Benjamin R. Donaldson Collection, Clarke Historical Library, Central Michigan University

Charles Benedict Driscoll Collection, Spencer Research Library, University of Kansas

J. H. Field Photographs, Special Collections, University of Arkansas Libraries

Charles J. Finger Papers (MC 639), Special Collections, University of Arkansas Libraries

Finger–Stone Correspondence (MC 449), Special Collections, University of Arkansas Libraries

May Massee Collection, William Allen White Library Special Collections and Archives, Emporia State University, Kansas

Henry C. Pitz Papers, Special Collections and University Archives, University of Oregon Libraries

M. C. Ragsdale Photograph Collection, Fort Concho National Historic Landmark, San Angelo, Texas

Conrad Richter Papers, Department of Rare Books and Special Collections, Princeton University Library

Digital Repositories

American Memory, Library of Congress (memory.loc.gov)

Ancestry.com

British Presence in Southern Patagonia (patbrit.org)

California Digital Newspaper Collection, University of California, Riverside (cdnc.ucr.edu)

Jane Cameron National Archives, Stanley, Falkland Islands (fig.gov.fk)

Chronicling America: Historic American Newspapers, Library of Congress (chroniclingamerica.loc.gov)

Find a Grave (findagrave.com)

FreeBMD (freebmd.org.uk)

Newspapers.com

Ohio Memory (ohiomemory.org)

Portal to Texas History (texashistory.unt.edu)

Ripley Bee Database, Union Township (Ohio) Public Library (http://uniontownship.advantage-preservation.com)

Union Township (Ohio) Public Library (ripleylibrary.com)

University of Alabama Historical Map Archive (alabamamaps.ua.edu)

University of Westminster Digitised Archive (westuni.websds.net)

Abbreviations

AD	*Arkansas Democrat*
ADS	*Arizona Daily Star* (Tucson, AZ)
AG	*Arkansas Gazette*
AML	University of Alabama Map Library
AN	Ancestry.com
AP	Associated Press
AW	*All's Well* (Charles J. Finger Papers)
BP	British Presence in Southern Patagonia (patbrit.org)
BRD	Benjamin R. Donaldson (Except where noted, correspondence with BRD is in the Benjamin R. Donaldson Collection.)
CBD	Charles B. Driscoll
CE	*Enquirer* (Cincinnati, OH)
CJF	Charles J. Finger
CJP	Charles J. Peer
CR	Conrad Richter (Letters from GWM to CR can be found in CR Papers.)
DFP	*Detroit Free Press*
DI	*The Dearborn Independent*
EEN	*Enquirer and Evening News* (Battle Creek, MI)
FD (FDD)	*Fayetteville Democrat* (also known as *Fayetteville Daily Democrat*)

"FF"   "Free Fantasia," CJF's column in *AW*
GGB   Gayeta Guest Book (CJF Papers)
GWM   George Washington Maddox
HCP   Henry Clarence Pitz (Letters from CJF to HCP are in the HCP Papers.)
HFL   Helen Finger Leflar
HT   *Home Tidings*, University of Westminster Digitised Archive
JGF   John Gould Fletcher
LAT   *Los Angeles Times*
PHC   Philip H. Cornick (Letters from CJF to PHC are in the PHC Papers;
       copies of some are in the CJF Papers.)
PM   *Polytechnic Magazine* (University of Westminster Digitised Archive)
PT   The Portal to Texas History
MJP   The Modernist Journals Project
NWAT   *Northwest Arkansas Times*
NYHT   *New York Herald Tribune*
NYPL   New York Public Library
NYT   *New York Times*
RB   *Ripley Bee*
RBCG   Robert Bontine Cunninghame Graham
RHD   Robert Hobart Davis
RM   *Reedy's Mirror*
SAP   *San Angelo Press*
SR   *Saturday Review of Literature*
UAL   University of Alabama Historical Map Archive (alabamamaps.ua.edu)
USFC   US Federal Census
WMR   William Marion Reedy (Letters from Reedy to Finger are in
       CJF Papers.)
WMS   Wilbur Macey Stone (Some letters between Finger and Stone are
       in Finger–Stone Correspondence, UA.)
WTC   West Texas Collection, Angelo State University

––––––––

Except where noted, letters, journals, manuscripts, photographs, and ephemera are in CJF Papers. Except where noted, demographic and genealogical information—such as census manuscripts, passenger lists, city directories, and grave marker inscriptions—was retrieved from Ancestry.com.

Introduction

1. Sedgwick, *Between Men*, 206.
2. CJF, "Olla Podrida," *SAP*, Feb. 18, 1903, 8.
3. Simpson, "C. J. Finger in Fayetteville."

4. "The Polytechnic Institute," *Times* (London), April 23, 1888.

5. "The Literary Society," *PM*, June 6, 1889, 332.

6. Hurley, *Circulating Queerness*, 223–24.

7. CJF, "Ebro."

8. Molesworth, "Ghost," 233–37; CJF, "Some Mischievous Thing," 119; Dellamora, *Masculine Desire*, 196; Showalter, *Sexual Anarchy*, 207; Brodie, *Devil Drives*, 304–09; Reade, *Sexual Heretics*, 30–31, 81; Furneaux, *Queer Dickens*, 171.

9. Gardner, *Reviewing the South*, 5, 9, 70–72. Also see Radway, *A Feeling for Books*, 254–55.

10. "American Impressionism: The Lure of the Artists' Colony, March 7, 2015–May 31, 2015," retrieved from Dayton Art Institute, daytonartinstitute.org.

11. Bozorth, *Auden's Games*, 30; Hurley, "Queer Traffic in Literature," 82–84.

12. Wigginton, *In the Neighborhood*, 6–8, 89, 96, 111, 134; Hurley, *Circulating Queerness*, 5; "FF," April–May 1923; CJF, *Ozark Fantasia*, 171; Shores, "Library." For another study of the circulation of direct and indirect literary and artistic influences in the interwar period, see Knighton, "William Faulkner's Illustrious Circles."

13. Gardner, *Reviewing the South*, 67.

14. Hurley, *Circulating Queerness*, 82, 90.

15. Haley, *Wolf*, 196–97.

Chapter 1

1. CJF, "Polytechnic Literary Society," *PM*, May 23, 1889; Whitman, *Democratic Vistas*; Mitchell and Leavitt, *Pages Passed*, xviii–xix; Jeffs, "Man's Words," 19–20, 30–31; Gifford, *Dayneford's Library*, 19, 113; Woods, *Gay Literature*, 176–77; Cocks, *Nameless Offences*, 11, 159; Martin, *Homosexual Tradition*, xvi–xvii; D'Emilio and Freedman, *Intimate Matters*, 127–29. On Whitman as a representative of the secret Arcadian places where men could share comradely love, see Fone, "This Other Eden," 31.

2. "The Literary Society," *PM*, June 6, 1889, 332; Martin, *Hero, Captain, Stranger*, 21, 38; Edwards, *Exotic Journeys*, 19.

3. Record for Charles Finger, Births, March 1868, retrieved May 1, 2018, from Free BMD Index, freebmd.org.uk; London, England, Electoral Registers; England, Select Marriages, 1538–1973; London, England, Marriages and Banns. Some records identify Finger's father as Charles Henry Christian Martin Finger. I refer to him as Martin to avoid confusion with his son Charles. Finger himself verified that his birth year was 1867 when he noted in his diary on December 25, 1891, that it was his twenty-fourth birthday. (CJF Journals, Dec. 25, 1891.) However, he indicated to Francis Galton's Anthropometric Laboratory in 1888 that he was born on December 25, 1868. By 1910 he pretended to have been born in 1872, five years after his actual birth. In 1929, writing to the vital records agency in London to ask for a copy of his birth certificate, he cited his own false claim to Galton.

(Record for CJF, 1910 USFC; CJF to Registry department, March 1, 1929.) In 1930 a book reviewer related that Finger was born in 1871. (Burris Jenkins, "Drift of the Day," *Monitor-Index and Democrat [Moberly, MO]*, Feb. 8, 1930, 4.) A reporter repeated this inaccuracy in 1936. (Irene Carlisle, "Finger Is Noted Literary Figure," *FD*, June 11, 1936, B8.) After Finger's death various reports gave the year of his birth as 1869 and 1871. (AP, "C. J. Finger, 71, Dies; Author of Juvenile Books," *NYHT*, Jan. 9, 1941, 22; "Charles J. Finger Funeral Rites Thursday at 3," *NWAT*, Jan. 8, 1941, 1, 7.)

4. Records for the Fingers' children in various collections, AN.

5. Row 112, List of Persons Entitled to Vote . . . Occupied within the In-Wards of the Parish of Saint George, Hanover Square, London, England, Electoral Registers; CJF, Empire Reporting Book; CJF Journals "Short Summary," 1890; CJF, *Seven Horizons*, 81; "FF," July 1931; Dubourg, *Violin*, 170; Rawson, "Gottfried Finger"; Izbicki, "London Polytechnics," 201.

6. "Royal Polytechnic Institution," *Illustrated London*, 1864, 112; "Fisbury Polytechnic," *Times (London)*, Dec. 13, 1887, 7; "From Our London Correspondent," *Manchester Guardian*, April 7, 1888, 7; Kershen, "Higher Education," 80; Strong, *Education, Travel*, 138; Simonis, *Street of Ink*, 1–2; Cook, *London*, 14; "Historic Regent Street Cinema to Be Restored," BBC News, website, Oct. 15, 2012. Finger practiced shorthand in a clothbound notebook, stamped "Empire Reporting Book" on the cover, that he labeled "Charles J. Finger Polytechnic 309 Regent Street." He made the first dated entry in the notebook on July 31, 1886. (CJF, Empire Reporting Book.) Students at the Polytechnic took classes in shorthand as training for elementary and advanced reporting. By 1888–89, there were four levels of shorthand instruction. ("Result of Examinations," *HT*, July 11, 1885, 17; "Preliminary Time Table of Classes," *PM*, May 23, 1889, unnumbered page.) Regarding my use of "*gay*," in 1995 James Gifford considered it an appropriate term in a study of "nascent American homosexual writing," which this work certainly is. (Gifford, *Dyneford's Library*, 3.) William Leap and Tom Boellstorff reached the same conclusion in 2004, believing *gay* was a good "referential shorthand for a broad range of same-sex desires, practices, and subjectivities." (Leap and Boellstorff, *Speaking*, 4.) As recently as 2011, Michael Bronski used "gay history" as a synonym for "queer history." (Bronski, *Queer History*, 1.)

7. Weeks, *Coming Out*, 34–35; Dellamora, *Masculine Desire*, 195–196; Showalter, *Sexual Anarchy*, 11–13; Gifford, *Dayneford's Library*, 13; Cook, *London and the Culture of Homosexuality*, 147; Strong, *Education*, 141; Milne-Smith, *London Clubland*, 6–8; Black, *Room of His Own*, 8–9, 19.

8. Peter Plain, "Saying Good-bye," *HT*, April 10, 1886, 343–44; "Institute Gossip," *PM*, July 26, 1888, 49–50; "Mr. Quintin Hogg . . .," *Manchester Guardian*, Dec. 12, 1888, 5; "Obituary: Mr. Quintin Hogg," *Times (London)*, Jan. 19, 1903, 6; "Memorial Notices," *Manchester Guardian*, Jan. 19, 1903, 6; "Late Mr. Quintin Hogg," *Manchester Guardian*, Jan. 21, 1903, 5; "Quintin Hogg," *Spectator*, Oct. 1, 1904, 480–82; Hogg, *Quintin Hogg*, 150, 260–63; Hyde, *Love*, 154; Reade, *Sexual*

Heretics, 29; Cohen, *Talk*, 39; David, "Class and Gender," 102, 106; Glynn, "Higher Education," 30; Pratt and Richards, "Higher Education," 49, 54–55; Cook, *London*, 37–39; Koven, *Slumming*, 234–36, 263, 279; Black, *Room of His Own*, 42; Strong, *Education*, 140–41.

9. CJP, "Mutual Improvement Society," *HT*, July 16, 1887, 21; CJP, "Mutual," *PM*, April 5, 1888, 179; CJP, "Mutual Improvement Society," *HT*, Oct. 15, 1887, 133, Dec. 3, 1887, 189; "Institute Gossip," *PM*, Sept. 12, 1889, 156; C. Loxston, "Polytechnic French Society," *PM*, Oct. 24, 1889, 261; R. J. Owen, "Radical Notes," *PM,* Oct. 31, 1889, 279; A. E. Hopkins and G. T. Wooderson, "Mutual Improvement Society," *PM*, Nov. 28, 1889, 339; A. E. Flower, "Boxing Club," *PM*, Nov. 28, 1889, 340; "Coming Events," *PM*, Dec. 26, 1889, 1; Albert J. Spalding, "Polytechnic Parliament," *PM*, Dec. 5, 1894, 321; CJF Journals, Jan. 16, 1891; Rose, *Intellectual Life*, 58–61, 65.

10. Record for Henry Somerfield, London, England, Church of England Births and Baptisms; "Members of the Institute," *HT,* March 1883, 68; CJP, "Mutual Improvement Society," *HT*, Feb. 26, 1887, 69; "Institute Gossip," *PM*, Jan. 15, 1892, 41–42; CJF, *Seven Horizons*, 136–37; CJF to Somerfield family, in Brooks, *Henry Somerfield*. Somerfield's father, John Smith Somerfield, was a newsagent in Marylebone Lane and later in Manchester Square. ("Qualified Physician or Surgeon Required," advertisement, *Lancet*, Jan. 31, 1874, page number unknown; "To Medical Teachers," advertisement, *Lancet,* March 28, 1885.) CJF referred to CJP as "C. J." in his diary. (CJF Journals, Jan. 11, 1890.)

11. "Mutual," *PM*, Sept. 27, 1888, 1999; "Radical Social," *PM*, March 14, 1889, 145; CJP and A. E. Hopkins, "Mutual," *PM,* March 21, 1889, 167; CJF, Empire Reporting Book, April 19–22 and Sept. 5–8, 1889; CJF Journals, "Short Summary," 1890; CJF, *Seven Horizons*, 89–91; Davis, *Over My Left Shoulder*, 218. Finger was known early in his life as Charlie or Charley but as a young adult was more widely known as C. J. (CJF Journals, June 6, 1891.)

12. CJP, "Mutual Improvement Society," *HT*, April 30, 1887, 149; "Polytechnic Institute," *Times (London)*, April 23, 1888, 14; Britannicus [pseud.], "London Letter," *Building Budget*, Nov. 30, 1888, 146–47; CJF, "London Johnny and the Claim-Jumpers"; Weeks, *Coming Out*, 41–42; Woods, *Gay Literature*, 6; Bozorth, *Auden's Games*, 16; Cocks, *Nameless Offences*, 4, 10; Cook, *London*, 124–25; Brake, "Deaths of Heroes," 174; Brake, *Print*, 15. The American poet Frederick Shelley Ryman wrote in his journal in 1883, and several other times, "No wife to scold me / No children to squall / God bless the gay man / Who keeps bachelor's hall." (Chudacoff, *Age of the Bachelor*, 235.) Another American writer, describing a group of friends at Harvard University in the 1890s who called themselves the Bachelor Maids, had a male character with the name Estelle exclaim, "I hope you will not think I was too gay, this afternoon!" (Gifford, *Dayneford's Library*, 132.) The article about the institute was reproduced again in a Pennsylvania report on industrial education. ("Polytechnic

Institute," in *Report . . . Made to the Legislature of Pennsylvania*, edited by Pennsylvania Commission on Industrial Education, 1891, 513–15.)

13. "Institute Gossip," *PM*, Nov. 29, 1888, 337–38; CJF, "Polytechnic Literary Society," *PM*, Dec. 20, 1888, 394; "Our Active List," *PM*, Dec. 15, 1897, 260; CJF, "Polytechnic Literary Society," *PM*, Dec. 20, 1888, 394.

14. "'Portrait of Mr. W. H.' by Oscar Wilde, 1889," retrieved Feb. 23, 2018, from British Library, bl.uk; "Arts and Crafts Exhibition Society," advertisement, *Times (London)*, Sept. 18, 1889, 1; Arts and Crafts Exhibition Society, Catalogue of the Second Exhibition, abstract, retrieved Feb. 22, 2018, from wmgallery.org .uk; H. Halliday Sparling, "Chicago Murders & Bloody Sunday," *Commonweal*, Oct. 26, 1889, 1; "FF," November 1925; CJF, *Tragic Story*, 6–8; CJF, *Seven Horizons*, 144–45; Oscar Wilde to W. A. S. Benson, May 16, 1885, in Hart-Davis, *Letters*, 174–76, 215n3, 217n2; Reade, *Sexual Heretics*, 28; Kelvin, *Collected Letters*, 730n2, 838n6; Mitchell and Leavitt, *Pages Passed*, 240; Goodway, *Anarchist*, 69; Cannadine, *Victorious Century*, 398. On references to Wilde in "name-dropping reminiscences," see Rupert Croft-Cooke quoted in Woods, *Homintern*, 32.

15. "Radical Social," *PM*, March 14, 1889, 145; CJF, "Polytechnic Literary Society," *PM,* Feb. 7, 1890, 71.

16. "Polytechnic Literary Society," *PM*, Oct. 24, 1889, 260; Cruikshank, *Loving Ballad*, 1–40; Chas. P. Johnson, "The Loving Ballad of Lord Bateman," *Athenaeum*, Jan. 21, 1888, 86; Kitton, *Minor Writings of Charles Dickens*, 70–74.

17. Record for Martin Finger, New York, Index for Naturalization filed in New York City*; SS Arizona*, Nov. 27, 1888, Passenger List; CJF Journals, Dec. 1889–Jan. 1890, Feb 7, 1890; CJF, *Seven Horizons*, 79–82.

18. CJF, *Seven Horizons*, 129–32.

19. Stevenson quoted in Buckton, *Cruising*, 68. On exotic locales in literature as utopian places of freedom, see Gifford, *Dayneford's Library*, 13–14, 27; Youngs, *Travel Writing*, 137.

20. *SS Wisconsin* Passenger List, July 5, 1889. An anonymous writer reported in *Polytechnic Magazine*, after CJP's return, on prospects for immigrants to New York. ("Institute Gossip," *PM*, Aug. 29, 1889, 124.) The following spring, CJP traveled to Madeira, probably on another reconnaissance for Hogg. (List of Arrivals and Departures by Colonial and Indian Steamers, *Colonies and India*, Aug. 20, 1890, 30.) By February 1892 CJP worked full-time for Hogg and organized Poly tours around Great Britain and to Europe and Chicago. In August 1892 an anonymous writer, probably CJP, described the Polytechnic Institute's travel program in a magazine that CJP helped edit. ("The Regent Street Polytechnic Trips," *Review of Reviews*, August 1892, 62–63.) Daniel Armistead Cauthorn was a native of Audrain County, Missouri. His family had ranches in Sutton County, Texas. (1900 USFC; Find a Grave Index; 1860 USFC;

Lackey, "Homestead: Cauthorns Settle in Texas after Journey from Missouri,"
San Angelo Standard-Times, Dec. 8, 2012.)

21. CJF Journals, "Short Summary," 1890; CJF, "Reflections," *RM*, Aug. 19, 1920,
640; CJF, *Seven Horizons*, 190–97; Bronski, *Queer History*, 42, 46; Rowbotham,
Edward Carpenter, 112.

22. Fodor's Travel, *London*, 202.

23. CJP, "Social and Educational Centers"; CJF, *Seven Horizons*, 190; Schults,
Crusader, 233, 251–52; "Our Active List," *PM*, Dec. 15, 1897, 260; Brake, King,
Luckhurst, and Mussell, *W. T. Stead*, xiv, 39; Cook, *Cook's Handbook*, 49.

24. Brooks, *Henry Somerfield*.

25. Simonis, *Street of Ink*, 106; Hart-Davis, *Letters*, 519n2; Hyde, *Cleveland Street*,
14, 19, 26, 47; Simpson, Chester, and Leitch, *Cleveland Street*, 5, 15, 22, 56–57,
8, 122, 130, 156; Dynes, *Homolexis*, 38; Dellamora, *Masculine Desire*, 196,
200, 206; Cohen, *Talk*, 91–93, 121–22; Gifford, *Dayneford's Library*, 5, 10–11;
Brake, *Print*, 138; Cook, *London*, 14, 42, 45, 50–51; Kaplan, *Sodom*, 167–71;
Copley, *Bloomsbury*, 3; Goodway, *Anarchist*, 70; Cannadine, *Victorious
Century*, 8.

26. CJF Journals, Jan. 6, 9, and Feb. 3, 1890.

27. CJF, "Unrecognized Golden Age," 410; CJF, *Seven Horizons*, 26–29, 65–66;
Anderson, *Dime Novel*, 57–58, 206–07; Knuth, *Children's Literature*, 52–53,
64–65; Ruppel, *Homosexuality*, 22.

28. CJF Journals, Jan. 6 and 11, 1890; Jones, *Merchants*, 258; Edmundson, *British
Presence*, 104–06.

29. "Institute Gossip," *PM*, Oct. 1, 1887, 109; R. Owen, Radical Party Whip, "Our
Parliament," *PM*, Sept. 6, 1888, 155; CJF Journals, Jan. 4, 6–8, and 11, 1890.
Arnold Fox was born in 1869. He and his family lived on High Street in London
in 1881. When they immigrated to New York in 1892, they indicated their home
was Sandbach, Cheshire, England. (1881 England Census; Record for Arnold
Fox, Index to Petitions for Naturalization filed in New York City.)

30. A. Rieder, "Literary Society," *PM*, Feb. 28, 1888, 124; "Literary Society," *PM*,
June 6, 1889, 332; A. E. Hopkins and G. T. Wooderson, "Mutual Improvement
Society," *PM*, Nov. 28, 1889, 339. CJF referred to Hyde as "Ted" in his diary.
(CJF Journals, Jan. 20, 1890.)

31. CJF Journals, Dec. 25, 1891; CJP, "Mutual Improvement Society," *HT*, Dec. 10,
1887, 196; S. C. Saxby, "Radical Library," *PM*, Jan. 23, 1890, 52.

32. CJF Journals, Feb. 10–18 and June 30, 1890; W. Vokes, "Polytechnic Literary
Society," *PM*, Feb. 20, 1890, 118; Brake, King, Luckhurst, & Mussell, *W. T. Stead*,
xiv, 39; Shores, "Library."

33. CJF Journals, Feb. 19, 1890; "Institute Gossip," *PM*, Feb. 27, 1890, 125–27; Chas.
Loxston, "Polytechnic French Society," *PM*, Feb. 27, 1890, 134; "Great Eastern
Railway," retrieved July 25, 2018, from Harwich & Dovercourt, harwichand
dovercourt.co.uk; Jones, *Merchants*, 258.

Chapter 2

1. CJF Journals, Feb.–March 1890; Irene Carlisle, "Finger Is Noted Literary Figure," *FD*, June 11, 1936, B8; Brodie, *Devil Drives*, 304–09; Reade, *Sexual Heretics*, 30–31, 81; Colligan, "Born Pederasts," 3–5; Furneaux, *Queer Dickens*, 171; Julia Kuehn, "Exoticism in 19th-Century Literature," Discovering Literature: Romantics and Victorians, retrieved Feb. 20, 2017, from British Library, bl.uk.

2. Findlay, *Directory*, 8; Dixie, *Patagonia*, 29; Maclaren, *Gold*, 661; Penrose, "Gold Regions," 692–94; Childs, *El Jimmy*, 51; Rector, *Chile*, 30.

3. CJF, *Valiant Vagabonds*, 216; "Plano Punta Arenas—1886," retrieved July 25, 2018, from the James Caird Society, archive.jamescairdsocietycom.

4. CJF Journals, April 6–7, 1890; Dixie, *Patagonia*, 30; Theodore Child, "Smyth's Channel and the Strait of Magellan: A Coasting Voyage in Southern Latitudes," *Harper's*, Feb. 1891, 456. CJF kept detailed journals for at least two periods during the next six years, records that provide context for the vivid stories he later told and wrote about Patagonia. The surviving journals are for the years 1890–91 and 1896. Finger may have kept a diary in pencil while traveling and copied the entries more neatly in journals with dated pages. Journal entries in 1890 support this theory: For April 28 he wrote that he was making the entry *while* watching a herd of 1,100 sheep, without even the benefit of a sheepdog, and that the animals occasionally began stampedes, yet the entry is perfectly neat, and the handwriting exactly matches the style and size of the entry on the facing page. For that day, the 29th, he wrote that rain forced him to return to Fish River House in the afternoon, where he cooked supper and wrote letters. Perhaps he made rough pencil notes each day and copied them into the journal on days when he could work indoors. On August 24 he wrote that in camp, he "read, wrote and arranged my notes."

5. Child, "Smyth's Channel," 274–75; Spears, *Gold Diggings*, 34–46; Carpenter, *South America*, 274–75; Childs, *El Jimmy*, 52–54.

6. CJF Journals, April 1890; "King Macrae Finds New Use for Bagpipes," article reproduced from *London Mail*, San Francisco Call, Jan. 15, 1905, California Digital Newspaper Collection; Edmundson, *British Presence*, 120–23; Carpenter, *South America*, 277–79; "Family MacRae–Stevenson," retrieved March 8, 2019, from BP.

7. Dixie, *Patagonia*, 60.

8. CJF Journals, April 17–May 7, 1890; Dixie, *Patagonia*, 60, 69, 73; Thomas A. Saunders, "Diary of a Sheep-drive from the Rio Negro to San Julian, Sept. 1888–March 1889," retrieved from BP; Childs, *El Jimmy*, 93; Carpenter, *South America*, 275–77; Rector, *Chile*, 106.

9. CJF Journals, April 16, May 10–11, 17, 24, and 29, and July 3, 1890; Popper, *Expedition*, 37; Gunn, "Recent Exploration," 319; Spears, *Gold Diggings*, 23; Carpenter, *South America*, 281–84; "King Macrae," *London Mail*, San Francisco Call, Jan. 15, 1905; Penrose, "Gold Regions," 683–86; Edmundson, *British Presence*, 120–23; Youngs, *Travel Writing*, 56.

10. Hydrographic Office, Admiralty, *South American Pilot,* 105.

11. CJF Journals, May 20–25, June 12, 16, and 26–27, and July 8, 1890; Popper, *Expedition,* 7–8; Spears, *Gold Diggings,* 10–11 and 34–46; Penrose, "Gold Regions," 687–94; Gunn, "Recent Exploration," 319–26; CJF, "Incongruity," 69; CJF, *Seven Horizons,* 348; CJF, "Single-Handed Travel to Patagonia in a V-8," review of *The Way Southward* by A. F. Tschiffely, "Books," *NYHT,* March 3, 1940, 3; Ansel, "European Adventurer," 99–100. Spiro's expedition with Popper became the subject of a short story, "Tierra del Fuego," by Francisco Coloane (1910–2002) and then a feature film based on that story, *Tierra del Fuego* (2000), directed by Miguel Littin, with Claudio Santamaria playing the part of Spiro.

12. Popper, *Expedition,* 7–8; Gunn, "Recent Exploration," 326; Maclaren, *Gold,* 661; CJF Journals, July–Sept. 1890; "FF," Jan.–Feb. 1926.

13. CJF Journals, Oct. 25, 1890, Summary of 1890, and Feb. 6, 1891; "Disasters at Sea," *Times (London),* Nov. 3, 1890, 7, Dec. 8, 1890, 11; "Institute Gossip," *PM,* Dec. 12, 1890, 373–74; Child, "Smyth's Channel," 442–60; Findlay, *Directory,* 55. The *Villarino* was an Argentine transport ship that supported scientific expeditions in 1884 and 1896. (Brebbia, *Patagonia,* 258; Hatcher and Scott, *Reports,* I: 13, I: 76, I: 201.)

14. See, for example, "Revolt in Chili," *Times (London),* Feb. 26, 1891, 5; "Chilean Trouble," *San Francisco Chronicle,* March 7, 1891, 1.

15. CJF Journals, Oct. 31–Nov. 4, 1890, Jan.–Feb. 1891; CJF, *Seven Horizons,* 359–60.

16. CJF Journals, November 1890 and January 1891; Childs, *El Jimmy,* 87, 110; "Cameron Family," retrieved March 16, 2018, from Jane Cameron National Archives, fig.gov.fk. John Cameron immigrated to the Falkland Islands and then Patagonia. His oldest daughter was Mary Ann (b. 1875). (British Families in Southern Patagonia, retrieved from BP.)

17. CJF Journals, Jan. 5, 28, Feb. 4, 14–15, and 17, 1891; Henry William Reynard and Charles Robert Reynard, "*Life of Henry L. Reynard,*" unpublished manuscript, 84, 86, 152, retrieved from BP; Spears, *Gold Diggings,* 31; Young, *Merry Banker,* 188; Childs, *El Jimmy,* 93; Moss, *Patagonia*; Ray, *West Coast,* 39.

18. CJF Journals, Feb.–July, Aug. 1, 30, Sept. 6–7, 24, and Dec. 6, 1891; "Chilean Trouble," *San Francisco Chronicle,* March 7, 1891, 1; "Institute Gossip," *PM,* Jan. 15, 1892, 41–42.

19. CJF Journals, Oct. 7, 12–13, 1891.

20. CJF Journals, Feb. 15, July 17, Oct. 7, 12–13, 1891; Row 54, St. James, Punta Arenas, Baptisms, and "Punta Arenas: Some 'British' Commercial and Industrial Interests," retrieved from BP; Childs, *El Jimmy,* 119; "Institute Gossip," *PM,* July 10, 1891, 17–18; "From Over the Water," *Quintinian,* May 1892, 3, November 1892, iv, and January 1893, v; "Institute Gossip," *PM,* May 1, 1895, 227.

21. CJF, *Charles J. Peer 1893,* pen-and-ink drawing; Henry L. Reynard, May 25, 1893; "FF," December 1932.

22. "From Over the Water," *Quintinian*, November 1892, iv; "Institute Gossip," *PM,* June 7, 1893, 411–13; CJF, "Dramatic Tale," review of *Magellan: His Life and Adventures* by Arthur S. Hildebrand, "Books," *NYHT,* Nov. 30, 1924, 3; CJF to BRD, Oct. 7, 1925; CJF, *Seven Horizons,* 333–36; Saunders, "Diary of a Sheep." Fernande Lataste was director of the National Natural History Museum in Santiago. ("Scientific News," *American Naturalist,* August 1889, 748–49.) An entry about a South American bird species in a book about field research in Patagonia refers to an 1893 survey on the Strait of Magellan and cites a report published in 1900 as Lataste, *Actes Soc. Sci. Chili,* III. (Hatcher and Scott, *Reports,* III: 419.)

23. CJF to May Massee, Dec. 22, 1922, May Massee Collection; Molesworth, "Ghost," 233–37; Showalter, *Sexual Anarchy,* 112; Chauncey, *Gay New York,* 18. Bevil Molesworth arrived in Punta Arenas by mid-January 1890, according to a letter from one of Henry Reynard's employees. (George E. Harris to Robert F. Reynard, Jan. 19, 1890, retrieved Aug. 15, 2017, from BP.) He was still in Punta Arenas on June 15, 1893, when he served as witness to a marriage ceremony. (Civil Registration, Magallanes: Some 'British' Marriages, retrieved from BP.) CJF used *queer* in a suggestive way as early as 1891 when he referred in his journal to "a queer little Frenchman." In 1903 he described "a queer old character" he met in New Mexico, comparing him to the "misanthropical old Frenchman" he met "on the Straits of Magellan." (CJF Journals, April 8, 1891; CJF, "Letters of Travel, No. 2," *SAP,* Aug. 5, 1903, 8.)

24. "From Over the Water," *Quintinian,* June 1894, 332, and February 1896, 74; Ernest Schumacher to CJF, July 21, 1926, and Oct. 17, 1926; records for Ernest Schumacher, 1940 USFC and California Death Index.

25. Carpenter, *South America,* 276; CJF, "Andrew Lang," 313; Ernest Schumacher to CJF, Oct. 17, 1926; Childs, *El Jimmy,* 86, 91.

26. Childs, *El Jimmy,* 88–89; "Selected Families and Individuals," retrieved April 9, 2015, from My Genealogy by Judith Lorraine Daft, garycolquhoun.com.au; "John MacLean, honorary sheriff: Official correspondence, 1902–1906," retrieved March 19, 2018, from BP. A clipping of the article about the ranch party, missing the headline and date, survived between pages of Finger's 1896 journal.

27. "From Over the Water," *Quintinian,* Feb. 1896, 74; CJF, "Forty Years in Patagonia," review of *El Jimmy, Outlaw of Patagonia* by Herbert Childs, *SR,* Aug. 1, 1936, 7.

28. "Institute Gossip," *PM,* July 24, 1895, 43–45.

29. "From Over the Water," *Quintinian,* Feb. 1896, 74; "Institute Gossip," *PM,* May 1, 1895, 227; Ernest Schumacher to CJF, Oct. 17, 1926.

30. CJF Journals, Feb. 15, 1896.

31. Record for Ernest Schumacher, 1920 USFC; Ernest Schumacher to CJF, Oct. 17, 1926; "FF," Nov. 1931.

32. CJF Journals, March 5, April 10–May 6, 1896; "Institute Gossip," *PM*, June 17, 1896, 295–97; CJF, *Seven Horizons*, 354–56.

33. CJP, "Social and Educational Centers"; "Social Centers of London," *Review of Reviews*, 1893, 113; records for C. J. Peer, England & Wales Marriage Index, 1901 England Census, and London, England, Births and Baptisms; Brooks, *Henry Somerfield*.

34. It is clear that CJP or CJF read the poem in the anthology *The Canterbury Poets: Songs of Freedom,* because someone pasted a clipping of a poem about Whitman on a blank page opposite it. (Shores, "Library"; Walt Whitman, "For You O Democracy," retrieved Oct. 8, 2017, from poetryfoundation.org.)

35. Cohen, *Talk*, 175–76; Dynes, *Homolexis*, 38; Sedgwick, *Between Men*, 216–17; Showalter, *Sexual Anarchy*, 3, 171; Gifford, *Dayneford's Library*, 120; Woods, *Gay Literature*, 3, 183; Buckton, *Secret Selves*, 190; Weeks, *Coming Out*, in Koven, *Slumming*, 269; Woods, *Homintern*, 40; Cannadine, *Victorious Century*, 398.

36. Passenger List, *SS Monarch*; "Institute Gossip," *PM*, July 1, 1896, 1.

Chapter 3

1. CJF Journals, July–Sept. 1896; "From Over the Water," *Quintinian*, June 1894, 332; "Institute Gossip," *PM,* July 29, 1896, 49–51; "Henry George Will Run," *Brooklyn Daily Eagle*, Oct. 6, 1897, 3; Phillipina Finger record, New York Marriage Index; Robert Wilhelm Bergmann records in New York Index to Petitions for Naturalization and 1900 USFC; CJF, *Seven Horizons*, 355–58; Finger, "Single Tax Town"; Barry Fox Stevens to JGF, Oct. 7, 1941, retrieved from AN; Graham, *Brenon*; Young, "Brenon," 118.

2. CJF, "Ebro," 471.

3. CJF Journals, Sept. 19–Oct. 8, 1896; "From Over the Water," *Quintinian*, Dec. 1896, 267; CJF, *Seven Horizons*, 359–60; CJF, "I Remember Another Texas"; Chauncey, *Gay New York*, 76–77; CJF, *Sapphire Skies*, 243–44; Carlson, *Woollybacks*, 110.

4. CJF Journals, Sept. 19–Oct. 8, 1896; "FF," November 1925; Tom Green County, *Chronicles*, I; 33, 251; Dalton, "Wagon Yards," 16–18; Byrns, "Tom McCloskey," 52, 55; "City Heritage, National History," retrieved July 26, 2018, from Fort Concho National Historic Landmark, fortconcho.com; Robert T. Hill, *Map of Texas* (Washington, DC: US Department of Interior, Geological Survey, 1899), UAL; Escal F. Duke, "San Angelo, Texas," retrieved July 26, 2018, from Handbook of Texas, tshaonline.org; "Chadbourne Street 1895" and "Interior of Arc Light Saloon," M. C. Ragsdale Photograph Collection, Fort Concho National Historic Landmark.

5. 1880 USFC; S. J. Grinnell, March 1, 1882, Grinnell Letters, WTC; CJF Journals,

Oct.–Nov. 1896; CJF, "From Over the Water," *Quintinian*, December 1896, 267; "Sonora and San Angelo," advertisement, *SAP*, Nov. 8, 1901, 3; "From the Ozona Courier," *San Angelo (TX) Standard*, Aug. 19, 1893, 1; HFL, "Autobiography," 2–3; CJF, *Distant Prize*, 305–06; Herbert Finger, "Dear Folks," Jan. 16, 1970; Carlson, *Woollybacks*, 108–09, 116; Carman, Heath, and Minto, *History and Present Condition*, 896; "Texas Ecoregions" and "Devils River State Natural Area," retrieved July 26, 2018, from Texas State Parks, tpwd.texas.gov.

6. 1900 USFC; "FF," Spring 1934; CJF, *Seven Horizons*, 360–61; Hodgson and Stamp, *Guide*; Tom Green County Historical Society, *Montage*, 65; Boyd Cornick Family Papers, finding aid; Tom Green County, *Chronicles*, I: 316; Rothman, *Living*, 153.

7. CJF Journals, Oct. 15 and Nov. 3, 1896. The *Enterprise* later was moved from San Angelo to Sherwood, Texas. (Tom Green County Historical Preservation League, *Tom Green County*, II: 132.)

8. "Institute Gossip," *PM,* Aug. 25, 1897, 75; Peterson, *Magazines*, 158; CJF, "How Lazy Sam Got His Rise: A Story of Patagonia," *Youth's Companion*, Aug. 26, 1897, clipping.

9. "Round About," *El Paso Herald*, July 10, 1897, 4.

10. CJF Journals, Aug. 7, 1896; "Institute Gossip," *PM,* Aug. 25, 1897, 75; CJF, "Patriots!" *Appeal to Reason*, Oct. 16, 1897, 2; CJF, Odds & Ends[:] A Collection of Extracts, Stray Thoughts, and Items of Wit & Wisdom[,] 1898." Finger recalled that he first saw the issue of *the Youth's Companion* containing his story, which was published in August 1897, while he was "in Mexico." (CJF, *Seven Horizons*, 359–60.)

11. "Institute Gossip," *PM,* Sept. 21, 1898, 102; CJF, "Books That Have Meant Most to Me." *Scholastic* Oct. 8, 1932, 11; CJF, "London Johnny," 118–19.

12. HFL, "Autobiography," 3; Leflar, "Memories," 1.

13. Appointments of US Postmasters, 1832–1971; "Institute Gossip," *PM,* May 10, 1899, 232–33; Jim Wheat, *Postmasters & Post Offices of Texas, 1846–1930*, retrieved July 16, 2019, from rootsweb.com.

14. Illinois College, *Catalogue*, 17; Photograph of Ferdinand Haberkorn; CJF, *Seven Horizons*, 362.

15. "Institute Gossip," *PM,* Aug. 16, 1899, 73–74; "Institute Gossip," *PM,* Oct. 25, 1899, 201; Foy, "Home Set to Music," 67; Roell, "Piano," 89.

16. Details that Finger mentioned years later match two government surveys of northern Ontario that took place in 1900. ("Geological Investigations in Western Ontario," *Engineering and Mining Journal*, June 23, 1900, 738; Hodgins and Hoyle, *Canoeing North*, 52; "FF," September 1924.)

17. Howard Payne College, *Twelfth Annual Catalogue*, 31; Illinois College, *Catalogue*, 17; 1900 USFC; Paddock, *History*, I: 358; 1900 USFC; James Dick, "David Wendel Guion," retrieved June 17, 2016, from Handbook of Texas, tshaonline.com.

18. "New People, Visitors and Newsmakers," *Ballinger (TX) Banner-Leader,* Jan. 26, 1901, retrieved July 26, 2018, from hiddenancestors.com; CJF, *One-Act Plays,* 24–25; Camann, *David Guion's Vision,* 6–9.

19. "FF," April 1932; Albums 9 and 10, M. C. Ragsdale Photograph Collection; Tom Green County Historical Preservation League, *Tom Green County,* I: 344; Kendall Curlee, "McArthur Cullen Ragsdale," June 15, 2010, retrieved Nov. 6, 2015, from Handbook of Texas Online, tshaonline.org.

20. "Oral Memoirs of David W. Guion," 11, 20, retrieved July 10, 2019, from Baylor University Institute for Oral History, contentdm.baylor.edu. The Cornick family probably moved from Knickerbocker to San Angelo by November 1901, as Boyd Cornick called then for expanded school facilities in San Angelo to prevent the spread of contagious diseases. ("To the Hon. County Judge . . . ," *SAP,* Nov. 1, 1901, 1.)

21. "Under the efficient management . . . ," *SAP,* March 12, 1902, 6; "Seventh Recital, C. J. Finger's Pupils, Saturday, March 22," *SAP,* March 26, 1902, 6; "Mr. Haberkorn . . . ," *SAP,* April 2, 1902, 3; "G. G. Odom . . . ," *SAP,* April 2, 1902, 8.

22. CJF to PHC, Jan. 8, 1902; "Finger–Haberkorn Affair," reproduced from *Ballinger (TX) Ledger, SAP,* Jan. 22, 1902, 7.

23. "Last Saturday at 3 o'clock . . . ," *SAP,* Nov. 29, 1901, 8; "San Angelo Music School," *SAP,* Dec. 6, 1901, 3; "Program of Concert," Dec. 28, 1901; "Grand Recital, Coleman Court House," program, Dec. 30, [1901]; "Program of Concert," Jan. 1, 1902; "Philharmonic," advertisement, *SAP,* Jan. 29, 1902, 2; "Ferdinand Haberkorn . . . ," *SAP,* Feb. 12, 1902, 1; "Mr. Haberkorn . . . ," *SAP,* April 2, 1902, 3; "Hutchinson, Kan.," *Violinist,* June 1912, 39; *Illinois College, Catalogue,* 17.

24. "C. J. Finger . . . ," *El Paso Herald,* June 25, 1901, 1.

25. Salis [pseud.], "Study in Egoism," *SAP,* April 16, 1902, 1; CJF, "Study in Egoism," *SAP,* April 23, 1902, 1; "In our next issue . . . ," *SAP,* April 23, 1902, 1; CJF, "Paderewski," *SAP,* April 30, 1902, 8.

26. CJF to PHC, Dec. 1901; "How about This P. E.?" *SAP,* Feb. 26, 1902, 2; "Entre Nous Club," *SAP,* April 16, 1902, 6; Jack Random [pseud.], "Ballinger's Grand Ball," *SAP,* Dec. 10, 1902, 7.

27. Hodgson and Stamp, *Guide;* CJF to PHC, December 1901.

28. Shores, "Library."

29. "Last Saturday at 3 o'clock . . . ," *SAP,* Nov. 29, 1901, 8; "San Angelo Music School," *SAP,* July 9, 1902, 5; "Philip Cornick," *SAP,* June 25, 1902, 3; "Sick," *SAP,* April 16, 1902, 3; CJF, "Requiescat: Sophie," *SAP,* Dec. 24, 1902, 2; *University of Tennessee Record,* Oct. 1903, 148, 254–55, 258, 261; "Class Officers Elected," *Courier-Journal (Lexington, KY),* Dec. 16, 1902, 4; CJF to PHC, Dec. 22, 1902, Jan. 15, [1903], and various undated letters; Cook, *London,* 124–25.

30. "W.O.W. Minstrels," *SAP,* April 16, 1902, 6; "Alamogordo News," *El Paso Sunday Times,* Aug. 24, 1902, 5; "San Angelo Abroad," *SAP,* Aug. 27, 1902, 5;

CJF, "Letters of Travel," *SAP*, Aug. 27, 1902, 8; Riskin, *Train Stops Here*, 128; Eidenbach, *Alamogordo*, 38–39; The Lodge Resort, "Brief History of the Lodge," retrieved from thelodgeresort.com. The line "arched green glory . . ." was from a poem that appeared in newspapers and magazines in 1890. (Edith Sessions Tupper, "Deep in the Woods," *Outing*, May 1890, 152.)

31. Fone, "This Other Eden," 13–14, 24, 32; Kellogg, "Introduction," 4; Borgeaud, *Cult of Pan*, 47, 74; Imko, "Pan and 'Homosexual Panic,'" 3, 5, 21.

32. "Dan Cauthorne . . . ," *SAP*, June 18, 1902, 8; CJF to Alice Finger, Sept. 23, 1902; "D. A. Cauthorn . . . ," *SAP*, April 30, 1902, 7; "Your Neighbors," *Mexico Missouri Message*, Sept. 7, 1905, 3; "For Rent," classified advertisement, *Muskogee (OK) Times-Democrat*, Oct. 5, 1907, 7; 1910 USFC; *Duluth 1918 Buyers' Guide*, 149, US City Directories; "Porter," *Muskogee (OK) Times-Democrat*, June 5, 1920, 15. On the connotation of *bachelor*, see Furneaux, *Queer Dickens*, 102–03. On YMCAs as sites for cruising in the early twentieth century, see Chauncey, "Christian Brotherhood," 296, and *Gay New York*, 156; Mjagkij, *Adrift*, 256.

33. Jack Random [pseud.], "Ballinger's Grand Ball," *SAP*, Dec. 10, 1902, 7; Radway, "Learned and Literary Print Cultures," 215. CJF referred in 1925 to the fact that Jack Random was one of his pen names. ("FF," Jan.–Feb. 1925.)

34. CJF, *Seven Horizons*, 147; Showalter, *Sexual Anarchy*, 106; Dellamora, *Masculine Desire*, 205; Weeks, *Coming Out*, 41–42; Fone, "This Other Eden," 29; Dynes, *Homolexis*, 37; Jeffs, "Man's Words," 19–20; Bruhm, "Roderick Random's Closet," 401–05; Chauncey, *Gay New York*, 103, 287; Gifford, *Dayneford's Library*, 10–103, 113; Buckton, *Secret Selves*, 173; Woods, *Gay Literature*, 5, 136, 154–55, 176–77; Ruppel, *Homosexuality*, 2; Smollett, Basker, Boucé, Seary, and Brack, *Roderick Random*, xv, xxxiv–xxxvii, 439n23–24. CJF's friend William Marion Reedy acknowledged that Jack Random was a "kinsman" of Roderick Random. (WMR to CJF.)

35. "Good Time Is Coming," advertisement, *SAP*, Dec. 24, 1902, 8; "Orient," advertisement, *SAP*, Dec. 31, 1902, 8; "S.A.M.S.," *SAP*, Jan. 14, 1903, 7.

36. Dynes, *Homolexis*, 62.

37. Whitman, "Glimpse," quoted in Jeffs, "Man's Words," 38; Mullins, "Stopping History," 7.

38. "The sight . . . ," *SAP*, Dec. 3, 1902, 5; Jack Random [pseud.], "Jack Random Wishes His Fellows a Happy New Year, Dedicated to Edward Carpenter—the True Man," *SAP*, Dec. 24, 1902, 4–5; "'Jack Random's' Contribution . . . ," *SAP*, Dec. 24, 1902, 2; "San Angelo Music School," advertisement, *SAP*, Dec. 31, 1902, 7; Buckton, *Secret Selves*, 164–65; Dellamora, *Masculine Desire*, 209; Brown, Introduction, 9.

39. "Mollie Random," *SAP*, Jan. 7, 1903, 4.

40. Lule Harper [pseud.], "Peep into a Bachelor's Scrap Book," *SAP*, Jan. 21, 1903, 7; Cook, *London*, 124–25.

41. "How about This P. E.?" *SAP*, Feb. 26, 1902, 2; "How's Angelo?" *SAP*, Jan. 28,

1903, 5. Although this report was anonymous, the first sentence mentioned "rumors of a S. A. M. S.," or San Angelo Music School, concert.

42. CJF, "Trend of Thought," *SAP*, Feb. 4, 1903, 8; CJF, "Olla Podrida," *SAP*, Feb. 18, 1903, 8; Carpenter, *Ioläus*, 23, 90, 130–31; Mitchell and Leavitt, *Pages Passed*, xiii; Shores, "Library."

43. CJF to Alice Finger, Sept. 23, 1902; People of the State of New York ex rel. the F. P. Bhumgara Company, Relator, against James L. Wells, et al., Defendants, in Court of Appeals of the State of New York, Appeal Book, 1904; "FF," September 1924. Minnie Bergman was a German immigrant like Robert, and she and George later lived near Robert Bergman and Alice Finger in New Jersey. (Certificate #20304, New York Marriage Index; 1910 USFC; New York, Index to Petitions for Naturalization; "10,000 Painters to Strike To-Day," *NYT*, April 1, 1907, 18.)

44. "Mr. C. J. Finger . . . ," *SAP*, Jan. 14, 1903, 3; Shores, "Library."

45. "In the Public Eye," *SAP*, Dec. 31, 1902, 10; "S. A. M. S.—The New Year's Reception," *SAP*, Jan. 7, 1903, 6; "S.A.M.S.," *SAP*, Jan. 14, 1903, 7; "Red Men to Organize," clipping, in CJF to PHC, Jan. 15, [1903]; "Degree of Pocahontas . . . ," *SAP*, Sept. 2, 1903, 2; Shores, "Library."

46. Smollett et al., *Roderick Random*, 39.

47. A jury in Tom Green County convicted a man on this charge in 1905, although he won an appeal by demonstrating that the young woman in question was not "chaste" at the time of their encounter. (State of Texas v. Emmal Garlos, District Court, Tom Green County, May term, 1905, WTC.)

48. CJF, "Mr. C. Ferguson . . . ," *SAP*, July 29, 1903, 6; Eidenbach, *Alamogordo*, 7. C. Ferguson was still on the Crockett County tax rolls in 1904. (Texas County Tax Rolls.)

49. "Club Rooms Furnished," *SAP*, July 22, 1903, 3; "Red Men Install," *SAP*, July 22, 1903, 3; "Degree of Pocahontas . . . ," *SAP*, Sept. 2, 1903, 2.

50. "C. J. Finger . . . ," *SAP*, July 22, 1903, 3; "Misses Nellie and Amelia . . . ," *SAP*, July 22, 1903, 6; CJF, "Letters of Travel, No. 1," *SAP*, July 29, 1903, 6; CJF, "Mr. C. Ferguson . . . ," *SAP*, July 29, 1903, 6; "CJF, "Letters of Travel, No 2," *SAP*, Aug. 5, 1903, 8; "Miss Amelia Ferguson . . . ," *Alamogordo (NM) News*, Aug. 8, 1903, 4; "CJF, "Letters of Travel, No 2," *SAP*, Aug. 5, 1903, 8; "Ferguson–Finger," *SAP*, Sept. 2, 1903, 6; Shores, "Library."

51. "Good Bye," *SAP*, Aug. 19, 1903, 3; "Change of Management," *SAP*, Aug. 19, 1903, 3; "P. E. Truly . . . ," *SAP*, Aug. 19, 1903, 4; "Ferguson–Finger," *SAP*, Sept. 2, 1903, 6.

52. "Trustee Sale Notice," *SAP*, Aug. 19, 1903, 8; Coleman National Bank *v.* C. J. Finger, No. 1395, District Court of Tom Green County, May Term, 1905, WTC.

53. "San Angelo Music School," advertisement, *SAP*, Sept. 2, 1903, 2; "Music School Recital," *SAP*, Oct. 28, 1903, 7; "San Angelo Music School," advertisement, *SAP*, Sept. 23, 1903, 3.

54. "T. S. Sharpe," *SAP*, Aug. 5, 1903, 8; "T. S. Sharpe . . . ," *SAP*, Sept. 30, 1903, 7; "Prof. C. J. Finger . . . ," *SAP*, Sept. 30, 1903, 8; "T. S. Sharpe . . . ," *SAP*, Oct. 7,

1903, 2; "Col. J. D. Sugg . . . ," *SAP*, April 28, 1904, 7; "T. C. Wynne . . . ," *SAP*,
Sept. 29, 1904, 7; "Another Party of Hunters Returns," *SAP*, Dec. 1, 1904, 1;
Record for T. S. Sharpe, 1940 USFC.

55. "Concho Club . . . ," *SAP*, Oct. 14, 1903, 7.

56. "Mrs. C. J. Finger . . . ," *SAP*, Nov. 4, 1903, 3; "There will be . . . ," *SAP*, Dec. 2,
1903, 3; "Red Men Elect Officers," *SAP*, Dec. 23, 1903, 10; Tom Green County
District Court, Citation, Coleman National Bank *v.* CJF, Jan. 13, 1904, WTC.

57. This is the birth date that appears in official records of Hubert Philip Finger's
death. (Michigan Department of Vital and Health Records; US Social Security
Death Index.) However, his grave marker in Missouri shows a birth date of
Feb. 21, 1904. (Find a Grave Index.)

58. "Federation of Labor," *SAP*, Dec. 30, 1903, 6; "Walk-Out Is Ordered," *SAP*,
Jan. 7, 1904, 3; Coleman National Bank *v.* CJF, No. 1395, District Court of Tom
Green County, May Term, 1905, WTC.

59. "CJF . . . ," *SAP*, Jan. 7, 1904, 7; CJF to PHC.

60. "Personal Mention," *Railway Age*, June 17, 1904, 1150; "Railway Club of
Alamogordo," program, June 12 and 13, 1904; "Notes and News," *Railway Age*,
Oct. 28, 1904, 634; "Alamogordo Railway Club," *Railroad Gazette*, Oct. 28,
1904, 137; Eidenbach, *Alamogordo*, 20.

61. "Link and Pin," *El Paso Herald*, Oct. 19, 1904, 5; "Alamogordo Railway Club's
Big Social a Success," *El Paso Herald*, Nov. 14, 1904, 3; "Local and So-Forth,"
Alamogordo (NM) News, Dec. 24, 1904, 3; "Big Balls," *Alamogordo (NM) News*,
Jan. 7, 1905, 3; "Members of Railway Club Included Everybody in Town 50 Years
Ago," *Alamogordo (NM) News*, Aug. 19, 1954, 28.

62. "Nobody deserves . . . ," *Alamogordo (NM) News*, April 8, 1905, 4; "Alamogordo
possesses . . . ," *Alamogordo (NM) News*, April 29, 1905, 4.

63. "News of Alamogordo," *El Paso Herald*, June 26, 1905, 8; "Railway Club and
Gen. Mgr. Simmons," *Alamogordo (NM) News*, Aug. 5, 1905, 1; "Mrs. C. J.
Finger . . . ," *Alamogordo (NM) News*, Aug. 12, 1905, 4. CJF sometimes spelled
their daughter's nickname "Kittie," but she signed the family guest book "Kitty
Finger." (GGB, Dec. 25, 1923.)

64. "About Railroad People," *El Paso Herald*, July 21, 1905, 5; CJF, *Seven Horizons*,
381; "News of Alamogordo," *El Paso Herald*, Aug. 2, 1905, 12, Aug. 3, 1905, 8;
"Local and So-Forth," *Alamogordo (NM) News*, Sept. 2, 1905, 4.

Chapter 4

1. "Personal Mention," *Railway Age*, Sept. 15, 1905, 333, and Oct. 26, 1906, 524;
"The stockholders . . . ," *Daily Public Ledger (Maysville, KY)*, March 23, 1908, 1;
"Name Receiver for Road," *CE*, Oct. 9, 1914, 5; CJF, "History Hath Its Lessons,"
Electric Railway Journal, Dec. 27, 1919, 1036–38; Zachman, *Historical Homes*;
personal observation, Aug. 22, 2017; Alison Gibson, Union Township (OH)
Public Library, personal communication.

2. 1920 USFC; record for Charles Joseph Finger Jr., US Social Security Death Index.

3. "Local Matter," *RB*, Nov. 8, 1911, 5; "Fruit Hill," advertisement, *CE*, Oct. 31, 1909, 33.

4. "Syndicate Wants C. G. and P. Road," *CE*, May 8, 1912, 5; "Railroads," *CE*, Aug. 22, 1913, 5; Hilton and Due, *Electric Interurban*, 3, 255.

5. "Back to Ripley," *RB*, Dec. 31, 1913, 1; "Again at the Helm," *RB*, March 4, 1914, 5; "Watch for Finger," *CE*, April 21, 1914, 11; HFL, "Autobiography," 3.

6. "Name Receiver for Road," *CE*, Oct. 9, 1914, 5; "Receivership Lifted," *Daily Public Ledger (Maysville, KY)*, Nov. 18, 1916, 4; "Public Notice," advertisement, *RB*, March 28, 1917, 4; "Local Matter," *RB*, Oct. 3, 1917, 5; "Notes of the Trade," *Waste Trade Journal*, June 15, 1918, 28; "Fare Increase Authorized," *CE*, Dec. 15, 1918, 9; "Interurban to Be Sold," *CE*, Jan. 2, 1919, 10; "Will Sell Railroad," *Evening Telegram (Elyria, OH)*, Jan. 4, 1919, 5; 1920 USFC; CJF to James Branch Cabell, Feb. 22, 1920, James Branch Cabell Collection; CJF, "Out of the Grip," *RM*, May 6, 1920, 373–75.

7. "Local Matter," *RB*, Sept. 4, 1907, 5; "Manufacturers!" advertisement, *Literary Digest*, June 27, 1908, inside back cover; "Discussion Club," *RB*, Oct. 14, 1908, 1, Nov. 25, 1908, 4; "Hall of Union Lodge, No. 71," newspaper clipping without title, Dec. 16, 1908; "Discussion Club," *RB*, Oct. 20, 1909, 1, Nov. 23, 1910, 1; "Decatur," *RB*, Jan. 25, 1911, 4; "Discussion Club," *RB*, April 12, 1911, 1; "Masonic Meeting," *RB*, June 10, 1914, 7; "Chautauqua Tickets," *RB*, Aug. 19, 1914, 1; "Debate," *RB*, March 17, 1915, 1; "Discussion Club," *RB*, Dec. 22, 1915, 1; "Big Event of the Year," *RB*, Aug. 23, 1916, 1.

8. "Mr. C. J. Finger . . . ," *RB*, Aug. 28, 1912, 5; "Mr. C. J. Finger . . . ," *RB*, Oct. 16, 1912, 7; "Local Matter," *RB*, Feb. 5, 1913, 11; Raitz and O'Malley, *Kentucky's Frontier Highway*, 14.

9. Jack Random [pseud.], "Admetus," *Railway World*, March 1915, 264–65.

10. Galbreath, "Claude Meeker," 604–09.

11. "At high noon . . . ," *Daily Public Ledger (Maysville, KY)*, Sept. 17, 1908, 3.

12. "Terminal Facilities in Tucumcari, N. M.," *El Paso Herald*, Jan. 9, 1904, 6; "Alamogordo Items," *El Paso Herald*, Aug. 1, 1907, 3; "Council's Last Session," *Tucumcari (NM) News and Tucumcari Times*, Sept. 26, 1908, 1; "Mrs. C. Ferguson," advertisement, *Tucumcari (NM) News and Tucumcari Times*, March 15, 1912, 5.

13. "Water Melon Resolution," *Tucumcari (NM) Times*, Aug. 21, 1909, 5; "Ripley," *CE*, Oct. 24, 1909, Sec. 4, 6; "Personal and Social Mention," *Tucumcari (NM) News and Tucumcari Times*, July 16, 1910, 7; 1910 USFC.

14. "Mr. C. J. Finger . . . ," *RB*, June 22, 1910, 5; "Local Matter," *RB*, June 29, 1910, 5; "Local Matter," *RB*, Aug. 24, 1910, 5.

15. Galbraith, *Chillicothe Presbytery*, 144; Hagedorn, *Beyond*, 41–42, 82; Young, "Underground Railroad," 10. As the town planned its centennial observance, a

newspaper noted, "Here Harriet Beecher Stowe wrote 'Uncle Tom's Cabin.'" ("Ripley to Have Big Centennial," *Portsmouth (OH) Daily Times*, Aug. 20, 1910, 17.)

16. CJF to Boyd Cornick, Jan. 20, 1911.

17. "Philip Cornick . . . ," *SAP*, March 9, 1905, 6; US Consular Registration Certificates; Cornick, "Land Value Taxation," 311; Hodgson and Stamp, *Guide*; CJF to PHC. CJF gave a speech about Mexico in 1911, drawing from "his personal knowledge and experience." ("Discussion Club," *RB*, May 17, 1911, 1.) He later recalled reading a book that was published in 1909 while he was in Mexico: "It was in Mexico, on the west coast, that I read 'The Man Shakespeare and His [Tragic] Life Story.'" (CJF to Frank Harris, letter to the editor, *Pearson's*, May 1919, 331–32; "Man Shakespeare," advertisement, *NYT*, Oct. 22, 1909, 27.) Much later, Finger referred vaguely to considering a job as general superintendent of a mine in Mexico. (CJF, *Seven Horizons*, 417.)

18. "Local Matter," *RB*, Aug. 17, 1910, 7; CJF to Boyd Cornick, Jan. 20, 1911.

19. Inside the back cover of the *English Men* volume on Samuel Johnson, CJF noted, "I bought this book in 1903 at San Angelo Texas when directing the conservatory of music." The analysis in this chapter of CJF's reading habits is based on my inventory of his personal library, which his family preserved at his home in Fayetteville, Arkansas. Bookstore labels, bookplates, and marks that CJF made in his books and pamphlets provide a rough idea of when he studied particular works. For example, many of the books he acquired in Ohio bear bookplates depicting a pirate. He made pencil notes in some volumes and tucked or even pasted clippings or pamphlets in some, revealing more about his interests. (Shores, "Library.")

20. CJF, "Dry Stuff," *RM*, Jan. 29, 1920, 75; CJF, "Out of the Grip," *RM*, May 6, 1920, 373–75.

21. CJF inscribed his copy of *A Miscellany of British Poetry* "Charles J. Finger[,] Allen Hotel. Delaware, O. 1919." The book had a preface dated September 1919, so he must have bought the book late in the year. The book by Masefield bore a sticker for the University Book Store on South Sandusky Street in Delaware, near the campus of Ohio Wesleyan University. CJF returned to Delaware in January 1920, staying long enough that a correspondent addressed a letter to him at the Allen. (A. Meyer to CJF, Jan. 10, 1920.)

22. Masefield, *Round House*, 193–99, 260–62. I found seven books by Masefield in CJF's library, and he referred to owning an eighth. ("FF," Jan.–Feb. 1925.)

23. Frederick, *William Henry Hudson*, 10.

24. CJF, *Wilde in Outline*, 8–9; Korte, *English Travel Writing*, 189n16; Wilson, *Hilaire Belloc*, 105; Goodway, *Anarchist Seeds*, 32; Burrow, "Queer Clubs," 114, 116–17.

25. Woods, *Homintern*, 32.

26. Vierek, *Candle*, 17, 19–20, 44; Gertz, *Odyssey*, 79; Elledge, *Masquerade*, xxxi; Slide, *Lost Gay Novels*.

27. CJF to Frank Harris, letter to the editor, *Pearson's,* May 1919, 331–32.

28. Carpenter, *Days and Dreams,* 97.

29. CJF, "Unrecognized Golden Age," 411.

30. Rowbotham, *Edward Carpenter,* 268.

31. Huneker, *Ivory,* 13.

32. CJF Journals, Sept. 8, 1890; "FF," March 1925 and Jan.–Feb. 1926; CJF, Introduction, *Collected Works of Joseph Conrad,* ix–x; CJF, *Seven Horizons,* 345–49, 440; CJF, *Give a Man,* 119; Conrad, *Heart of Darkness,* 67, 78, 105, 107–08, 121, 133, 151, 154; Showalter, *Sexual Anarchy,* 112; Hodges, "Deep Fellowship"; Hynes, "Art of Telling," xvi; Harpham, *One of Us,* 112; Casarino, "Sublime of the Closet," 228, 241, 243; Harpham quoted in Ruppel, "Girl!" 167n1; Ruppel, *Homosexuality,* 1–2, 33, 27, 55. The Conrad scholar Peter Lancelot Mallios speculated that CJF and editors of other small literary magazines in the South were inspired by HLM's essay "The Sahara of the Bozart" to study and evoke Conrad. However, there is a chronological problem with Mallios's assumption about CJF. "Sahara of the Bozart" did not receive wide circulation until the release in November 1920 of *Prejudices, Second Series,* but CJF was writing in a Conradian style by 1919, when his editor William Marion Reedy praised his story "Incongruity" as "good Finger and good Conrad." (WMR to CJF, Jan. 14, 1920.) Mallios also garbled some facts, erroneously indicating CJF devoted the entire issue of *AW* in August 1924 to Conrad. CJF included lengthy remarks about Conrad in his column "Free Fantasia" and reprinted a poem by F. W. Bateson, "Ulysses," as an implicit tribute to Conrad. However, he dedicated that issue to the composer David W. Guion and devoted much of his column to a boat trip down the James River in Missouri, an account much more Whitmanesque than Conradian. Mallios even weirdly wrote that Finger was married to "the editor of a 1925 edition of Conrad's and Ford's *The Inheritors.*" (Mallios, *Our Conrad,* 269, 271–72, 303; "FF," August 1924, 4–7.)

33. "Stewart Kidd," retrieved May 4, 2018, from Social Networks and Archival Context, socialarchive.iath.virginia.edu.

34. Bender, *Sea-Brothers,* 83–84; Lundquist, *Jack London,* 5–7; Berman, Introduction, vii, xii; Haley, *Wolf,* 45–46, 278–79; Editors, "Jack London," July 20, 1998, retrieved May 4, 2018, from *Encyclopaedia Britannica,* britannica.com.

35. CJF to PHC; Margaret Germann, "Wandering in Many Lawless Lands, C. J. Finger Got Material for Tales," *Dallas Morning News,* May 11, 1924.

36. T. R. H., "Cincinnati Interurban Electric," letter to the editor, *Rural New Yorker,* Oct. 29, 1904, 779; "Bruce's Spellbinders Have Another Very Busy Day; Dempsey Issues a Rebuke," *CE,* July 20, 1913, 13; Samuel Danziger, "Singletax and American Municipalities," *National Municipal Review,* Oct. 1915, 616–21; Stanley E. Bowdle, "Herbert Bigelow," *Public,* Jan. 19, 1912, 52. Bigelow lived on Five Mile Road in Fruit Hill, and his office was at 514 Main, one block from

the CG&P office. (1910 USFC; Cincinnati, map, 1912, University of Alabama Historical Map Archive; *Williams's Cincinnati Directory,* June 1912, 232.)

37. CJF, *Seven Horizons,* 408–11.

38. "Announcements," *CE,* Aug. 27, 1911, Section 3, 8; "Mrs. Herbert S. Bigelow . . . ," *CE,* Nov. 17, 1912, Section 4, 6; "Political Gossip," *CE,* April 27, 1913, 9; "Charter Campaign Closes; All Ready for the Vote," *CE,* July 29, 1913, 10; 1920 USFC; Oberlin College, *Catalogue,* 275. Margaret Naomi Doane Bigelow did not appear in a Cincinnati city directory after 1915. By 1920 she and Herbert were separated. Twenty years later, they were still married but did not live together. When Margaret was on her deathbed in Columbus, Ohio, in 1941, Herbert went to her side. (*Cincinnati, Ohio, City Directory, 1917,* 240; 1920 and 1940 USFC; AP, "Mrs. Bigelow Dies," *Washington C. H. (OH) Record-Herald,* April 11, 1941, 1.)

39. "Ripley," *CE,* April 19, 1914, 52; "Watch for Finger," *CE,* April 21, 1914, 11; "Ripley," *CE,* May 24, 1914, 60; 1920 USFC.

40. National Civil Liberties Bureau, *Outrage*; Herbert S. Bigelow, "Bigelow's Patriotism," advertisement, *CE,* Dec. 2, 1917, 32; Shapiro, "Herbert Bigelow Case," 108–10; CJF, *Seven Horizons,* 490–11; Brierton, Smith, and Wright, "Over There," 14; Shapiro, "Herbert Bigelow Case," 115; "Secretary Married to Bigelow," *CE,* June 17, 1942, 1.

41. Christian Lorentzen, "Can Short Stories Still Shock?" *New York,* Jan. 7, 2016, retrieved May 24, 2016, from vulture.com.

42. "Wanted," advertisement, *RB,* Sept. 6, 1916, 5; "Local Matter," *RB,* May 3, 1916, 7; CJF to Nellie Finger, carbon copy; Shores, "Published Works."

43. "Ohio River & Columbus RR," *Poor's and Moody's Manual Consolidated* 18, I: 702.

44. "Local Items," *Border Vidette (Nogales, AZ),* March 22, 1913, 3; "City and Environs," *LAT,* May 11, 1914, 8; US City Directories; "Local News," *Border Vidette (Nogales, AZ),* Feb. 19, 1916, 3; "Local Matter," *RB,* Oct. 25, 1916, 7.

45. "Jack London's Death Sudden; Caused Stir Here Few Years Ago," *Sandusky (OH) Star-Journal,* Nov. 23, 1916, 1, 2; "Ashes of Jack London," *CE,* Nov. 27, 1916, 14; CJF, "Some Mischievous Thing," 119.

46. New York State Census, 1915, AN; "Art Students League," *Brooklyn Daily Eagle,* Feb. 2, 1915, 5; "Calendar of Special New York Exhibitions," *American Art News,* May 26, 1916, 6.

47. CJF, "Life in Porvenir," letter to the editor, *Public,* June 1, 1917, 536.

48. London, *Revolution,* 305–06.

49. CJF Journals, Jan. 4, Feb. 2, and May 3, 1891; "Chilean Trouble," *San Francisco Chronicle,* March 7, 1891, 1.

50. CJF to Frank Harris, letter to the editor, *Pearson's,* May 1919, 331–32.

51. Frank Harris, "With Our Readers," *Pearson's,* May 1919, 332.

52. CJF, "Plain Words on the Railroad Deficit," *Public,* Aug. 30, 1919, 933–34;

CJF, "Evolution in Transportation"; CJF, "History Hath Its Lessons"; Shores, "Library."

53. "Authors Hear Charles Finger," *FD*, May 6, 1921, 1; CJF, *Seven Horizons*, 418; Leflar, *"Memories,"* 9.

54. "Mrs. Ferguson Dies," *Tucumcari (NM) News and Tucumcari Times*, Jan. 17, 1913, 1. The purchaser of the Gilliland house in June 1914 was recorded as Nellie, not C. J. ("Local Matter," *RB*, April 15, 1914, 7; "Ripley," *CE*, May 24, 1914, 60; "Transfers of Real Estate," *RB*, June 10, 1914, 1.)

55. "From the Workshop of Mr. H. G. Wells," *RM*, April 1, 1920, 272–73.

56. Carl Sandburg, "Finger and His Songbook," *SR*, Dec. 3, 1927, 373–74; Gunn, "John W. Gunn Visits"; "Profits in Lambs if Handled in Right Way," *FD*, March 20, 1920, 2.

57. Nan Lawler, "Will Lighton (1866–1923)," March 4, 2015, retrieved Feb. 3, 2017, from Encyclopedia of Arkansas, encyclopediaofarkansas.com.

58. Carpenter, *Days and Dreams*, 151, 302, 305; Brown, Introduction, 13; Cook, *London*, 133; Koven, *Slumming*, 235; Rowbotham, *Edward Carpenter*, 7, 111; Knuth, *Children's Literature*, 86–87.

59. "Local and Personal," advertisements, *Tucumcari (NM) News and Tucumcari Times*, Nov. 6, 1919, 5; CJF, "Neglected Open Secret," review of *The Place of Agriculture in Reconstruction* by James B. Morman (1919), *Public*, Nov. 29, 1919, 1121.

60. The transaction on December 23, 1919, was traced in a 1944 deed transfer. (St. Louis–San Francisco Railway Company to C. J. Finger Jr., Jan. 15, 1944, retrieved Nov. 19, 2014, from www.co.washington.ar.us/Information /Chronicle.) Finger mentioned construction on the Fayetteville property as early as January 14, 1920. (WMR to CJF, Jan. 14, 1920.) A census enumerator recorded in February 1920 that Christopher Ferguson and May A. Ferguson lived in Prairie Township, Washington County, Arkansas. (1920 USFC.) Nellie and Herbert apparently traveled to Arkansas on March 27 or April 3. (A. Meyer to CJF, April 3, 1920; WMR to CJF, April 7, 1920.) Finger wrote to Nellie around April 1920 that he was not "very keen" to sell their Cleveland house "until I have seen the place," apparently referring to the Arkansas property. (CJF to Nellie Finger, carbon.)

61. London, *Revolution*, 308–09; "Life on a California Ranch Described by Jack London," *NYT*, April 9, 1916, 81; "Jack London's Death Sudden; Caused Stir Here Few Years Ago," *Sandusky (OH) Star-Journal*, Nov. 23, 1916, 1, 2; "Notable Year in the World of Fiction," Book Review, *NYT*, Nov. 26, 1916, 502–06; Laymon [pseud.], "From the Book Pile," *RM*, Aug. 12, 1920, 630; "Current Opinion Hails Finger as Peer of E. A. Poe," *FD*, Aug. 30, 1924, 1, 5; Taliaferro, *Tarzan Forever*, 128.

Chapter 5

1. "Reedy on Christmas," *SAP*, Dec. 30, 1903, 1.

2. Kunitz and Haycraft, *Twentieth Century Authors*, 1155–56; McKinney, "William Marion Reedy," 431; Putzel, *Man in the Mirror*, 6–7.

3. WMR to CJF, Feb. 14, 1916, and Aug. 1, 1919; CJF, "R. B. Cunningham Grahame [*sic*]" *RM*, Nov. 27, 1919, 836; CJF, "Impressions from Cleveland," *RM*, Dec. 18, 1919.

4. WMR to CJF, Jan. 14 and 28, 1920; Dzwonkoski, *American Literary Publishing Houses*, 61; Greene, *Damned*, 93.

5. HLM, *My Life*; Mayfield, *Constant Circle*, 9–10, 19; Riggio, *Dreiser–Mencken Letters*, 330, 380; Earle, "Pulp Magazines," 200; Hamilton, "American Manners," 236; Crowther, *Infuriating American*, 5.

6. HLM to CJF, Oct. 30, 1919, and Jan. 12, [1920], letters folded and pasted inside CJF's copy of Mencken's *Prejudices, First Series* (Shores, "Library"); Mayfield, *Constant Circle*, 49, 62, 85.

7. Edwards, *Exotic Journeys*, 139. The issue included "Village Nocturne" by McClure, "Porcelain and Pink (A One-Act Play)" by Fitzgerald, and "Variations on a Theme by Havelock Ellis" by Van Vechten.

8. Huneker, *Ivory*, 12–13.

9. CJF, "Incongruity," 75.

10. WMR to CJF, Jan 14, 1920; CJF, "Ma-Ha-Su-Ma," 219; Hurley, *Circulating Queerness*, 52.

11. CJF, "Some Mischievous Thing," 120, 126.

12. CJF, *Hints on Writing Short Stories*. In 1921 the cross-dressing theater critic Alexander Woollcott called the characters in a "curiously effeminate comedy" "odd folk." (Fone, *Stonewall*, 265–66; Thomas Meehan, "At Last the Star of the Show," review of *The Wit, World, and Life of Alexander Woollcott* by Howard Teichmann, Book Review, *NYT*, May 16, 1976, 7.)

13. Jack Random [pseud.], "Odd Thoughts," *RM*, Feb. 5, 1920, 93, and Feb. 19, 1920, 124–25; Young, *Disarming*, 246–47.

14. WMR had published and praised Dreiser in the *Mirror*. (Loving, *Last Titan*, 134, 282.)

15. CJF to Nellie Finger, carbon.

16. "Books of the Day," *RM*, June 10, 1920, 483–85; Kennerley quoted in Bruccoli, *Mitchell Kennerley*, 42. The same issue carried a large advertisement by a bookstore in St. Louis for Conrad's new book. ("Rescue: Joseph Conrad's Latest Romance," advertisement, *RM*, June 10, 1920, 476.) On the narrative frame as a device for introducing ambiguity, see Showalter, *Sexual Anarchy*, 82–83.

17. Belloc, *First and Last*, 18–19; Cunninghame Graham, *Gaucho Laird*, 325–26.

18. CJF, "Ebro," 469.

19. Rowbotham, *Edward Carpenter*, 89–90; "Percival Chubb, Leader, 1912–1933," retrieved from Ethical Society of St. Louis, ethicalstl.org.

20. Austen, *Playing the Game*, 9–10; Cook, *London*, 26; Nissen, *Manly Love*, 26.

21. Tolstoy, *Kreutzer Sonata*, 3, 31.

22. "Why He Foreswore Cards," *El Paso Daily Herald*, July 7, 1897, 3, *Salt Lake (UT) Herald*, June 16, 1897, 7, *Estherville (IA) Daily News*, June 24, 1897, 15, *Sterling (IL) Standard*, July 15, 1897, 14, *Galveston (TX) Daily News*, June 7, 1897, 4, *Massillon (OH) Item*, May 18, 1898, 2, *Philipsburg (MT) Mail*, Aug. 20, 1897, 3, *Lebanon (PA) Daily News*, July 28, 1897, 3, *Naugatuck (CT) Daily News*, July 1, 1897, 7.

23. "Jacob Gordin and 'The Kreutzer Sonata,'" *Current Literature*, October 1906, 420–21; "Kreutzer Sonata / Herbert Brenon [motion picture]," retrieved Oct. 13, 2016, from Performing Arts Encyclopedia, Library of Congress, memory.loc .gov; "'Nazimova' at the Diamond," *Evening Review (East Liverpool, OH)*, Dec. 30, 1916, 2; "War Brides," advertisement, *Wilmington (OH) Daily News*, Nov. 10, 1917, 6.

24. Galsworthy, *Little Man*, 78; Shores, "Library."

25. Child, "Smyth's Channel," 453–54.

26. Weeks, *Coming Out*, 42; Sedgwick, *Epistemology*, 203; Woods, *Gay Literature*, 14; Cook, *London*, 39; Huneker, *Ivory*, 20.

27. CJF, "Out of the Grip," *RM*, May 6, 1920, 373–75; Frederick O'Brien, "Little Fling at Mr. Finger," letter to the editor, *RM*, June 10, 1920, 476; "FF," January 1932.

28. CJF, "Ebro," 469, 471, 473, 483; Childs, *El Jimmy*, 66, 70. CJF did not record meeting Hyslop in his journal, but he probably knew of him since baptism records refer to Samuel Hyslop being in Punta Arenas in October 1890, whereas the first published reference to Hyslop seems to have been in 1931, a decade after "Ebro." ("Some British Baptisms," retrieved from BP; Barrett and Barrett, *Yankee in Patagonia*, 81.)

29. Levin, *Gay Novel*, 74; Gifford, *Dayneford's Library*; Bozorth, *Auden's Games*, 30; Ruppel, *Homosexuality*, 91–92; Gunn, *Gay American Novels*, 3.

30. William Henry Hudson to RBCG, June 29 and Aug. 5, 1920, in Curle, *Letters*, 103, 105–06. The editor of Hudson's letters to RBCG incorrectly read Hudson's handwritten reference to the story's title as "Ehrs."

31. WMR's biographer Max Putzel identified the author of the Elmer Chubb letters as Edgar Lee Masters (*Man in the Mirror*, 281–82), but WMR asked CJF, "Are you Elmer Chubb?" (WMR to CJF, April 3, 1920). CJF later recalled that WMR wrote sonnets under the name of Chubb. ("FF," Jan.–Feb. 1925.)

32. CJF, "Card from Elmer Chubb, Ph.D., LLD," *RM*, July 8, 1920, 547–48; "Divine Wrath," *RM*, July 22, 1920, 579–80.

33. WMR to CJF, May 10, 1920; WMR, "Temblor," *RM*, Aug. 19, 1920, 639.

34. WMR to CJF, Jan. 14, 28, Feb. 5, 12, April 7, and May 28, 1920; Alma Meyer to CJF, Jan. 2 and April 3, 1920; Flanagan, "Reedy of the *Mirror*," 143–44.

35. CJF, "And Now, 1927," *AW*, January 1927, inside cover.

36. US Ordnance Department, *Big Gun*, 12, 48; Cullum and Holden, *Biographical Register*, 1217; Robson, "Administrative and Supply Functions," 246; Braim, *Test of Battle*, 46–47, 69; Office of the Adjutant General, *Awards*, 739; Mathias, *Amazing Bob Davis*, 314; R. Jackson Marshall III, "Wildcat Division," Jan. 1, 2006, retrieved Oct. 11, 2016, from NCpedia.org; American Battle Monuments Commission, *81st Division*, 11. GWM's parents were George Taylor Maddox (1848–97) and Mary H. Leigh Maddox (1861–83). (Gravestones for George Taylor Maddox and Mary H. Maddox in Owenton and Maddox Cemetery, Turkey Foot, Scott County, Kentucky, retrieved Aug. 8, 2017, from findagrave .com.)

37. "Infantry Officers," *Army and Navy Register*, Dec. 21, 1918, 719; Cullum and Holden, *Biographical Register*, 1217; *Army–Navy–Air Force Register and Defense Times*, March 12, 1921, 260; Laurie and Cole, "Role of Federal Military Forces," 297–99.

38. CR to GWM, April 21, 1936.

39. "Athletes of Army Put Rank Aside at 3-Day Games," *St. Louis Post-Dispatch*, July 3, 1920, 10; "City Celebrates '4th' Tomorrow," *Courier-Journal (Louisville, KY)*, July 4, 1920, 1; CJF, "Reflections," *RM*, July 22, 1920, 577; Photograph of GWM by RHD, RHD Papers.

40. CJF, "Reflections," *RM*, July 22, 1920, 577, and Aug. 19, 1920, 640–41; J. A. Symonds to Edward Carpenter, Jan. 21, 1893, quoted in Tsuzuki, *Edward Carpenter*, 126.

41. WMR to CJF, July 28, 1920; CJF, "William Marion Reedy," *RM*, July 29, 1920, 587; Putzel, *Man in the Mirror*, 282.

42. "Reedy Funeral to Be Held at County Home Wednesday," *St. Louis Post-Dispatch*, July 30, 1920, 2; CJF, "Reflections," *RM*, Aug. 12, 1920, 624–25; CJF, "In My Master's Workshop," *RM*, Aug. 5, 1920, 604–05.

43. Jack Random [pseud.], "In Ye Good Olde Days," *RM*, Aug. 12, 1920, 629; Laymon [pseud.], "From the Book Pile," *RM*, Aug. 12, 1920, 630.

44. CJF, "Reflections," *RM*, Aug. 19, 1920, 640–41.

45. Henry H. Wilson, "Unpalatable Realism," letter to the editor, *RM*, Aug. 12, 1920, 630; CJF, "Reflections," *RM*, Aug. 12, 1920, 640–41; "Reedy Who Made the Mirror," *Fourth Estate*, Aug. 14, 1920, 17; Margie Reedy to CJF, Aug. 21, 1920; "New Name—A New Owner," *RM*, Sept. 2, 1920, 671. On WMR's marriage to Margaret Chambers, see "William Marion Reedy," *Public*, Dec. 15, 1911, 1259–61.

46. Hodgson and Stamp, *Guide*.

47. CJF, "Jack Random," *RM*, Aug. 26, 1920, 660–61; US Ordnance Department, *Big Gun*, 12, 48; Dynes, *Homolexis*, 33. George Sylvester Viereck, one of the writers Finger studied, was known for having a framed violet, taken from Oscar Wilde's grave, in his office. (Gifford, *Dayneford's Library*, 87–89.)

48. "New Name—A New Owner," *RM*, Sept. 2, 1920, 671.

Chapter 6

1. CJF wrote in 1921 that he had 120 acres "under orchard and garden cultivation." (CJF, "No Promise on the Farms for the Unemployed," letter to the editor, *Nation*, Sept. 21, 1921, 321.) However, a magazine writer who visited Gayeta in 1923 wrote that it was 110 acres. (Gunn, "John W. Gunn Visits.")

2. "Local Train Service to Be Cut One-Third," *FD*, Dec. 6, 1919, 1; Rand McNally, Arkansas, map, in *Ideal Atlas of the World*, 1916, AML. The Fayetteville newspaper referred to "the Ferguson lawn" that was "at the foot of Mount Kessler" and "on the way to Farmington." ("Spend a cool evening...," *FD*, July 29, 1922, 3.) WMR's widow addressed a letter to Finger at "Gayeta Lodge." (Margie Reedy to CJF, Aug. 21, 1920.)

3. Elbert Hubbard, "Editor's Note," *Roycroft*, Aug. 1918, 230; Smith, "Michael Monahan," 24–25; Niven, *Carl Sandburg*, 122–24; Flanagan, "Reedy of the *Mirror*," 142; Quinan, "Roycroft," 1, 9.

4. "FF," May 1926; HFL, "Cartograph," 1937. London, *Little Lady*, 2, 11, 17, 38, 82, 108, 111. Perhaps coincidentally, the Fingers' house resembled London's cottage at Beauty Ranch, as well as the first Ripley house, in having a single, large upstairs window and white exterior paint with dark trim. (The Beauty Ranch, photograph album, retrieved July 14, 2017, from Huntington Digital Library, hdl.huntington.org.)

5. CJF, *Thoreau*, 6–10; CJF, *Seven Horizons*, 433; CJF to Hubert Finger, Jan. 29, 1938, courtesy of Charles Joseph Leflar; Leflar, "*Memories*," 4; Gunn, "John W. Gunn Visits."

6. Gifford, *Dayneford's Library*, 36–37; CJF, *Seven Horizons*, 422–23, 432.

7. Tebbel and Zuckerman, *Magazines in America*, 216–18.

8. Kaestle and Radway, "Reading in Situ," 473; Gardner, *Reviewing the South*, 57.

9. Garvey, "Ambivalent Advertising," 172; Rubin, "Making Meaning," 513; Radway, "Learned and Literary Print Cultures," 199.

10. CJF, *Ozark Fantasia*, 95–96; CJF, *Seven Horizons*, 436–37.

11. "FF," April–May 1923.

12. Buckton, *Cruising*, 8; Woods, *Homintern*, 2; Henry James quoted in Gifford, *Dayneford's Library*, 36–37. On "coterie manuscript culture," see Bozorth, *Auden's Games*, 32, 282n11.

13. "FF," December 1924; CJF, "And Now, 1927," *AW*, January 1927, inside cover; CJF to BRD, Feb. 6, 1929.

14. Leflar, "*Memories*," 11.

15. Theodore Dreiser to CJF, Feb. 16, 1921; George Sterling to CJF, April 12, 1921; Starrett, "Starrett's Chicago Letter"; Vincent Starrett to CJF, Aug. 29, 1920, note folded inside Finger's copy of Starrett's *Arthur Machen*. (Shores, "Library.")

16. "Story on Arkansas in July 'The Guide,'" *FD*, July 19, 1921, 3.

17. Conrad, "Secret Sharer," 122, 131, 135, 140; Conrad quoted in Harpham, *One of Us*, 113; Ruppel, *Homosexuality*, 71.

18. Korte, *Travel Writing*, 104; Smith, "Michael Monahan," 24–26; Hoffman, Allen, and Ulrich, *Little Magazine*, 237, 258. "Free Fantasia" was the title of an essay by E. Belfort Bax, one of the celebrities in the William Morris circle in London in the 1880s. (E. Belfort Bax, "Free Fantasia on Things Divine and Human," *Today*, no. 59 (October 1888): 101–13; Wright, "Valiant Dead," 35–36.) CJF used the phrase in a letter to Philip Cornick in 1901. (CJF to PHC, Oct. 18, 1901.)

19. "Experience Meeting," *Writer's Monthly*, May 1922, 450–55.

20. CJF, "Lizard God," 208, 211.

21. Dorothy Hoskins, "Post Magazine's Literary Corner," *Houston Post*, July 17, 1921, 47; Christopher Morley to CJF, July 21, 1921; "All's Well," advertisement, *Drama*, December 1921, ii; "'All's Well' Listed One Nation's Best Magazines," *FD*, Dec. 27, 1921, 1.

22. WMR, "Reflections," *RM*, May 20, 1920, 403–05; "If railroads lay off . . . ," *FD*, April 26, 1921, 1; "Social and Personal," *FD*, May 7, 1921, 4; "At Large among the Literati with the Book Worm," *FD*, Nov. 15, 1921, 3; "Editor of 'All's Well' Writes of Arkansans," *FD*, June 2, 1921, 2; "Finger Named among Seven Best Writers," *FD*, Dec. 19, 1921, 1.

23. James Branch Cabell to CJF, Dec. 14, 1920, letter folded and affixed to the inside front cover of Finger's copy of *Jurgen: A Comedy of Justice* (Shores, "Library"); George Sterling to CJF, April 12 and May 2, 1921; CJF, *Choice of the Crowd*, vii; Bolton Hall to CJF, April 18, 1921; "Story on Arkansas in July 'The Guide,'" *FD*, July 19, 1921, 3; Silas Bent to CJF, Nov. 23, 1921; Dedication, *AW*, December 1925, 1.

24. George Jean Nathan to CJF, May 23, 1921, letter folded inside CJF's copy of Mencken's *A Book of Prefaces* (Shores, "Library"); HLM, "South Begins to Mutter," *Smart Set*, August 1921, 139, 141. HLM encouraged CJF to launch *AW* and sent him his home address in Baltimore for a subscription. (HLM to CJF, Dec. 14, 1920.) Mencken's *Prejudices II*, containing the essay "Sahara of the Bozart," was published in October 1920. (HLM to Theodore Dreiser, Aug. 20, 1920, in Forgue, *Letters*, 191.) The historian Brooks Blevins observed the "Bozart" essay was one of very few places when Mencken even noted the existence of Arkansas. (Blevins, *Arkansas/Arkansaw*, 74.)

25. Niven, *Carl Sandburg*, 113–14; Sutton, *Carl Sandburg*, 134.

26. "Carl Sandburg, Noted Poet, Here April 4th," *FD*, March 16, 1921, 1; "Gossip Shop," *Bookman*, July 1921, 471–80; Leflar, "*Memories*," 2; Haas and Lovitz, *Carl Sandburg*, 103.

27. "Authors Hear Charles Finger," *FD*, May 6, 1921, 1; "Editor of 'All's Well' Writes of Arkansans," *FD*, June 2, 1921, 2; Mrs. K. G. Tallqvist, "Why Is Charles J. Finger—Realist?" *AD*, date unknown, reprinted in "At Large among the Literati with the Book Worm," *FD*, Nov. 15, 1921, 3; "FF," April–May 1925.

28. Carl Sandburg to CJF, June 27, 1921; "Gossip Shop," *Bookman*, July 1921, 471–80; Matson, *Children's Book Reviews*, 35.

29. "Dr. Virgil Jones . . . ," *FD*, Nov. 30, 1915; Miami University, *Catalogue*, 11; "Boy Scouts . . . ," *FD*, Dec. 28, 1918; 1920 USFC; "Social and Personal," *FD*, Jan. 20

and April 15, 1921; "Stunt Night Program at Chapel at 8 P.M," *FD*, May 14,
1921; "Attention Scouts," *FD*, Sept. 22, 1921; UA, *Razorback,* 1922; "Services Set
for Ex-Head of Crane Campus," *Chicago Tribune*, Nov. 8, 1969, sec. B. A small
newspaper item about the impromptu gathering mentioned "Murray Hill," but
there apparently was no Murray Hill in Fayetteville. If Finger himself provided
the list of guests to the newspaper, he could have mistakenly written "Murray
Hill" instead of "Murray Sheehan"; the former was a writer who was featured in
the *Bookman* in 1920. ("Gayeta Lodge . . . ," *FD*, April 26, 1921, 1; Murray Hill,
"Murray Hill on His Travels," *Bookman*, September 1920, 40–46.)

30. William C. Lengel, "Men and Women Who Make Our Mediums: Bob Davis
of *Munsey's*," *Advertising and Selling*, Jan. 24, 1920, 8–10; "Fayetteville," *AD*,
Oct. 23, 1921, 2; "With the Movies," *Daily Courier-Gazette (McKinney, TX)*,
Nov. 21, 1921, 8; "At the Alhambra," *Elwood (IN) Call Leader*, Dec. 3, 1921, 6;
Martin B. Dickstein, "On the Screen," *Brooklyn Daily Eagle*, Feb. 13, 1924, 10A.

31. "Glee Club's First Concert, or, Club Gets Stoned!" Feb. 20, 2011, retrieved
Nov. 9, 2015, from Miami University Glee Club History, mugleeclubhistory
.squarespace.com; Murray Sheehan, "Fate," *Harvard Monthly*, November 1916,
182; Murray Sheehan, "Boulevard St. Michael," *Bruno's Weekly*, Feb. 12, 1916;
Sheehan, "Wind," in CJF, *Choice of the Crowd*, 24. On the editor Guido Bruno's
interest in Oscar Wilde, see Wetzsteon, *Republic of Dreams*, 362.

32. "Story on Arkansas in July 'The Guide,'" *FD*, July 19, 1921, 3.

33. Leflar, *"Memories,"* 3.

34. "Mr. Sheehan Building Bungalow Home Here," *FD*, Dec. 27, 1921, 1; "Writer
Builds a 'Hermitage,'" *AD*, Jan. 1, 1922, 23; "Import Tamworth Sows," *AG*,
Feb. 5, 1922, 12; "Goes in for Grapes," *AG*, March 11, 1922, 7; "Professor Builds
Bungalow," *AD*, March 19, 1922, Magazine and Society Section, 6; Margaret
Gordon, ed., "Writers of the Day," *Writer*, April 1922, 59; CJF to PHC, May 18,
1922; "Fair Awards," *FD*, Oct. 2, 1922, page unknown; "FF," Oct.–Nov. 1922.

35. Wappell and Simpson, *Once upon Dickson*, 292; J. H. Field photographs, 1899–
1931, finding aid.

36. "Arkansas Gains Distinction in Work of 'News' Editor for the General
Federation," *AD*, Feb. 19, 1922, Magazine and Society Section, 5; Mrs. K. G.
Tallqvist, "Fayetteville—Mecca for Writers," *AD*, Nov. 20, 1921, 6; Mrs. K. G.
Tallqvist, "South Wind Blows the Bait in the Fishes Mouth," *AD*, July 16, 1922,
Magazine and Society Section, 5; Kay Tallqvist, "By Gossamer Threads to Fame,
Wins Arkansas," *AD*, Nov. 26, 1922, Magazine and Society Section, 5; Lessie
Read, "What Women Talk About," *FD*, Dec. 28, 1923, 3.

37. "Famous Galloway College Has Notable Commencement," *AG*, June 10, 1902,
4; "National Chautauqua Bureau, Cleveland, Ohio: Season 1912," advertisement,
Luyceumite and Talent, September 1911, 9–10; "Social and Personal," *FD*, May 15,
1923, 4; *SS Caronia*, Dec. 28, 1924; "FF," April 1932; CJF, *Ozark Fantasia*,
303–04; "FF," May 1932; CJF to WMS, March 15, 1933; Michigan Death Records
retrieved from findagrave.com.

38. Record for William J. Baerg, US World War I Draft Registration Cards; Eddie Dry, "William J. Baerg (1885–1980)," Oct. 20, 2009, retrieved Jan. 10, 2018, from Encyclopedia of Arkansas, encyclopediaofarkansas.net; Dillard, *Statesmen*, 184.

39. Gilstrap, "To Remembered Happiness," 13–14.

40. Baerg saved a copy of the issue of *the Double Dealer* that contained the story "The Tooth." (William J. Baerg Collection.)

41. CJF, "Tooth," 221, 226.

42. CJF, "Very Satisfactory God," 71, 76–78.

43. Beatrice Vaughan Dale, "Emperor Jones, review," *Double Dealer*, Aug.–Sept. 1921, 112–13; Mallios, *Our Conrad*, 302, 436n104.

44. "Finger Named among Seven Best Writers," *FDD*, Dec. 19, 1921, 1; "At Large among the Literati with the Book Worm," *FD*, Jan. 8, 1923, 3; CJF, "O'Brien on Short Story Writers," *AW*, January 1923, 2; O'Brien, *Best Short Stories of 1920, 1921, 1922*, and *1924*; Joselyn, "Edward Joseph O'Brien," 3–4, 9, 15; Kunitz and Haycraft, *Twentieth Century Authors*, 1037; Updike and Kenison, *Best American Short Stories*, 808; Christian Lorentzen, "Can Short Stories Still Shock?" *New York*, Jan. 7, 2016, retrieved April 11, 2018, from nymag.com.

45. Cowley, *Exile's Return*, quoted in Woods, *Homintern*, 186; Wald, *Revolutionary Imagination*, 22; Sascha A. Sussman, "Half a God," *Brooklyn Sunday Eagle, Book Section*, May 1, 1927, 19.

46. Howe, *Memoirs of the Harvard Dead*, II: 243–55; Bristow, *American Pandemic*, 43–44; Wald, *Revolutionary Imagination*, 50, 126; *Mirrors of Venus* quoted in Alan M. Wald, "John Wheelwright's Life and Career," retrieved July 15, 2016, from Modern American Poetry, english.illinois.edu.

47. "Fifty Years Ago," *NWAT*, July 5, 1974, 4; W. C. Cobb, "Wonderfully Adventursome [sic] Life Revealed in Book," review of *Bushrangers* by CJF, *Tennessean (Nashville, TN)*, Jan. 4, 1925, 44; CJF to BRD, Feb. 24, 1925; CJF, *Seven Horizons*, 55–56; Allan Gilbert Jr., "Classical Antiquity, circa 1927," *NWAT*, Sept. 29, 1967, 7.

48. "Murray Sheehan Is School Head," *Hamilton (OH) Daily News*, May 1, 1926, 15; Untitled editorial, *FD*, Oct. 28, 1926, 2; Sheehan, *Half-gods*, 3, 13, 34, 57–58, 141, 160, 208, 273–74, 377–78; "Murray Sheehan's Book Published," *Hamilton (OH) Daily News*, April 9, 1927, 2; "'Half Gods' from Pen of Murray Sheehan Praised by New York Reviewers," *Hamilton (OH) Daily News*, April 22, 1927, 14; "Modern Centaur," review of *Half-gods* by Murray Sheehan, *SR*, May 14, 1927, 820; "Genesis Reinterpreted," review of *Eden* by Murray Sheehan, *SR,* Feb. 4, 1928, 569–70; "Prince until He Was Yanked from Princeton," *Santa Cruz (CA) News*, June 17, 1933, 9; report of Murray Sheehan's death, Naples, Italy, July 12, 1963.

49. CJF, "Eric," 54, 59; "CJF, "Some Mischievous Thing," 119; Mullins, "Stopping History," 10.

50. CJF, "Shame of Gold," 756; Glenn Frank to CJF, Jan. 7, 1922; Ohmann, "Diverging Paths," 103–04; "Editor Addresses Short Story Class," *Columbia*

Spectator, July 29, 1921, 1; William Henry Hudson to RBCG, July 31, 1922, in Curle, *Letters*, 111.

51. CJF, "Jade Piece," 181–82.

52. CJF, "My Friend Julio," 325, 329, 337; Gifford, *Dayneford's Library*, 125, 131; Cook, *London*, 132.

53. CJF could have seen the word *spottgeist* in the essay "A Free Fantasia" by E. Belfort Bax.

54. CJF, "My Spottgeist," 112, 114; Fone, "This Other Eden," 21–22; Austen, *Playing the Game*, 33–34; Fone, *Stonewall*, 220–21. CJF used the word *spottgeist* a third time in a 1923 story, "Where the Foam Flies."

55. Emanuel Julius, "Sachet Powders versus Corned Beef and Cabbage," *Appeal to Reason*, Feb. 10, 1917, 3; Sutton, *Carl Sandburg*, 155. CJF sent a letter to the *Appeal* in 1897. (CJF, "Patriots!" *Appeal to Reason*, Oct. 16, 1897, 2.)

56. Herder, "American Values," 289–90; Rubin, *Making of Middlebrow Culture*, 232; Rose, *Intellectual Life*, 131–32; Price, "Whitman in Selected Anthologies"; Christy Birney, "Haldeman-Julius Collection," finding aid, 2004, retrieved Sept. 14, 2015, from K-State Libraries University Archives & Manuscripts, lib.k-state.edu; Amherst College Archives and Special Collections, "Haldeman-Julius 'Little Blue Book' Collection, 1919–1947," finding aid, 2008, retrieved April 11, 2018, from en.wikipedia.org; "Greatest Prison Poem Ever Written," advertisement, *Appeal to Reason*, Feb. 22, 1919, 2; "Publishers Change Name," *Girard (KS) Press*, Feb. 16, 1922, 1; Shores, "Library."

57. "Girard News," *Sun (Pittsburg, KS)*, May 23, 1920, 3; Mrs. K. G. Tallqvist, "Fayetteville—Mecca for Writers," *AD*, Nov. 20, 1921, 6; "League of American Pen Women Welcomes Poet of New School to Arkansas," *AD*, Jan. 15, 1922, Magazine and Society Section, 5; CJF, "Dime Culture," *Appeal to Reason*, March 4, 1922, 2.

58. "Rockford," *Cook County (IL) Herald*, June 9, 1916, 3; "Growth of an Idea," reprinted from *Kansas City Post*, *Appeal to Reason*, June 18, 1921, 2; "Dust," *Oakland (CA) Tribune*, July 10, 1921, Amusement Section, 4; Herder, "American Values," 289–93; D'Emilio and Freedman, *Intimate Matters*, 265–66; DeGruson, Introduction; Price, "Whitman in Selected Anthologies."

59. "Appeal Readers, Meet Mr. Finger," *Appeal to Reason*, Feb. 11, 1922, 2; "Original Magazine," *Appeal to Reason*, March 4, 1922, 4; CJF, "Reflections of a Boss," *Appeal to Reason*, April 1, 1922, 1; "Important Announcement on Our Future Book Publishing Plans," *Appeal to Reason*, April 1, 1922, 4; CJF, "No Surface Ripple," review of "Infant in the News Sheet" by Herman George Scheffauer, *Appeal to Reason*, April 15, 1922, 4; CJF, "Appeal Writer Interviews Bishop Brown—Fascinating Story of His Life and Views," *Appeal to Reason*, May 13, 1922, 1, 2; "Subs for Life and Letters Pouring in at Rate of 1,000 per Day," *Appeal to Reason*, July 15, 1922, 2; "Haldeman-Julius Breaks Another Precedent," *Kansas City Kansan*, Oct. 22, 1922, 12B; "What the People Read," *Iola (KS)*

Daily Register, April 21, 1923, 4; Haldeman-Julius, *My Second Twenty-Five Years*, 77–80; Schultz and Joshi, *Shadow of the Unattained*, 41, 306.

60. "Upton Sinclair's Suppressed Masterpiece 'Russia: A Challenge' in Pamphlet Form," advertisement, *Appeal to Reason*, April 19, 1919, 2; CJF, "Dime Culture," *Appeal to Reason*, March 4, 1922, 2; CJF, *One-Act Plays*, 7–8; Johnson and Tanselle, "Haldeman-Julius Little Blue Books," 7–8; Dzwonkoski, *American Literary Publishing Houses*, 176; Kansas Historical Society, "Haldeman-Julius House," September 2014, retrieved July 23, 2017, from Kanspedia, kshs.org.

61. CJF, "Charles J. Finger Writes Pen Portrait of E. Haldeman-Julius," *Appeal to Reason*, July 8, 1922, 4; "Interesting Experiment," *Appeal to Reason*, Sept. 9, 1922, 3.

62. "I Take Pen in Hand to Remind You," *AD*, June 4, 1922, Magazine and Society Section, 5; CJF to May Massee, Dec. 22, 1922, May Massee Collection; "Haldeman-Julius a Visitor Here," *FD*, March 28, 1923, 1; John W. Gunn, "John W. Gunn Visits," 1–4; CJF, *Seven Horizons*, 437–39; Haldeman-Julius, *First Hundred Million*, 180; "Haldeman-Julius Publications, Little Blue Books," finding aid, retrieved Aug. 19, 2016, from Kent State University Special Collections and Archives, library.kent.edu; Barrett-Fox, *Feminism, Socialism, and Pragmatism*; Shores, *"Published Works."* Murray Sheehan's Little Blue Book titles and their numbers were *Hints on News Reporting* (342), *Story of Painting* (387), *Hints on Scenario Writing* (437), *Story of Architecture* (468), *Story of Music* (403), and *History of Sculpture* (466).

Chapter 7

1. Vining, "May Massee," vi, viii; Harrison, "May Massee," 463–64; Dzwonkoski, *American Literary Publishing Houses*, 366; Eddy, *Bookwomen*, 104; Marcus, *Minders*, 71–72, 86, 91, 95; Carl Sandburg to May Massee, Sept. 3, 1921, image of letter in Hodowanec, *May Massee Collection*, 287; Massee, "Reminiscences," 30, 35.

2. May Massee to CJF, Dec. 19, 1922, and CJF to May Massee, Dec. 22, 1922, both in May Massee Collection.

3. "Army Announces Long Detached Officers' List," *Leavenworth (KS) Times*, Jan. 10, 1922, 2; "Fort News," *Leavenworth (KS) Times*, July 7, 1922, 5; "FF," Oct.–Nov. 1923; CJF, *Seven Horizons*, 436–37; "Answers to Queries," *St. Louis Post-Dispatch*, Aug. 6, 1923, 21; "New Commander Assigned to Jefferson Barracks," *St. Louis Post-Dispatch*, April 14, 1924, 19; "Trip to Gasconade River Region," *St. Louis Post-Dispatch*, May 10, 1925, Feature Section, 2. "History of Jefferson Barracks," retrieved Sept. 26, 2016, from Jefferson Barracks Community Council, jbccstl.org.

4. Dynes, *Homolexis*, 101; Chauncey, "Christian Brotherhood," 295; Canaday, *Straight State*, 77–78; "John Edgar Hoover," Dec. 6, 2016, retrieved from Encyclopedia of World Biography, www.encyclopedia.com; Bronski, *Queer History*, 143–44. CJF mentioned GWM's secretive nature in a letter. (CJF to

BRD, June 8, 1927.) A writer who accompanied RHD on a three-month road trip in 1941 described most of the persons they encountered by their full names but never fully identified GWM, calling him "Sep" Maddox. (Mathias, *Bob Davis*, 312–22.)

5. Irvin S. Cobb, "Laughing around the World," *Evening News (Harrisburg, PA)*, Aug. 31, 1927, 10; RHD to W. M. Davidson, carbon copy, Jan. 19, 1938, RHD Papers; Mathias, *Bob Davis*, 312–22; "Prosecutors Here Ready to Enforce Revamped Dry Law," *St. Louis Star*, June 23, 1923, 1.

6. "FF," Aug.–Sept. 1923.

7. Charles Erskine Scott Wood, "My Comrade," *AW*, Aug.–Sept. 1923, 8.

8. FF, Oct.–Nov. 1923; Van Vechten, *Peter Whiffle*, 8; George Sterling to Clark Ashton Smith, April 9, 1924, in Schultz and Joshi, *Shadow*, 240.

9. GWM to CJF; "At Large among the Literati with the Book Worm," *FD*, June 28, 1923, 5; "Art Notes," *DFP*, Dec. 16, 1923, 8.

10. CJF, *Highwaymen*, 219.

11. "FF," Oct.–Nov. 1922 and Feb.–March 1923; CJF, "Utopia in Arkansas"; C. L. Edson, "Arkansas: A Native Proletariat," *Nation*, May 2, 1923, 515–16; CJF, "At Little Rock," *AW*, June–July 1923, 2–3; CJF "Where the Foam Flies."

12. "At Large among the Literati with the Book Worm," *FD*, Aug. 25, 1923, 6; "Sheriff Willmann of St. Louis County Will Be in Command of Merged Forces at Grounds," *St. Louis Post-Dispatch*, Sept. 30, 1923, 76; "Air Program Set for Sunday to Be Given Tomorrow," *St. Louis Post-Dispatch*, Oct. 2, 1923, 2.

13. Marcus, *Minders*, 92; Larson, *Scene Design*, 72; Bragdon, *More Lives*, 203–05.

14. "Recitals of the Week," *Brooklyn Daily Eagle*, Oct. 21, 1923, B3; *Williams's Cincinnati Directory, 1922*, 650; "FF," Oct.–Nov. 1923; Sheehy, Richardson, Hass, and Atmore, *Letters*; Maxwell Aley to CJF, Oct. 9, 1923. The publishing world knew Aley as "Max." ("Periodical Notes," *Publishers Weekly*, April 23, 1921, 1264.)

15. Tebbel and Zuckerman, *Magazine in America*, 204–05; "Carl Clinton van Doren," retrieved Feb. 5, 2019, from New Netherlands Institute, newnetherlands institute.org.

16. Leslie Nelson Jennings, "Stranger," *Century*, Oct. 1923, 893.

17. John V. A. Weaver, "Personally Conducted," *Brooklyn Daily Eagle*, Nov. 10, 1923, 3; "Art Notes," *DFP*, Dec. 16, 1923, 8; "Guy Holt, Book Publisher, Dies," *Brooklyn Daily Eagle*, April 23, 1934, 3; "Guy Holt," retrieved Oct. 19, 2016, from the Greenwich Village Bookshop Door, norman.hrc.utexas.edu.

18. Vining, "May Massee," ix; Harrison, "May Massee," 463–64.

19. Hoffman, Allen, and Ulrich, *Little Magazine*, 237, 245.

20. Gunther, *Learned Hand*, 140–41; Geddes, *Miracle*, 204, 208–11; Kenneth MacGowan, "Centre of the Stage: The Artist Takes It for Lack of Great Actors," *Theatre Arts*, April 1921, 91–92; Larson, *Scene Design*, 72–73; Bragdon, *More Lives*, 203–05.

21. Theodore Dreiser to CJF, Feb. 16, 1921; CJF, *England in Shakespeare's Time*, cited in Gunn, "John W. Gunn Visits"; John M. Maxwell, "Sir George Somers, None Other Than the 'Faire Friend' of the Procreation Sonnets of William Shakespeare," *AW*, April 1921, 100–07; John M. Maxwell, "Who Juggled the Hamlet Letters and Why?" *AW*, June 1921, 123–34; "Reader's Notes," *Indianapolis Star*, March 25, 1921, 6; HLM, "South Begins to Mutter," *Smart Set*, Aug. 1921, 139, 141; Brander Matthews to CJF, Aug. 3, 1921; Newlin, *Theodore Dreiser*, 220; Elias, *Letters*, I: 269, I: 347; Rusch and Pizer, *Theodore Dreiser*, 272n2; "Guide to the John M. Maxwell Papers," Charles Deering McCormick Library of Special Collections, Northwestern University.

22. GGB; Riggio, *Dreiser: Letters to Women*, II: 181–82. McCoy later moved to New York and was a researcher for Dreiser. ("Esther McCoy," Dictionary of Art Historians, retrieved Dec. 19, 2016, from dictionaryofarthistorians.org.)

23. CJF, "Paul Honore's Work as Wood Engraver," *DI*, July 4, 1925.

24. "Varied Art at State Fair," *DFP*, Sept. 3, 1922, Part 5, 3; "Detroit Conservatory of Music," advertisement, *Etude*, July 1921, 486; "Name Winners in State Contest," *DFP*, April 16, 1922, 79; "Detroit Conservatory of Music," advertisement, *DFP*, Sept. 2, 1923, Automotive Section, 12.

25. Leila E. Bracy, "Development of American Painting," *DFP*, July 24, 1921, 67.

26. "Frank Brangwyn," advertisement, *Times (London)*, Nov. 21, 1910, 1; World War I Draft Registration Card for Paul Honoré; Bracy, "Development"; Paul, "Paul Honoré," 2.

27. CJF, *Ozark Fantasia*, 335–36.

28. Mitchell Kennerley, "Free Lance," *RM*, Aug. 5, 1920, 607; "FF," Oct.–Nov. 1922 and Feb.–March 1923; "Anderson Galleries," advertisement, *NYT*, Dec. 12, 1922, 7; CJF, "Some Books I've Read," *AW*, June–July 1923, 10–11; "At Large among the Literati with the Book Worm," *FD*, June 28, 1923, 5; Putzel, *Man in the Mirror*, 171–72, 282–87; Austen, *Playing the Game*, 15; Bruccoli, *Mitchell Kennerley*, 4–8, 40, 46, 141; Shores, "Library."

29. "FF," Aug.–Sept. 1923 and January 1924; CJF to WMS, Feb. 4, 1924.

30. CJF to May Massee, Nov. 12, 1923; "FF" Jan. 1924; "Art Notes," *DFP*, Dec. 16, 1923, 4–8; "Christmas Book Number—Lists—Reviews," *Brooklyn Daily Eagle*, Dec. 15, 1923, 3.

31. "In Lawless Lands," advertisement, *AW*, March–April 1924, 10; Margaret Germann, "Wandering in Many Lawless Lands, C. J. Finger Got Material for Tales," *Dallas Morning News*, May 11, 1924; "Primitive Stories," review of *In Lawless Lands* by CJF, *Rochester (NY) Democrat and Chronicle*, June 22, 1924, 52; CJF, *Seven Horizons*, 439; Bruccoli, *Mitchell Kennerley*, 151–64.

32. "New Commander Assigned to Jefferson Barracks," *St. Louis Post-Dispatch*, April 14, 1924, 19; "Foreign," *Marthasville (MO) Record*, April 18, 1924, 7; CJF, *Ozark Fantasia*, 294–95; GGB. All quotations of Finger regarding the April 1924 trip are from "FF," May–June 1924.

33. "FF," Aug.–Sept. 1926; CJF, *Ozark Fantasia*, 117; Amiel and Ward, *Amiel's Journal*; Carpenter, *Ioläus*, 97; Collins, *Doctor Looks*, 234–36; Fremantle, *Protestant Mystics*, 256; Hurley, *Circulating Queerness*, xii. Finger mentioned planning to read "Jean Jacques Rousseau by Henri-Frederic Amiel." ("FF," Aug.–Sept. 1923.) This was a 1922 edition of a lecture on Rousseau that Amiel gave in 1878.

34. CJF, "From the Workshop of Mr. H. G. Wells," *RM*, April 1, 1920, 272–73; GWM to CR, March 16, 1943; Forgue, *Letters*, 117n5; Davies and Moore, *Letters*, 63n1; Shores, "Library." On Janvier's interest in bodybuilding, see Meredith Janvier, "Eugen Sandow; A Personal Recollection," reprinted from *Sun (Baltimore, MD)*, *Santa Cruz (CA) News*, Oct. 20, 1925, 3.

35. Angela Jill Cooley, "John Hollis Bankhead II," Jan. 9, 2008, and G. Wayne Dowdy, "William B. Bankhead," Oct. 8, 2007, both retrieved Dec. 14, 2016, from Encyclopedia of Alabama, www.encyclopediaofalabama.org; GWM to CR. RHD later referred to Henry Bankhead as "Fat Jack." (RHD to CJF, Jan. 3, 1928.)

36. "Army and Navy," *Washington (DC) Times*, Nov. 2, 1914, 12; "Army and Navy Changes of the Day," *Washington Post*, July 31, 1915, 5; "News from the Islands," *Army and Navy Register*, Sept. 2, 1916, 305; "Officers Announced for Camp Jackson," *Greenville (SC) Daily News*, Sept. 3, 1917, 8; A. W. C., "Charles J. Bailey," retrieved Oct. 11, 2016, from externalapps.westpointaog.org.

37. "Army," *Army and Navy Register*, Sept. 20, 1922, 334; record for the Bankheads, 1925 New York State Census.

38. "Departure of Capt. and Mrs. Bankhead," *Constitution (Atlanta, GA)*, Dec. 29, 1914, 7; C. M. Stanley, "Bankhead Comes Home to Honor Sister," *Montgomery Advertiser–Alabama Journal*, Sept. 19, 1954, 3B; Frances Osborn Robb, "Tallulah Bankhead," Jan. 16, 2008, retrieved Dec. 27, 2016, from *Encyclopedia of Alabama*, encyclopediaofalabama.net; "Tallulah Bankhead," Jan. 27, 2019, retrieved Feb. 14, 2019, from *Encyclopaedia Britannica*, britannica.com; Robert Gottlieb, "Dah-ling: The Strange Case of Tallulah Bankhead," *New Yorker*, May 16, 2005, retrieved May 9, 2018, from newyorker.com.

39. Van Doren quoted in Hilton and Due, *Electric Interurban*, 250–51.

40. C. V. D., "Baresark in Arkansas," *Century*, Aug. 1924, 574–75. Van Doren signed a publicity photograph of himself for CJF "To Finger[,] an honest man, from Carl Van Doren."

41. Kluger and Kluger, *Paper*, 324; Rubin, *Middlebrow Culture*, 62–64, 83–85.

42. Shores, "Published Works."

43. CJF, "Fascination of the Criminal," review of *A Library of Crime* and *Famous Crimes and Criminals* by C. L. McClure Stevens, *Famous Judges and Famous Trials* by Charles Kingstone, and *Unsolved Murder Mysteries* by Charles B. Pearce, "Books," *NYHT*, May 16, 1926, 12; CJF, "Destiny Dealer," review of *Wild*

Bill Hickok by Frank J. Wilstach, "Books," *NYHT*, Nov. 28, 1926, 5–6; Hurley, *Circulating Queerness*, xiii.

44. "May Sinclair Is Here," *Des Moines Sunday Register*, May 11, 1924, E-5; "FF," November 1925; John V. A. Weaver, "Personally Conducted," *Brooklyn Daily Eagle*, March 8, 1924, 5. The Brevoort was the location for many literary functions. (Kellner, *Carl Van Vechten*, 140; Wetzsteon, *Republic of Dreams*, 344.) The evening with Sinclair probably was an informal gathering since the PEN Club's annual dinner was not until May 13. ("All Eyes on Fannie Hurst at Writers' Annual Dinner," *Brooklyn Daily Eagle*, May 14, 1924, 22.)

45. Dorothy G. Van Doren, "Gentlemen Robbers All!" *Forum*, May 1924, 701–02.

46. "Book Plates on Show," *Brooklyn Daily Eagle*, May 12, 1908, 28; "Random Impressions in Current Exhibitions," *New York Tribune*, Feb. 8, 1920, Sec. III, 5; CJF to WMS, June 1, 1923; "FF," January 1924; CJF to WMS, Feb. 4 and 14, 1924; "Wilbur Macey Stone Papers," finding aid, J. Murrey Atkins Library, University of North Carolina, Charlotte, retrieved Oct. 22, 2015, from specialcollections.uncc.edu; "Mostly Letters about Bookplates," Nov. 29, 2012, retrieved Nov. 12, 2014, from My Sentimental Library, blog.mysentimental library.com; WMS quoted in Dan Piepenbring, "Nude Bookplates: Should They Exist?" *Paris Review*, April 15, 2016, retrieved Aug. 5, 2017, from theparisreview .org; Rare Book & Manuscript Library General Manuscript Collection, 1789–2013, finding aid, Columbia University Libraries, retrieved Aug. 5, 2017, from findingaids.cul.columbia.edu. CJF sloppily referred to meeting "Colonel Jack Bankhead . . . in West [*sic*] Orange." (FF, November 1925.)

47. Nissen, *Manly Love*, 36; Whitman quoted in Jeffs, "Man's Words," 36; Woods, *Gay Literature*, 156.

48. Michael Monahan, "Letter," *AW*, May–June 1924, 9–11.

49. CJF, "Andrew Lang," 311–24; CJF, *Hints on Writing Short Stories*; Donald Davidson, "O'Brien's Best Story Anthology Is Out," *Tennessean (Nashville, TN)*, Jan 11, 1925, Firing Line Section, 10; Stevenson, "Beach of Falesá," 148, 183; Menikoff, *Robert Louis Stevenson*, 97; Buckton, *Cruising*, 8, 237; Shores, "Library."

50. Anne Carroll Moore, "Storyteller of True Romance," "Books," *NYHT*, Oct. 26, 1924, 6; Harry Hansen, "Drowsy Tales," review of *Tales of Silver Lands* by CJF, "Books," *NYHT*, Oct. 26, 1924, 6; Leonore St. John Power, "New Books for Children," *Outlook*, Nov. 12, 1924, 410–12; "Tales from Silverland," illustration, *Brooklyn Life*, Nov. 8, 1924, 13.

51. CJF, "Paul Honoré as Artist," *AW*, Sept. 1924, 3; "FF," Oct. 1924.

52. Bracebridge Hymyng, "Jack Harkaway and the Bushrangers," *Wide Awake Library*, Dec. 20, 1895, 1–22; "Manners in the Bush," caption, *St. Louis Post-Dispatch*, Dec. 13, 1924, 4; "Books We Have Read," *Century*, January 1925, 429–32; "In Brief Review," *Bookman*, May 1925, 357–64.

53. H. W. Roland to CJF, Feb. 2, 1924; CJF to H. W. Roland, Feb. 5, 1924; BRD to CJF, March 24 and April 16, 1924; and CJF to BRD, March 25, 1924, all BRD Collection; Woeste, *Henry Ford's War*, 47.

54. CJF, "Paul Honore's Work."

55. Boswell, "Frank Brangwyn," 171; Horner, "Biography," 32, 35; Horner and Naylor, *Frank Brangwyn*, 54, 90, 159, 160; Miller, "Swiftness, Vigour and Exuberance," 102.

56. Harry Hansen, "First Reader," *Minneapolis Morning Tribune*, Aug. 24, 1926, 10; RHD, "Literati under the Lens," *Bookman*, August 1929, 625, 630; "Guide to the Harry Hansen Papers, 1898–1977," retrieved March 2, 2015, from University of Chicago Library, lib.uchicago.edu. Hansen's Little Blue Book was *Carl Sandburg, The Man and His Poetry* (1925).

57. Sandburg, *Abraham Lincoln*, I: 264, 276.

58. CJF, "Romantic Rascal," review of *Memoirs of the Notorious Stephen Burroughs*, "Books," *NYHT*, Nov. 2, 1924, 5; "FF," December 1924; CJF to BRD, Dec. 19, 1924, and March 7, 1925; "Literary Spotlight VII: Sherwood Anderson," *Bookman*, April 1922, 157–62.

59. Haas and Lovitz, *Carl Sandburg*, 90, 96, 106; Penelope Niven, "Carl Sandburg's Life," Feb. 2000, retrieved April 10, 2017, from Modern American Poetry, english.illinois.edu; Penelope Niven, "Carl Sandburg Biography & Timeline," retrieved April 7, 2017, from Thirteen Media with Impact, thirteen.org.

Chapter 8

1. "United Service," *NYT*, April 6, 1898, 4; "Gives Her Heart to a Hero of Peking," *Call (San Francisco, CA)*, Aug. 15, 1901, 3; "Martial Law Ends in Kentucky City," *Logansport (IN) Daily Tribune*, Feb. 22, 1920, 2; "Army Officers to Be Assigned to New Posts," *Santa Ana (CA) Daily Register*, Oct. 29, 1924, 10; Summerall and Nenninger, *Way*, 25, 64, 66, 87, 129, 171, 175, 189, 199, 208, 214–15, 224.

2. "Fractured His Skull," *Nashville (TN) American*, July 29, 1903, 7; "John G. Long's Death Caused by Accident," *Washington (DC) Times*, Aug. 10, 1903, 2; "Will of John C. Long Offered for Probate," *Washington (DC) Times*, Aug. 11, 1903, 10; "Will of John C. Long," *Times-Democrat (New Orleans, LA)*, Aug. 12, 1903, 7; "Body Brought Here," *Evening Star (Washington, DC)*, Aug. 19, 1903, 5. Bankhead took several leaves of absence when Stickney returned to the US. ("To Forces of Land and Sea," *Sun [Baltimore, MD]*, Sept. 28, 1903, 2; "Army Orders," *Evening Star [Washington, DC]*, Nov. 25, 1903, 3; "Whirl of Society," *Inter Ocean [Chicago, IL]*, Nov. 27, 1903, 6; "Bankhead-Stickney," *Greenville [SC] Daily News*, Dec. 11, 1903, 2; "Bride Once Honored by the Khedive," *Courier-Journal [Louisville, KY]*, Dec. 18, 1903, 4.) Alice's son, whom she named John Long Bankhead, supposedly claimed in adulthood that he was born in South Carolina in October 1904, but the only source for this seems to have been his wife. (Records for John Long Bankhead in Virginia Death Records

and Social Security Death Index.) However, Alice was not in South Carolina
by October 1904 but with Henry in Manila. ("Many People Are on Sheridan,"
Pacific Commercial Advertiser [Honolulu, HI], Feb. 10, 1904, 7; *Manchuria*
passenger list, April 7, 1905; "Manchuria Makes a Record Voyage," *Pacific
Commercial Advertiser [Honolulu, HI]*, April 1, 1905, 7.) Other evidence suggests
John was born in October 1903. (Goodridge, *William Brockman Bankhead*.)
After Alice died a reporter in Ottawa related that John was born in 1903. This
could have been a typographical error or Bankhead's mistake in an interview
with the reporter, or Bankhead could have decided to hint at the truth. (C. J. K.,
"Popular Veteran of US Embassy Col. Bankhead Leaving Ottawa," *Ottawa
Journal*, May 29, 1948, 7.)

3. "Corp Commanders Are Given New Assignments," *EEN,* Dec. 5, 1924, Section
   Two, 9; record for GWM, New York Marriage Index; "Today's Events," *Olean
   (NY) Evening Herald,* Jan. 16, 1925, 3

4. "Women in Wartime," *Chicago Daily Tribune*, April 9, 1918, 15; "Red Cross
   Motor Corps in Need of More Workers," *EEN,* May 3, 1919, 4; "Celebrate
   First Drive of Yanks in the Great War," *Chicago Daily Tribune*, May 29, 1920,
   5; "First Division Men in Anniversary Meet," *Daily Pantagraph (Bloomington,
   IL)*, May 29, 1920, 1; "First Division Notes," *Army and Navy Register*, July 24,
   1920, 102; "First Division Circus Stunts Thrill Crowd," *Chicago Daily Tribune*,
   Aug. 20, 1920, 3; World War History and Art Museum, "Circus Goes to War,"
   retrieved May 25, 2017, from wwham.com.

5. Records for Martha Wright in 1900, 1910 USFC, Michigan Divorce Records,
   and Arizona Select Marriages.

6. Summerall and Nenninger, *Way*, 192–93.

7. "Alumni: '06," *Princeton Alumni Weekly*, March 26, 1913, 483; US Consular
   Reports of Marriages; US Social Security Applications and Claim Index;
   Gardner, *Calhoun County*, 922–24; *SS Chiyo Maro* passenger list, June 8,
   1914; *SS Empress of Asia* passenger list, Aug. 26, 1916; "Orchestra to Be Heard
   over WKBP on Monday Well Known in Community," *EEN,* Jan. 1, 1927, 14;
   "Brilliant Event," *EEN*, Nov. 17, 1918, 6.

8. "Corps Chooses Lieutenant," *EEN,* Oct. 23, 1918, 7; "Mother's Love Overrules
   Law," *EEN,* Dec. 6, 1922, 14; record for Helen Coyle, Michigan Divorce Records.

9. "Drove a War Tank, Flew among Clouds," *EEN,* May 12, 1919, 1; "Country Club
   Activities," *EEN,* May 23, 1919, 6; "Formal Opening at Country Club," *EEN,*
   May 31, 1919, 6; "Will Take a Vacation," *EEN,* June 28, 1919, 2.

10. "Of Local Interest," *EEN,* Jan. 6, 1920, 3; "Coyle Hallock Wedding," *EEN,*
    Jan. 8, 1920, 6; "Society," *EEN,* March 8, 1920, 6; AP, "Bride Legally Irrespon-
    sible before Union," *Daily Sun (San Bernardino, CA)*, Dec. 8, 1922, 1; AP,
    "Woman Irresponsible for Her Acts Just before Her Marriage, Court Decides,"
    Topeka (KS) Daily Capital, Dec. 8, 1922, 1; "Coyle Alimony Case Amended,"
    EEN, April 25, 1923, 10.

11. Canaday, *Straight State*, 86–87; Robert B Leflar, "Charles J. & Helen Finger

Works," unpublished manuscript, courtesy of Robert B Leflar. This was an epigram by Walter Savage Landor (1775–1864), an English poet. ("Walter Savage Landor," retrieved Sept. 27, 2016, from poetryfoundation.org.)

12. "Box Holders at the Derby," *Courier-Journal (Louisville, KY)*, May 20, 1923, 28; "Feminine Fashions Vie with Horses at Derby," *Courier-Journal (Louisville, KY)*, May 17, 1925, 4, 32; "Hotel Arrivals," *Arizona Republic (Phoenix, AZ)*, May 25, 1925, 13. All quotations of CJF concerning the April 1925 trip with Maddox are from "FF," April–May 1925.

13. CJF to BRD, Aug. 14, 1925. The phrase is part of "Imri," an obscure pseudonymous poem that appeared in the *Southern Literary Messenger* in 1840 and can be interpreted as the tragedy of lesbian lovers whose "hearts . . . keep their sacred trust unsullied by this world's foul spreading stain." (Egira, "Imri.") Perhaps CJF found a copy of the issue when browsing for used books. I could find no link between "Imri" and Prime-Stevenson's novel *Imre: A Memorandum*.

14. "FF," March 1926; Showalter, *Sexual Anarchy*, 79–84; Anderson, *Dime Novel*, 194; Knuth, *Children's Literature*, 63.

15. "Midland County Courthouse: Passionate Partnership Confronts a Modern Challenge," abstract, *35th Annual Statewide Preservation Conference*, May 13–16, 2015, retrieved July 28, 2018, from Michigan Historic Preservation Network, mhpn.org.

16. CJF, *Spreading Stain*, 3, 83, 123, 204–05, 232, 235–36; CJF, "Unrecognized Golden Age," *American Mercury*, April 1930, 409; CJF, *Seven Horizons*, 29. Someone eventually returned Maddox's copy of *Stain* to Gayeta. (Leflar, "Charles J. & Helen Finger Works.")

17. "FF," October 1925.

18. Johan J. Smertenko, "Short Stories the World Over," *Nation*, April 22, 1925, 469–71; "FF," November 1925; Alpern, *Freda Kirchwey*, 20, 41–54; Tebbel and Zuckerman, *Magazine in America*, 204–05; Robert L. Gale, "Dorothy Van Doren," American National Biography Online, retrieved Oct. 7, 2015, from WorldCat.org; Mary Ryan Gallery, "Hugo Gellert," retrieved Oct. 7, 2015, from maryryangallery.com; Hagen, "New Yorker"; Roger Angell, "Snaps: 1925–1935," *New Yorker*, Feb. 23–March 2, 2015, 20; John Margolis, "Joseph Wood Krutch as Cultural Critic," retrieved Oct. 7, 2015, from columbia.edu.

19. Mathias, *Bob Davis*, 3, 321; Lewis, *Silver Kings*; Moskowitz, *Under the Moons*, 316–18, 402; Taliaferro, *Tarzan Forever*, 113; Locke, *Ocean*, 17; Osborne, "Publication of *Victory*"; Oskison, *Tales*, 128; Roy Le Notre, "Those Who Walk in Darkness," *Book News*, Dec. 1917, 119–20; "Major and Minor," *Musical Leader*, Aug. 22, 1918, 181; WMR, "Reflections," *RM*, Jan. 22, 1920, 54; Lengel, "Men and Women," 8–10; O. O. McIntyre, "In New York," *Palm Beach (FL) Post*, April 6, 1929, 4; RHD, *Over My Left Shoulder*, v.

20. Driscoll, *O. O. McIntyre*, 293–97; Greg Daugherty, "Odd McIntyre: The Man Who Taught America about New York," April 24, 2011, retrieved April 11, 2018, from Smithsonian.com; O. O. McIntyre, "New York Day by Day," *Pittsburgh*

Press, Feb. 12, 1922, Additional News Section, 8; O. O. McIntyre, "New York Day by Day," *Daily Democrat (Tallahassee, FL)*, Feb. 10, 1930, 4. On the Davis–Cobb friendship, see Moskowitz, *Under the Moons*, 342–43, and Ellis, *Irvin S. Cobb*, 6, 20, 100, 166.

21. "William Griffith Weds," *Editor and Publisher*, July 3, 1909, 2; CJF, *Seven Horizons*, 447–48.

22. CJF, "All's Well Picture Gallery," *AW*, Oct.–Nov. 1922; RHD, "Literati under the Lens," *Bookman*, August 1929, 625–40; RHD, *Man Makes His Own Mask*; Locke, *Ocean*, 18.

23. RHD to CJF, July 1, 1925; "Current Opinion," retrieved Sept. 4, 2016, from the Joseph Conrad Periodical Archive, conradfirst.net; Hall, *Baltimore*, 749–50. In naming some of the men that the four friends so honored, RHD mentioned CJF first, along with Ernest Boyd and Paul Honoré. (William Amelia, "Mencken Offers Bible," *Evening Sun [Baltimore, MD]*, Jan. 30, 1973, A10.)

24. CJF to BRD, June 15 and 29, 1925; Lewis, *Henry Ford*, 142.

25. "FF," June–July 1925.

Chapter 9

1. Matson, *Children's Book Reviews*, 8, 24–25; Marcus, *Minders*, 71–72, 86; Massee, "*Reminiscences*," 30; Harrison, "May Massee," 463–64.

2. Massee, Introduction, xvi; Bone, *Children's Stories*, 65; "At Large among the Literati with the Book Worm," *FDD*, Aug. 25, 1923, 6; "FF," June–July 1925.

3. CJF, *Silver Lands*, 6, 31, 59, 88, 96, 105.

4. *New York Herald Tribune*, "Stuart P. Sherman," advertisement, *Chicago Daily Tribune*, Sept. 18, 1924, 15.

5. Moore, *Roads to Childhood*, 42; Matson, *Children's Book Reviews*, 31–32.

6. Anne Carroll Moore, "Storyteller of True Romance," "Books," *NYHT*, Oct. 26, 1924, 6.

7. Matson, *Children's Book Reviews*, 61; Smith, *History of the Newbery*, 52–53; "Bostwick to Attend Meeting," *St. Louis Post-Dispatch*, June 29, 1924, 8. One of the new at-large members of the Newbery selection committee was Mary Gould Davis of New York, who worked for Moore at the New York Public Library. ("Radio Broadcasting News," *Portsmouth [NH] Herald*, July 31, 1924, 3; "Friday Book Review," *Akron [OH] Beacon Journal*, Dec. 7, 1923, 4.)

8. "Newbery Medal and Honor Books, 1922–Present," retrieved Aug. 9, 2017, from Association for Library Service to Children, ala.org.

9. CJF, Introduction, *Collected Works*.

10. CJF to BRD, July 14, 1925.

11. "Major" to CJF, telegram, July 9, 1925. All quotations of CJF concerning this trip are from "FF," Aug.–Sept. 1925.

12. George Sterling to CJF, April 12 and Oct. 26, 1921; George Sterling to HLM,

Sept. 5, 1921, in Joshi, *From Baltimore*, 142; George Sterling to James Branch Cabell, Aug. 14, 1921, in Maurice Duke, "Letters of George Sterling to James Branch Cabell," *American Literature* 44 no. 1 (March 1972): 146–53, retrieved Feb. 25, 2015, from George Sterling, george-sterling.org; "FF," June–July 1923; Margaret Germann, "Wandering in Many Lawless Lands, C. J. Finger Got Material for Tales," *Dallas Morning News*, May 11, 1924; Schultz and Joshi, *Shadow*, 313–18.

13. CJF, *Ozark Fantasia*, 263; Hamburger, *Two Rooms*, 288.

14. Sterling to HLM, March 24 and July 1, 1925, in Joshi, *From Baltimore*, 209, 213; Noel, *Footloose*, 311; Kunitz and Haycraft, *Twentieth Century Authors*, 1341–42; Haley, *Wolf*, 127–28, 189–90, 198.

15. Sterling to HLM, Aug. 6, 1925, in Joshi, *From Baltimore*, 215.

16. Hoag, *San Francisco Blue Book*, 280; Real estate listing for 2615 Larkin Street, San Francisco, retrieved March 28, 2015, from zillow.com; "Daughter of Late Jack London to Address Club," *Woodland (CA) Daily Democrat*, May 7, 1925, 8; "Joan London Will Talk to Mothers' Club," *Oakland (CA) Tribune*, Sept. 11, 1925, 7; Joshi, *From Baltimore*, 258n36.

17. *Public*, Jan. 7, 1916, masthead; Sara Bard Field, "Reedy's Last Party," *AW*, June 1921, 114; George Sterling, "Ballad of the Swabs," *American Mercury*, October 1925, 140–41; Putzel, *Man in the Mirror*, 283; Hamburger, *Two Rooms*, 288.

18. CJF, *Seven Horizons*, 444–45; Hobson, *Serpent*, 148; Larson, *Summer*, 163–64; Hamburger, *Two Rooms*, 157–58, 190; Wood et al., *Heavenly Discourse*, 23–25; Charles Erskine Scott Wood to CJF.

19. Edward F. O'Day, "George Sterling," *San Francisco Water*, July 1928, 9–13; CJF to WMS, Aug. 9, 1937; Noel, *Footloose*, 80–83, 107–08; Gifford, *Dayneford's Library*, 103–04; Edwards, *Exotic Journeys*, 50; Schultz and Joshi, *Shadow*, 306; London and Wichlan, *Complete Poetry*, 64; Haley, *Wolf*, 162–64, 189, 196–97; Labor, *Jack London*, 153, 244. Sterling's likely bisexuality is a winking matter in most biographies. See, for example, Gregory and Zaturenska, *History of American Poetry*, 57.

20. CJF, *Seven Horizons*, 444–46. A photograph of the mask exists in the CJF papers at the University of Arkansas Libraries, but the mask itself seems to have been lost, perhaps in a fire at the home of HFL. Another cast of London's death mask was photographed at London's widow's home in 1955. (*Hansel Mieth and Otto Hagel Photograph Collection*, 30, retrieved July 10, 2019, from Center for Creative Photography, creativephotography.org.) CJF later gave the photograph of Sterling to his friend Fielding P. Sizer of Monett, Missouri, who annotated it by writing "Sterling to Finger" at the top and "Finger to Sizer" at the bottom and saving it inside a copy of Sterling's 1923 collection, *Selected Poems*, along with a clipping of CJF's review of that book in *All's Well*. At some time this book and its associated ephemera became part of CJF's library. (Shores, "Library.")

21. CJF, "Eric," 59; "FF," May 1926; Stuart Olivier, "Book of a Very Dear Friend," *Springfield (MO) Leader*, Nov. 30, 1927, 16; O. O. McIntyre, "In New York," *Palm Beach Post*, April 6, 1929, 4; CJF, *Seven Horizons*, 345–46; Gifford, *Dayneford's Library*, 23–24; Cocks, *Nameless Offences*, 11, 197. W. D. Howells, writing in the *Atlantic Monthly*, characterized Charles Warren Stoddard's *South-Sea Idyls* "as the drollery of a small number of good fellows who know each other familiarly, and feel that nothing they say will be lost or misunderstood in their circle." (Howells quoted in Crowley, "Editor's Introduction," xxvii.)

22. Dreiser to George Sterling, July 25, 1925, in Elias, *Letters,* II: 427; CJF, *Ozark Fantasia*, 265; Kunitz and Haycraft, *Twentieth Century Authors*, 1341–42; Mayfield, *Constant Circle*, 109.

23. CJF to BRD, July 20 and Aug. 6, 1925; "FF," November 1925.

24. CJF to WMS, Nov. 6, 1925.

25. HFL, "Autobiography," 8; John Cowper Powys to CJF, March 13, [1926].

26. "FF," Jan.–Feb. and April 1926; CJF, *Ozark Fantasia*, 94, 303–04.

27. CJF to BRD, undated, and CJF to BRD, received Dec. 22, 1924.

28. "Country Club of Old English Type," *DFP*, Sept. 14, 1924, Part Six, 1; CJF to BRD, Jan. 26 and March 11, 1926; Carl Van Doren, "Roving Critic," *Century*, April 1926, 763–68; "Carl Sandburg to Be Feature at Jewish Council," *DFP*, April 11, 1926, 5; "FF," May 1926; CJF, *Ozark Fantasia*, 259; Barkun, *Racist Right*, 33–34; Bryan, *Henry's Lieutenants*, 37–38; Woeste, *Henry Ford's War*, 25, 90–92, 118.

29. "Authors Coming to Town Next Week!" *St. Louis Post-Dispatch*, May 8, 1926, 13.

30. "FF," May 1926; "Booksellers Want No Literary Censor," *St. Louis Post-Dispatch*, May 11, 1926, 19; CJF, "In the Ozarks a Free Fantasia," *DI*, Nov. 6, 1926, 16.

31. BRD to CJF, June 11, 1926; CJF, *Ozark Fantasia*, 35–43; Michael B. Dougan, "Opie Pope Read (1852–1939)," Sept. 23, 2009, retrieved July 29, 2018, from Encyclopedia of Arkansas, encyclopediaofarkansas.net.

32. Gardner, *Reviewing the South*, 64.

33. "Crowd of 5000 Stares at Writers on Authors' Night, Hears Itself Criticised," *St. Louis Post-Dispatch*, May 13, 1926, 1.

34. CJF to WMS, Dec. 14, 1938; Prince, *American Daredevil*, 43, 58, 65–67, 77; Greene, *Damned*, 16–17.

35. "FF," Aug.–Sept. 1926.

36. CJF and Paul Honoré, illus., "In the Ozarks a Free Fantasia," *DI*, Nov. 6, 1926, 16–18; CJF and Paul Honoré, illus., "Ozarks: An Alabaster Labyrinth," *DI*, Nov. 27, 1926, 16–18; Cooper, *Authors and Others*, 60; HFL, "Guest Book," 19; Leflar, "Memories," 6.

37. "Delightful Day at Happy Hollow," *FD*, July 3, 1916, 3; "400 Attend Opening of Campus Cafeteria; Club to Open Friday," *FD*, Jan. 2, 1922, 1; "William R. Lighton Dies at Hollywood," *FD*, Jan. 26, 1923, 1; "Rotary Club Supper to Formally Open the Green Tree Inn," *FD*, June 6, 1923, 1, 6; "Social and Personal,"

FD, June 9, 1923, 4; "Green Tree Inn," *FD*, June 16, 1923, 3; "Social and Personal,"
FD, June 20, 1923, 3; "Miss Elizabeth Ellis . . . ," *FD*, Aug. 1, 1923, 5; "Social and
Personal," *FD*, Nov. 30, 1923, 3; "Society and Personal Mention," *FD*, May 29,
1926, 3; "Miss Ann Coyle . . . ," *FD*, Aug. 23, 1926, 6; Nan Lawler, "Will Lighton
(1866–1923)," March 4, 2015, retrieved Feb. 3, 2017, from Encyclopedia of
Arkansas, encyclopediaofarkansas.net.

38. "FF," Aug.–Sept. 1926.

39. CJF to Paul Honoré, undated, BRD Collection; "Beautification of City Chief
Aim of League," *Galveston (TX) Daily News*, Nov. 3, 1926, 7; CJF, "Texas Cities
on the Gulf," *DI*, Dec. 3, 1927.

40. Gulf Park by-the-Sea, *1924–25 Calendar*, 10. It is not evident that Richard G.
Cox and Maddox's friend William N. Cox of Louisville were related.

41. CJF, *Sapphire Skies*, 273–74; Doris M. Reed, "Letters of Vachel Lindsay in the
Lilly Library at Indiana University," *Indiana University Bookman*, 1960, 21–63.
A photograph of Richard G. Cox and Vachel Lindsay posing with a large group
of students in the large live oak at Gulf Park College appeared in an Illinois
newspaper in August 1924, coincidentally on the same page as a review of
Finger's book *Highwaymen*. (John T. Frederick, "Gallant Rogues" and "Oak Tree
Is Poetry Classroom," caption, *Jacksonville [IL] Daily Journal*, Aug. 16, 1924, 4.)

42. Blotner, *Faulkner*, I: 392; Holditch, "William Faulkner," 32; Carolyn G.
Hanneman, "John Peebles McClure (1893–1956)," Oklahoma Historical Society,
2009, retrieved Feb. 18, 2019, from okhistory.org.

43. "FF," December 1926 and April 1930; Scott, *Natalie Scott*, 240, 242, 259–60;
Reed, *Dixie Bohemia*, 17, 84, 111, 162–63. It is possible that Finger and McClure
ran into Faulkner, a good friend of McClure's who lived around the corner
from him on St. Peter Street. Max Putzel, who wrote biographies of WMR and
Faulkner, speculated that Faulkner based the character of Major Ayers in his
second novel, *Mosquitoes*, on Finger. (Putzel, *Genius of Place*, 17n3.) However,
Mosquitoes already was at the publisher when Finger visited McClure, and
Faulkner was working with William Spratling on a collection of short pieces
about the French Quarter crowd that they published as *Sherwood Anderson &
Other Famous Creoles*. (Robbins, "Double Dealer," 86–92; Blotner, *Faulkner*, I:
393–94, I: 524, I: 534.)

44. CJF, "Beauvoir and the Gulf Coast," *DI*, Dec. 10, 1927.

45. "FF," December 1926; "Post Card History of Gulfport from the Collection of
Paul Jermyn," retrieved May 15, 2018, from the Historical Society of Gulfport,
historicalsocietyofgulfport.org; Gifford, *Dayneford's Library*, 27, 131; Furneaux,
Queer Dickens, 105–06, 141.

46. RHD to CJF, Nov. 26, 1926.

47. Helen Maddox, Dec. 25, 1926, GGB.

48. CJF, "Affair at the Inn: A Christmas Story," manuscript, BRD Collection; CJF,
"Affair at the Inn," 22–23, 31; Rubin, *Middlebrow Culture*, 217.

49. "Gulf Park College," advertisement, and CJF, "And Now, 1927," *AW*, January 1927, inside cover.

50. CJF to BRD, January or February, received Feb. 28 and March 19, 1927, and March 17 and 24, 1927.

Chapter 10

1. Leflar, *"Memories,"* 11.

2. CJF to BRD, written by hand on the back of a page of manuscript and received April 29 and June 8, 1927; Rusch and Pizer, *Theodore Dreiser*, 80; Shores, "Library."

3. "FF," Oct.–Nov. 1926; CJF, *Ozark Fantasia*, 117; Ellen Compton, "Charles Morrow Wilson (1905–1977)," April 21, 2007, retrieved April 25, 2018, from Encyclopedia of Arkansas, encyclopediaofarkansas.net; CJF to BRD, June 30, 1927; "Charles J. Finger . . . ," *Neosho (MO) Daily Democrat*, July 11, 1927, 2.

4. "New Business Manager Elected by Traveler," *FD*, Oct. 26, 1921, 2; "Among the New Books," *Bremen (IN) Enquirer*, Sept. 25, 1930, 6; Wilson, *Acres of Sky*, 5, 8; "FF," June 1931; 1940 USFC; Blevins, *Arkansas/Arkansaw*, 95–96.

5. CJF, *Ozark Fantasia*, 27–29; Blevins, *Arkansas/Arkansaw*, 79; CJF to BRD, written by hand on the back of a page of manuscript; CJF to BRD, received April 29 and June 8, 1927; "Baltimorean Buys Missouri Paper," *Sun (Baltimore, MD)*, May 14, 1927, 22; "Waste Basket," *Springfield (MO) Leader*, Nov. 24, 1927, 12; Stuart Olivier, "Book of a Very Dear Friend," *Springfield (MO) Leader*, Nov. 30, 1927, 16; CBD, "World and All," *Emporia (KS) Gazette*, Feb. 22, 1928, 2; "Books in Brief," *Nation*, June 13, 1928, 673; CBD, "All Things Considered," *Minneapolis Star*, Jan. 25, 1929, 24; Rusch and Pizer, *Theodore Dreiser: Interviews*, 80; Shores, "Library."

6. May Lamberton Becker, "Reader's Guide," *SR*, Nov. 5, 1927, 291; Rebecca Hourwich, "What Books Shall My Small Child Read," *Nation*, Nov. 16, 1927, 546–48.

7. "Adventurers All!" advertisement, *Boys' Life*, Nov. 1927, 65; "Latest Works of Fiction," Book Review, *NYT*, Oct. 16, 1927, 23.

8. Guion, "Sail Away for the Rio Grande"; "Artists Who Will Entertain during Federation Meet," *Waxahachie (TX) Daily Light*, April 21, 1925, 3; Edward Moore, "Three Pianists of Marked Merit on Sunday Bill," *Chicago Daily Tribune*, Dec. 6, 1926, 37.

9. Sandburg, *American Songbag*, xvii; "Finger and His Songbook," *SR*, Dec. 3, 1927, 373–74.

10. Stanley Walker, "Some Frontier Ballads That Are Fit to Print," reviews of *Frontier Ballads* by CJF and *Texas and Southwestern Lore* by J. Frank Dobie, ed., Book Review, *NYT*, Nov. 13, 1927, 5.

11. "New Books," *SR*, Nov. 17, 1928, 380.

12. Edd Winfield Parks, "Shifting Horizons of Life," review of *Seven Horizons* by CJF, *Tennessean (Nashville, TN)*, April 27, 1930, Automotive Section, 5.

13. CJF, "Ebro," 482; "FF," Jan.–Feb. 1925.

14. Jack Random [pseud.], "Odd Thoughts II," *RM*, Feb. 19, 1920, 124–25; CJF to James Branch Cabell, Feb. 22, 1920, James Branch Cabell Collection; CJF to BRD, undated and Feb. 19, 1925; BRD to CJF, March 9, 1925; C. A. Newman, "My Meeting with Charles J. Finger: Squire of the Ozarks at Home—Some Intimate Glimpses," *DI*, May 2, 1925, 14–15; "Novelist Scores 'Smut Writers,'" *Courier-Journal (Louisville, KY)*, May 20, 1925, 4; "FF," June–July 1926; Smith, *Chicago's Left Bank*, 11–13.

15. "FF," July 1924; "Check List of New Books," *American Mercury*, March 1928, 20; "Check List of New Books: Folk-Lore," *American Mercury*, July 1928; Rubin, *Making of Middlebrow Culture*, 48, 54–55; Eddy, *Bookwomen*, 119–20; Radway, "Learned and Literary Print Cultures," 222–23.

16. CJF to BRD, Sept. 21, 1924, and BRD to CJF, Sept. 30, 1924, March 9, 1925, and Sept. 4, 1926.

17. "FF," Jan.–Feb. and March 1925.

18. CJF to BRD, Feb. 19, March 21, and May 6, 1925, September and October 1926; BRD to CJF, March 9 and 30, 1925; CJF, "Paul Honore's Work"; "FF," Aug.–Sept. and November 1925, April, Aug.–Sept., and December 1926; George Sterling to HLM, Jan. 6, 1926, and HLM to George Sterling, Jan. 11, 1926, in Joshi, *From Baltimore to Bohemia*, 223–25; CJF, "Single Taxers Who Are Substantial Business Men," reprinted from *AW*, *Land and Freedom*, Nov.–Dec. 1926, 195; Kunitz and Haycraft, *Twentieth Century Authors*, 1276–77; Hobson, *Serpent in Eden*, 49.

19. CJF to William J. Cameron, Nov. 24, 1923, BRD Collection; "About *Dearborn Independent*," Chronicling America: Historic American Newspapers, chroniclingamerica.loc.gov; Barkun, *Religion and the Racist Right*, 31–34; Woeste, *Henry Ford's War*, 90–92, 155, 321.

20. "From the Workshop of Mr. H. G. Wells," *RM*, April 1, 1920, 272–73; "'All's Well' Scores Propagandists," *AD*, Dec. 11, 1921, 5; CJF, *Hints on Writing Short Stories*, 19; CJF, *Mark Twain*, 5–6; Haldeman-Julius, *First Hundred Million*, 206–07.

21. "FF," October 1924 and April–May 1925; CJF to BRD, undated and received Dec. 21, 1925; CJF, *Ozark Fantasia*, 35–43; Lewis, *Public Image of Henry Ford*, 143; Woeste, *Henry Ford's War*, 143, 168.

22. "FF," December 1924; CJF to BRD, Jan. 30, Feb. 17, 19, and March 14, 1925; BRD to CJF, Feb. 16, 1925.

23. "Ford Admits Jew Charges Are Not True," *DFP*, July 8, 1927; Barkun, *Religion and the Racist Right*, 34; Woeste, *Henry Ford's War*, 168, 271, 275, 292.

24. "Mr. Charles J. Finger . . . For Year 1924 and 1925" and "Following Manuscripts Purchased from Charles J. Finger," BRD Collection.

25. CJF to BRD, undated, Aug. 10 and Sept. 7, 1927, received Sept. 29, 1927, and Jan. 15, 1928; BRD to CJF, Oct. 14, 1927, and Feb. 10, 1928; Barkun, *Religion*

and the Racist Right, 41. CJF wrote in his memoir that another writer plagia-
rized *Highwaymen* and CJF sued the publisher, eventually winning two-thirds
of the royalties for the book. CJF's friend CBD, a syndicated columnist,
referred to the dispute twice. In a March 1931 column, he wrote that he disliked Joseph Gollomb because Gollomb wrote a book, "purporting to be all
fact, which was found to contain the remarkable adventures of some imaginary
highwaymen previously and originally written about by Charles J. Finger, who
didn't claim his characters were historical." In 1932 CBD noted "Charles J.
Finger . . . caught a thief who stole a whole book from him, mixing up fictional
and historical characters. The thief had to pay." (CJF, *Seven Horizons*, 440–41;
CBD, "World and All," *Lansing [MI] State Journal*, March 25, 1931, 6, and
Aug. 25, 1932, 6.)

26. CJF to Oscar [*sic*] Garrison Villard, Dec. 31, 1927, carbon; Oswald Garrison
Villard to CJF, Jan. 7, 1928; Charles Morrow Wilson, "Americans We Like:
Charles J. Finger, Literary Adventurer," *Nation*, Sept. 5, 1928, 219–21; Humes,
Oswald Garrison Villard, 41.

27. CJF, "Easeful Executive," *American Mercury*, June 1929, 202–08; "FF,"
October 1932 and February 1933; CJF, "Demon Prejudice," *AW*, February 1933,
3–6; Mayfield, *Constant Circle*, 78; Hamilton, "American Manners," 239.

28. George F. Thomson to CJF, Jan. 3, 1928.

29. CJF to BRD, undated; Shores, "Published Works."

30. "FF," Jan.–Feb. and Oct.–Nov. 1926, April 1930, and June 1932; Kittie Finger to
BRD, July 16, 1926, BRD Collection; University of Arkansas, *Razorback, 1927*,
69; "Novelist to Get Degree," *LAT*, June 14, 1928, 1; Leflar, "*Memories*," 11; "Past
Scroll of Honor Recipients," retrieved Sept. 21, 2017, from Knox College,
knox.edu.

31. CJF to BRD, Summer 1928; "Society and Personal Mention," *FD*, July 19, 1928, 3.

32. CJF, *Heroes*, v; RBCG, "Preface," vii–viii.

33. Turner, *Marketing Modernism*, 87.

34. Mary Graham Bonner, "Children's Book Week," reproduced from *New York Sun*,
Reading (PA) Times, Nov. 13, 1928, 9; Henry Beston, "Traffic and Discoveries,"
review of *Heroes from Hakluyt* by CJF, "Books," *NYHT*, Nov. 18, 1928, 8;
Benjamin March, "Brave Heroes, High Seas, Adventure," review of *Heroes from
Hakluyt* by CJF, *DFP*, Dec. 2, 1928, Part Four, 4; Rachel Field, "Gossip Shop," *SR*,
Dec. 8, 1928, 484, 486; "Scarab Club Notes," *DFP*, Nov. 25, 1928, Part Four, 5.

35. Margaret Stute, "Woman's Page," *Canyon (TX) News*, Feb. 9, 1928, 16; Cooper,
Authors and Others, 57.

Chapter 11

1. "Competitions," *CE*, May 26, 1928, 8; Kate Coplan, "Week at Pratt Library," *Sun
(Baltimore, MD)*, May 27, 1928, Section 2, 13; "Publishing News," *CE*, Dec. 15,
1928, 8. Longmans, Green evidently only awarded this prize twice, the second

time to Laura Adams Armer for *Waterless Mountain*, which also received the Newbery Medal. ("'Waterless Mountain' Wins John Newbery Medal Award," *Indianapolis Sunday Star*, May 1, 1932, Part Five, 9.)

2. "Sorosis' Last Meet," *Topeka (KS) State Journal*, June 11, 1897, 2; "Boro Woman's Club Holds Book Day," *Brooklyn Daily Eagle*, Nov. 25, 1924, 10; "Interesting Things in Print," *Public Libraries*, Dec. 1922, 649–50; "Noted Authors to Participate in Store Book Fair," *Brooklyn Daily Eagle*, Oct. 30, 1927, 12B; May Lamberton Becker, "Reader's Guide," *SR*, Nov. 5, 1927, 291, April 6, 1929, 867, April 13, 1929, 891.

3. HFL, "Autobiography," 8–16; *FD*, May 24, 1929.

4. "C. J. Finger," *PM*, June 1929, 125; CJF, "Golden Horseman," review of *A Vanished Arcadia* by RBCG, "Books," *NYHT*, March 1, 1925, 3; CJF, "A Bas Monotonous Ways," review of *Doughty Deeds* by RBCG, "Books," *NYHT*, Feb. 14, 1926, 1–2; Milton Bronner, "Absolute Home Rule Now Demanded of Britain," *Muncie (IN) Evening Press*, Feb. 11, 1929, 3; Cunninghame Graham, *Gaucho Laird*, 343–45.

5. "Defence of Trafalgar Square," *Times (London)*, Nov. 14, 1887, 6; CJF, "Book's the Man," review of *Thirty Tales and Sketches* by RBCG, *SR,* Sept. 28, 1929, 177–78; Thompson, *William Morris*, 488–94; Curle, *Letters*, 8, 12; Cunninghame Graham, *Gaucho Laird*, 314, 325–26.

6. CJP, "Mutual Improvement Society," *HT*, Nov. 19, 1887, 172–73; "French Society," *HT*, Nov. 19, 1887, 172; Carpenter, *Days and Dreams*, 254–56.

7. "Harold Bell Wright Treasures a Poem Dedicated to Him by a Tulsa Woman— Mrs. Ben Blakeney," *Tulsa (OK) Daily World*, April 6, 1919, C3; "Society and Personal Mention," *FD*, July 19, 1928, 3; Hill, *Oklahoma*, 16.

8. "Charles Driscoll, Columnist, Dead," *NYT*, Jan. 16, 1951, 29. The Cornicks and the Driscolls lived near each other in Yonkers. (1925 New York State Census; US City Directories.) One hint that Cornick and Driscoll were friends was an anonymous jibe in a journal devoted to Henry George's tax policy, which both Boyd and Philip Cornick espoused, expressing "regret" at Driscoll's "lack of intelligence on the subject" but adding, "that does not interfere with long established friendships." ("Comment and Reflection," *Land and Freedom*, Jan.–Feb. 1933, 3–4.)

9. CBD, columns of various titles in *Emporia (KS) Gazette*, Feb. 22, 1928, 2; *Minneapolis Star*, Jan. 25, 1929, 24; *Indianapolis Star*, Aug. 12, 1929, 6; *Harrisburg (PA) Telegraph*, Aug. 5, 1929, 8; Aug. 9, 1929, 8; Aug. 26, 1929, 12; *Morning Call (Laurel, MS)*, Aug. 23, 1929, 4; *Minneapolis Star*, Sept. 21, 1929, 18; *Coshocton (OH) Tribune*, Feb. 5, 1940, 7; "About Milton's Cottage," retrieved Sept. 19, 2017, from miltonscottage.org; "Thomas Gray, English Poet," retrieved Oct. 13, 2017, from Encyclopedia Britannica, britannica.com; Gregory Woods, "Gay Literature: An Introduction," retrieved Oct. 13, 2017, from gregorywoodspoet.blogspot.com.

10. CJF, "Picaresque," review of *Pearls, Arms and Hashish* by Henri de Monfried as told to Ida Treat, "Books," *NYHT*, Nov. 9, 1930, 10; CJF, "As Tomlinson Sees

the World," review of *Out of Soundings* by H. M. Tomlinson, "Books," *NYHT*, March 29, 1931, 3.

11. "Old Books in New Boards," *CE*, Dec. 15, 1928, 8; Schmidt, *Making Americans*, 33; Shores, "Library."

12. "Charles J. Finger," photograph and caption, *Brooklyn Daily Eagle*, Oct. 9, 1929, 12; "Charles J. Finger Writer; Baltimore *Sun* Archive Photo," photograph, retrieved Jan. 12, 2013, from ebay.com.

13. "Juvenile Books Named by Guild," *Binghamton (NY) Press*, Sept. 21, 1929, 7; "Merger of Two of the Juvenile Book Clubs Is Announced," *Galveston (TX) Daily News*, Oct. 6, 1929, 6; "Primary School Students Entertain Parents and Teachers," *Denton (MD) Journal*, April 10, 1937, 1; Radway, *Feeling for Books*, 200.

14. May Lamberton Becker, "Reader's Guide," *SR*, Nov. 16, 1929, 420, 422; May Lamberton Becker, "Christmas Books for Boys and Girls," *Bookman*, December 1929, 440–45.

15. Agatha L. Shea, "English Archer Makes Voyage with Magellan," *Chicago Tribune*, Oct. 5, 1929, 13; CJF, "Author Recalls He Was Boy, So Succeeds," *Chicago Tribune*, Nov 16, 1929, 13.

16. Dudley Cammett Lunt, "Art of Adventure," review of *Courageous Companions* by CJF, "Books," *NYHT*, Nov. 24, 1929, 8; Hodowanec, *May Massee Collection*, 61–63, 73.

17. Hansen, "Literary Lobbies," 162; Tolppanen, *Churchill*, 192.

18. HCP to CJF, Jan. 11 and Feb. 19, 1927; Herbert Corey, "Manhattan Days and Nights," *Courier-Journal (Louisville, KY)*, Oct. 14, 1929, 6; CBD, "World and All," *Harrisburg (PA) Telegraph*, Nov. 25, 1929, 10; Richard Massock, "About New York," *Fairbanks (AK) News-Miner*, Jan. 9, 1930, 4; Richard Massock, "About New York," *Corsicana (TX) Daily Sun*, April 14, 1930, 6; CJF, *Footloose*, 101.

19. "Army Orders," *El Paso Herald*, Sept. 27, 1929, 7; "Fort Ethan Allen," *Burlington (VT) Free Press and Times*, Oct. 3, 1929, 8; AP, "Stock Prices Lower; Trade Fairly Quiet," *St. Louis Post-Dispatch*, Oct. 26, 1929, 1; "FF," April 1930; GWM to RHD, with a pencil note "April 1930?" RHD Papers; record for GWM, 1930 USFC.

20. CJF to BRD, received Dec. 22, 1924, January and Feb. 19, 1925, and Jan. 18, 1926; Robert Dunne, "Sherwood Anderson (1876–1941)," retrieved Nov. 29, 2019, from Encyclopedia Virginia, encyclopediavirginia.org.

21. RHD to CJF, Feb. 17, 1926; John Cowper Powys to CJF, March 13, [1926].

22. E. Schumacher to CJF, July 21, 1926.

23. CJF to BRD.

24. CJF, "Grand Old Lady of Virginia City, Nev.," review of *Suns Go Down* by Flannery Lewis, "Books," *NYHT*, April 4, 1937, 1; Musselwhite, *Partings Welded Together*, 153–54; Hynes, "Art of Telling," xii; Fone, *Stonewall*, 207; Edwards, *Exotic Journeys*, 13; Bergman, *Gay American Autobiography*, xviii–xix.

25. CJF, *Seven Horizons*, 53–55; Belloc, *On Everything*, 25; Copley, *Bloomsbury*, 12; Henry S. Salt, "Edward Carpenter and Brighton," retrieved Oct. 21, 2015, from HenrySalt.co.uk.

26. Orens, "Stewart Headlam," 233; CJF, *A Man*, 10; CJF, "Book's the Man," review of *Thirty Tales and Sketches* by RBCG, *SR,* Sept. 28, 1929, 177–78; CJF, *Seven Horizons*, 157, 183–88.

27. CJF Journals, Feb. 14, 1890; CJF, *Seven Horizons*, 197–206; Gair, "Gender and Genre," 134, 138–39.

28. CJF, *Seven Horizons*, 251–52.

29. CJF Journals, Feb. 20 and March 4, 1890; Dynes, *Homolexis*, 101; Rowbotham, *Edward Carpenter*, 151–52.

30. Jeffs, "Man's Words," 38; Cocks, *Nameless Offences*, 168; Colligan, "Born Pederasts," 12; Carpenter, *Ioläus*, 156; Glass, *Authors*, 99–100.

31. Aldrich, *Colonialism*, 107; Showalter, *Sexual Anarchy*, 79–80; Buckton, *Cruising*, 216; Ruppel, *Homosexuality*, 43.

32. CJF, *Seven Horizons*, 223–24; Carpenter, "Peak of Terror," in *Narcissus and Other Poems* (1873), excerpted in Reade, *Sexual Heretics*, 142–43; Gifford, *Dayneford's Library*, 21–22.

33. "FF," May–June and July 1924.

34. Buckton, *Cruising*, 7.

35. Garrison, "Walt Whitman," 624; Wilde, *Collected Poems*, 70; CJF, *Seven Horizons*, 226; Shores, "Library."

36. CJF, *Seven Horizons*, 260, 266–67; Carpenter quoted in Rowbotham, *Edward Carpenter*, 151–52; Austen, "Stoddard's Little Tricks," 74.

37. "Yahgan," review, *Nature*, April 21, 1892, 578.

38. CJF Journals, May 24, 1890.

39. CJF, *Seven Horizons*, 268, 450.

40. CJF to Harry E. Maule, June 18, 1927, copy, BRD Collection; CJF, Introduction, *Seven Horizons*, manuscript, January 1930; "Harry E. Maule, Editor, Dead at 84," *NYT*, April 9, 1971.

41. "Modern Sea Wolf," advertisement, *Publishers' Weekly*, April 5, 1930, 1; Harry E. Maule to CJF, April 11, 1930.

42. Lewis Gannett, "Books and Other Things," *NYHT*, April 5, 1930, 11; I. M. P., "Turns with a Bookworm," "Books," *NYHT*, April 6, 1930, 19; Edwin P. Norris, "From Stuffy Mayfair Childhood Finger Wanders into 'Seven Horizons' of Life," review of *Seven Horizons* by CJF, *Philadelphia Record*, April 12, 1930, photocopy of clipping.

43. Jerome Coignard, "Very Small Talk," *Brooklyn Daily Eagle*, Jan. 22, 1930, 22; Harvey Fergusson, "CJF Himself," "Books," *NYHT*, April 13, 1930, 3–4.

44. "Notes of a Rapid Reader," review of *Seven Horizons* by CJF, *SR*, April 26, 1930, 983; Harry Hansen, "Floyd Dell Viewing Sex and Life from Common Sense Standpoint," *DFP*, April 20, 1930, Part Four, 8; Edd Winfield Parks, "Shifting Horizons of Life," review of *Seven Horizons* by CJF, *Tennessean (Nashville, TN)*, April 27, 1930, Automotive Section, 5; O. O. McIntyre, "O. O. M'Intyre's Impressions," *Ogden (UT) Standard-Examiner*, April 27, 1930, 16; Richard

Massock, "Literary Guidepost," *Tribune-Republican (Greeley, CO)*, Sept. 10, 1930, 10.

45. Rose C. Feld, "From Victorian London to the Ozarks of Arkansas," review of *Seven Horizons* by CJF, Book Review, *NYT*, May 18, 1930, 3.

46. CJF, "French Cook," review of *Captain Cook* by Maurice Thiery, "Books," *NYHT*, May 4, 1930, 13; Stephen Winik, "Charles J. Finger: Gallant Rogue or Hidden Folklorist?" *Folklife Today*, July 18, 2019, retrieved July 19, 2019, from blogs.loc.gov.

47. Margaret Wallace, "Seven Horizons," *Bookman*, June 1930, 346–47; Löhrke, "Beyond His Horizons," *Nation*, Sept. 3, 1930, 249–50; Joe Gould, "Stagecoaches, Etc.," *New Republic*, Oct. 1, 1930, 187–88, all reviews of *Seven Horizons*.

48. Barry Fox Stevens (Mrs. Albert Mason Stevens) to JGF, Oct. 7, 1941, retrieved Feb. 5, 2015, from Ancestry, www.ancestry.com.

49. Leflar, *"Memories,"* 9.

50. "Developments in City and Community within Week," *EEN*, Oct. 6, 1929, 7; "FF," April 1930; HFL, "Autobiography," 16.

51. "FF," June 1930; Anne Trubeck, "Book Boys," February 2005, retrieved Oct. 22, 2015, from ClevelandMagazine.com.

Chapter 12

1. Record for Charles A. Newman, 1881 England Census; CJF Journals, May 7, 1891; Charles A. Newman to CJF, Dec. 9, 1924; "FF," Oct. 1930.

2. CJF, *Sapphire Skies*, 86–89; GWM to RHD, with a pencil note "April 1930?"; RHD to GWM, April 18 and June 3, 1930, carbon copies, RHD Papers.

3. Philip R. Bishop, "Biography of Mosher," retrieved Oct. 30, 2017, from thomasbirdmosher.net. Mosher's edition of "The Jolly Beggar" was not in CJF's library at the time of my inventory, but he did have nineteen volumes of Mosher's Bibelot series of anthologies. (Shores, "Library.")

4. "Ode to the Printing Press," *School News and Practical Educator*, December 1911, 177.

5. Fairholt, *Gog and Magog*, 21.

6. "Ode to the Majujah," handwritten and typed manuscripts, RHD Papers. Circumstantial evidence suggests the third pair of friends whom Maddox named in the poem, "Chambers and Boyd," were Robert W. Chambers and Ernest Boyd, two prolific writers who lived in Greenwich Village. (O. O. McIntyre, "New York Day by Day," *Akron [OH] Beacon Journal*, Jan. 23, 1924, 4; "Ernest Augustus Boyd," retrieved July 7, 2018, from the Greenwich Village Bookshop Door, norman.hrc.utexas.edu.) Davis mentioned Chambers in *Munsey's* in 1905 and said Boyd was one of the early inductees of the New Face Club. ("Literary Chat," *Munsey's*, February 1905, 717; William Amelia, "Mencken Offers Bible," *Evening Sun [Baltimore, MD]*, Jan. 30, 1973, A10.) The names Irvin Cobb and Robert W.

Chambers appeared consecutively in a list of contributors to *the American Angler* in 1919, and the names Ernest Boyd and Robert W. Chambers appeared consecutively in a list of writers who signed a manifesto against censorship in 1927. ("Remarkable Symposium," *American Angler*, March 1919, unnumbered page; AP, "Authors Combine to Fight Censors," *Constitution [Atlanta, GA]*, May 1, 1927, 16A.)

7. GWM to RHD and RHD to GWM, Jan. 24, Feb. 25, and April 18, 1930, all carbon copies in RHD Papers; "Lecture Date Changed," *Daily Times (Davenport, IA)*, Feb. 20, 1930, 15; Hart-Davis, *Hugh Walpole*, 275; Florence Elizabeth Buttolph, "College Club Will Offer Diversity of Attractions," *DFP*, Jan. 9, 1927, Part Four, 8.

8. "FF," October 1930.

9. "FF," October 1930; CJF, *Sapphire Skies*, 265–72; "Bloodiest Trail in Arizona History Is Now Scenic Route," *ADS*, April 21, 1929, 5, 22; Arizona, Southwestern, and Borderlands Photograph Collection, University of Arizona Libraries, Special Collections; Arreola, *Postcards*, 21.

10. CJF, *Sapphire Skies*, 186–87.

11. Tennyson, "Ulysses," retrieved Oct. 27, 2017, from poetryfoundation.org.

12. CJF to Kitty Finger Helbling, Oct. 15, 1930, courtesy of Charles Leflar.

13. CBD, "World and All," *Lansing (MI) State Journal*, Aug. 6, 1930, 6, Nov. 21, 1930, 6, Dec. 16, 1930, 6; "Omansky in Akron to Visit Mother," *Akron (OH) Beacon Journal*, Dec. 25, 1935, 1; CBD, "New York Day by Day," *San Bernardino Sun*, Jan. 1, 1939, 20.

14. Description of the copy of the book retrieved Oct. 19, 2017, from bebooks .com.

15. "FF," October 1930; David T. Field, "Railway Publicity," *International Railway Journal*, March 1911, 10–11; CJF, *Sapphire Skies*, 4, 8, 48, 56, 62–63.

16. From a jacket blurb for *Footloose in the West*.

17. Bruce Catton, "Beauty or Industry," editorial, *Daily Times* (New Philadelphia, OH), March 18, 1931, 2; Bruce Catton, "Book Survey," *Olean (NY) Evening Times*, April 3, 1931, 13; "About Places," *Chicago Daily Tribune*, April 11, 1931, 13; "Spring Travel Made Enticing," *LAT*, April 19, 1931, Part III, 14; May Lamberton Becker, "Reader's Guide," *SR,* May 30, 1931, 869–70.

18. "Get the most out of your trip West and South!" advertisement for *Adventure under Sapphire Skies*, *SR*, June 6, 1931, 883; "Check List of New Books," *American Mercury*, September 1931, iv.

19. CBD, "World and All," *Lansing (MI) State Journal*, Oct. 14, 1931, 4; Edna Lou Walton, "Burly Giant of American Myth," review of *The Saginaw Paul Bunyan* by James Stevens and *A Paul Bunyan Geography* by CJF, Book Review, *NYT*, Feb. 14, 1932, 10.

20. Gulf Park College, *Sea Gull, 1931*, unnumbered page.

21. Mary Graham Bonner, "Stirring, Worth-while Books Are Obtainable," *Pittsburgh Press*, Sept. 23, 1927, 31; "Recent Books for Boys and Girls," *LAT*, Nov. 17, 1929, Part III, 17; "Books You May Wish to Own," *DFP*, Jan. 6, 1930, 10; "Library

Notes," *Simpson's Daily Leader-Times (Kittanning, PA)*, May 24, 1931, 8; "New Books Are Added at Library Saturday," *Lansing (MI) State Journal*, July 3, 1931, 7; "Library Notes," *Kerrville (TX) Mountain Sun*, Aug. 20, 1931, 4; "Fall Books at Harrisburg Library," *Harrisburg (PA) Telegraph*, Aug. 20, 1931, 7. For details of HCP's distinguished career, see Matthew Lavelle, "Henry Clarence Pitz," 2007, retrieved May 25, 2017, from the Pennsylvania Center for the Book, pabook.libraries.psu.edu.

22. "FF," July and November 1931; "Bookman's Corner," *Green Bay (WI) Press-Gazette*, May 14, 1932, 5; Record for death of Christopher Ferguson, California Department of Public Health, Office of the State Registrar of Vital Statistics; "John Edward Borein: The Vault Collection," retrieved Oct. 23, 2015, from Santa Barbara Historical Museum, santabarbaramuseum.com.

23. "FF," November 1931.

24. CJF, *Footloose*, 258–59.

25. "FF," June 1931 and Jan. 1933; US City Directories; "John Walter Maddox," obituary, *Gospel Advocate*, Jan. 26, 1956, 94, retrieved Aug. 8, 2017, from "History of the Restoration Movement," therestorationmovement.com.

26. CJF, *Footloose*, 291–92.

27. CJF to BRD, undated; "Motor Travelogue of West by Robust Writer Is Praised," *Oakland (CA) Tribune*, April 3, 1932, 24; "About Places," *Chicago Daily Tribune*, April 9, 1932, 16; "Group of Recent Books," *LAT*, April 24, 1932, Part III, 12; May Lamberton Becker, "Reader's Guide," *SR*, April 30, 1932, 705. An excerpt of the *NYT* review appeared in "The Bookman's Corner," *Green Bay (WI) Press-Gazette*, May 14, 1932, 5.

28. CJF to WMS, Dec. 23, 1931.

29. Leflar, "*Memories*," 13; James Keddie to CJF, June 24, 1932; CJF, "FF," June 1932.

30. CJF to WMS, Dec. 23, 1931; CJF, "FF," March 1932.

31. RHD to GWM, carbon copy, Jan. 24, 1930, RHD Papers; "'Dude' Ranch to Be Located Near Johnson, Arizona," *ADS*, June 29, 1922, 3; "Donnee's Dude Ranch," advertisement, *ADS*, Feb. 21, 1925, 13; "Suburban Home," advertisement, *ADS*, March 10, 1926, 10; "Douglas," *Arizona Republican (Phoenix, AZ)*, Jan. 5, 1930, 19; "Douglas," *ADS*, Feb. 6, 1930, 6; "Farm Problem Discussed for State Bankers," *ADS*, Nov. 8, 1930, 1, 16; "Thanksgiving Party at Ranch," *ADS*, Nov. 23, 1930, 11; "Ranch House Party Today," *ADS*, Nov. 27, 1930, 11; "Custer Tea Shop Cake Has Its Place in Battle Creek History," *EEN*, Feb. 14, 1956, 13; "History," retrieved Oct. 27, 2017, from Circle Z Ranch, circlez.com; Lisa Waite Bunker, "Early Years of the Patagonia Public Library," retrieved Oct. 27, 2017, from patagoniapubliclibrary.org.

32. CJF, *Ozark Fantasia*, 91–92; HFL, "Autobiography," 5.

33. CJF to WMS, Dec. 21, 1930, Finger–Stone Correspondence.

34. "Hacienda Los Encinos," advertisement, *ADS*, Nov. 2, 1930, 7; "Many Guests at Ranch Luncheon," *ADS*, Dec. 9, 1930, 9; "Social Events," *ADS*, Nov. 11, 1930, 11; "Social Events," *ADS*, Dec. 4, 1930, 11; "Large Party at Guest Hacienda,"

ADS, Dec. 7, 1930, Sec. 2, 1; "Leaving for Douglas Visit," *ADS*, Dec. 21, 1930, Sec. 2, 1.

35. "Motoring to Ranch Today," *ADS*, Jan. 18, 1931, Sec. 2, 1; "Social Events," *ADS*, Feb. 8, 1931, 11; "Luncheon Party at Guest Ranch," *ADS*, Feb. 8, 1931, 11; GGB.

36. Joyner, "Sketches."

37. CJF to WMS, Dec. 23, 1931; "Topics of Tucson," *ADS*, April 23, 1933, 3; "Los Encinos Opens for Winter Season," *ADS*, Oct. 8, 1933, 12.

38. CJF to Hubert Philip Finger, courtesy of Charles Leflar.

39. J. Omansky, "Experiment in Publishing," *AW*, April 1932, 27–28.

40. William Griffith to CJF, Dec. 26, 1932.

41. CJF, "Dinner, Debt, and Resurrection," *AW*, December 1932, 23–26; "Table Talk," retrieved Oct. 24, 2015, from Encyclopaedia Britannica, britannica.com.

42. CR mentioned in a letter in April 1933 that GWM had had poems published in *the Atlantic*. (Johnson, *Conrad Richter*, 141.)

43. CJF to James Keddie, Dec. 26, 1932; "FF," January 1933; Joyner, "Christmas Eve and Christmas Day."

44. "FF," January 1933.

Chapter 13

1. "Worker at Library Handles Volumes Written by Father," *Akron (OH) Beacon*, Aug. 5, 1930, 21.

2. "FF," March 1933; CJF to BRD; CJF to WMS, March 15, 1933; CJF to James Keddie, March 25, 1933; Leflar, *"Memories,"* 22.

3. CJF to James Keddie, May 9, 1933; CJF, "Fine Gentleman," *AW Quarterly*, Autumn 1933, 16–17.

4. "FF," January and April 1932; CJF, "New Light on Zebulon Pike," review of *Zebulon Pike's Arkansaw Journal* by Stephen Harding Hart and Archer Butler Hulbert, "Books," *NYHT*, Jan. 8, 1933, 5; CJF to Hubert Finger, April 10, 1933, courtesy of Robert B Leflar; "FF," Feb.–March 1935; CJF to PHC.

5. James Keddie to CJF, June 8 and 24, Sept. 13, Nov. 16, and Dec. 24, 1932, Jan. 26 and 28, March 14, May 15, and July 21, 1933; CJF to H. H. Bellows, Jan. 2 and Feb. 17, 1933; KFR (Keddie's assistant) to CJF, May 6, 1933; CJF to James Keddie, May 9, 1933; "FF," May 1932; CJF, "Fine Gentleman," *AW Quarterly*, Autumn 1933, 16–17.

6. Whitman, *Selected Poems*, 146–47.

7. "Charles J. Finger Writer; Baltimore *Sun* Archive Photo," photograph, retrieved Jan. 12, 2013, from ebay.com; George Currie, "Passed in Review," *Brooklyn Daily Eagle*, Dec. 27, 1933, 10; Edward M. Kingsbury, "Mr. Finger Rides at Double-Quick through Literature," review of *After the Great Companions* by CJF, Book Review, *NYT*, Jan. 21, 1934, 2; W. N., "Stranded Victorian," review of *After the Great Companions* by CJF, *LAT*, Jan. 21, 1934, Part II, 6; CJF to WMS, Feb. 8,

1934; Brennan and Clarage, *Who's Who of Pulitzer Prize Winners*, 165; Shores, "Published Works."

8. Dzwonkoski, *American Literary Publishing Houses*, 8–10. D. Appleton and its successor firm, D. Appleton-Century, published at least thirteen books by Davis. (WorldCat.)

9. "Great Rovers," review of *The Distant Prize* by CJF, Book Review, *NYT*, May 5, 1935, 13; Lewis Gannett, "Books and Things," *NYHT*, May 6, 1935, 13; W. N., "Some Were Rascals," review of *The Distant Prize* by CJF, *LAT*, May 12, 1935, A6; "Checklist of New Books," *American Mercury*, Aug. 1935, 507.

10. Conroy, "Mingling with the Ungodly," 193; Furneaux, *Queer Dickens*, 217–18.

11. CJF, *Valiant Vagabonds*, 8, 198–99; Katherine Woods, "Great Vagabonds of a Dozen Centuries," review of *Valiant Vagabonds* by CJF, Book Review, *NYT*, Nov. 8, 1936, 4; "Lives of Great Men Sometimes Remind," *LAT*, Nov. 15, 1936, IV-A-14.

12. "Librarians' Convention Ends Today," *News-Palladium (Benton Harbor, MI)*, Oct. 19, 1935, 3; CJF to HCP, Nov. 19, 1935, and Jan. 3, 1936.

13. "When Guns Thundered at Tripoli," review of *When Guns Thundered at Tripoli* by CJF, *Kirkus*, Oct. 7, 1937; Gardner, *Reviewing the South*, 261; Claiborne Smith, "Our History," retrieved July 2, 2018, from kirkusreviews.com.

14. "William Rose Benet," advertisement, *FD*, April 6, 1936, 6; Uncle Walt [pseud.], "Ozark Moon," *FD*, April 29, 1936, 2.

15. Christopher Morley to CJF, June 12, 1936, courtesy of Charles Leflar; CJF, "Forty Years in Patagonia," review of *El Jimmy, Outlaw of Patagonia* by Herbert Childs, *SR*, Aug. 1, 1936, 7; CJF, "Old Southwest," review of *Early Americana and Other Stories* by CR, *SR*, Aug. 8, 1936, 7.

16. CJF, *Magic Tower*, 42–43, 71–72, 80–81; *Catalog of Copyright Entries, New Series: 1934*, Part 1, 1358; record for Kings Arms Press in Firms Out of Business, retrieved May 10, 2015, from Harry Ransom Center and University of Reading Library, norman.hrc.utexas.edu. Someone eventually returned GWM's copy of *Magic Tower* to Gayeta. (Leflar, "Charles J. & Helen Finger Works.")

17. James Keddie to CJF, Nov. 16, 1932, and Jan. 12 and 28, 1933; CJF to James Keddie, Dec. 30, 1932; CJF to H. H. Bellows, Jan. 2, 1933; H. H. Bellows to CJF, Feb. 17, 1933; CJF, "Western Books," *AW*, Winter 1934, 22.

18. "Charles J. Finger Is Monett Speaker; Prize Award Judge," *FD*, April 25, 1934, 1; "FF," Sept.–Oct. 1935; "Art Display at Democrat," *FD*, Oct. 19, 1934, 1; CJF to HCP, Jan. 3, 1936; CJF to James Keddie.

19. Cady, "Art Comes to Cape Ann," 10–12; Recchia, *Artists*, A12, A20; Cate McQuaid, "In Rockport, Artists Kept the Depression at Bay," *Boston Globe*, Aug. 24, 2010, retrieved Jan. 31, 2017, from archive.boston.com.

20. "FF," Autumn 1934; "Omansky in Akron to Visit Mother," *Akron (OH) Beacon Journal*, Dec. 25, 1935, 1; CBD, "World and All," *Lansing (MI) State Journal*, April 29, 1937, 8.

21. GWM to CR, Dec. 8, 1935; HFL, 1935 cartograph; "Bankhead Appointed," *Montreal Gazette*, June 17, 1933, 1; GWM to CR, undated, Dec. 8, 1935, May 19, 1936, and June 19, 1938; W. N., "California Boyhood," review of *Tree Toad* by RHD, *LAT*, Nov. 17, 1935, III-7; "Popular Veteran of US Embassy Col. Bankhead Leaving Ottawa," *Ottawa Journal*, May 29, 1948, 7. HFL's cartographs became a family tradition that she maintained after marrying and having children.

22. Jack, "America's Forgotten Regionalist," v, 8; "Papers of Jay Sigmund," finding aid, University of Iowa Libraries, Special Collections Department; Carlson, "Bard of the Wapsipinicon," unpaginated.

23. Dennis, "Grant Wood Works on Paper," 38; Herring, "Regional Modernism," 1; Philip Kennicott, "Wonderfully Queer World of 'American Gothic's' Grant Wood," *Washington Post*, March 2, 2018.

24. Frederic Newlin Price, "Making of an Artist," *Sun (Baltimore, MD)*, Jan. 20, 1935, Sunday Magazine Section, 6; "FF," *AW*, Sept.–Oct. 1935; Evans, *Grant Wood*, 195–96, 204, 207, 212–13, 354n204; Hommerding, "Gay as Any Gypsy Caravan," 391.

25. CJF, *Distant Prize*, unnumbered page; "FF," June–July and Sept.–Oct. 1935; M. Jagendorf to CJF, Nov. 22, 1935; CJF, "End of Act," *AW Quarterly*, Winter 1935, 33–35; CJF to WMS, Dec. 14, 1938.

26. "New Books Received," *Brooklyn Daily Eagle*, Nov. 6, 1936, 20; John C. Winston, "Twelve New Books I've Picked Out for 12 Good Children I Know," advertisement, *Chicago Tribune*, Dec. 5, 1936, 19; Agatha L. Shea, "Much Interest in Fiction for the Teen Ages," *Chicago Daily Tribune*, Dec. 12, 1936, 19; Wendell Phillips Dodge Jr., "Passed in Review," *Brooklyn Daily Eagle*, Jan. 9, 1937, 14; Grace R. Osgood, "'A Dog at His Heels,' by Charles J. Finger," *Washington Post*, March 3, 1937, 9; Anne T. Eaton, "New Books for Boys and Girls," Book Review, *NYT*, June 13, 1937, 10.

27. "Facts and Fun for Children," *LAT*, Nov. 1, 1936, III-8; John Selby, "Reading and Writing," *Corsicana (TX) Daily Sun*, Nov. 3, 1936, 2; "On Display in Good Book Week," *Garrett (IN) Clipper*, Nov. 5, 1936, 1; Houghton Mifflin, "By the Author of 'Green Light,'" advertisement, *LAT*, Nov. 15, 1936, IV, 2; Ellen Lewis Buell, "New Books for Boys and Girls," Book Review, *NYT*, Dec. 20, 1926, 11; "Ellen L. Buell, 84, a Times Editor," obituary, *NYT*, Nov. 1, 1989.

28. GGB, Jan. 8, 1927; JGF to CJF, Jan. 20 and Feb. 8, 1927; Frederic J. Haskin, "Answers to Questions," *Salt Lake (UT) Tribune*, Dec. 19, 1935, 34; "We Meet Our Publishers," *School and Home*, Dec. 1936, 52; JGF, *Autobiography*, 391, 395; Johnson, *Fierce Solitude*, 218–22; Ben Johnson, "John Gould Fletcher (1886–1950)," retrieved Feb. 6, 2013, from Encyclopedia of Arkansas, encyclopediaofarkansas.net.

29. Lockie Parker to CJF, Jan. 17, Feb. 3, March 10 and 21, 1936; Howard Simon to HFL, March 1, 1936.

30. Shores, "Published Works."

31. Irene Carlisle, "Finger Is Noted Literary Figure," *FD,* June 11, 1936, B8.

32. "Lansing Woman's Story Is First in Collection of Prize-Winners," *State Journal (Lansing, MI),* Jan. 30, 1936, 13; "Gossip of the Book World," *LAT,* July 12, 1936, III-8; Ross Eugene Braught to CJF, May 20, 1936; Helen L. Hoke to CJF, June 21, 1936; CJF to Helen Hoke, June 24, 1936; CJF, "Out of Our Own West and Out of France," review of *The Shadow of Half Moon Pass* by E. M. Baker et al., "Books," *NYHT,* Nov. 15, 1936, 10.

33. "CJF Recordings," catalog records, June 5, 1937, retrieved July 1, 2018, from Library of Congress Online Catalog, loc.gov; CJF to Ross Braught, carbon, Aug. 11, 1937; Winik, "Charles J. Finger: Gallant Rogue or Hidden Folklorist?".

34. Barbara Nolen to CJF, May 14, 1937; Ulrich, *Periodicals Directory,* 107; "Book World," *LAT,* June 27, 1937, III-8.

35. "*Chimney-sweep Tower,*" review of *Chimney-sweep Tower* by Rita Kissin and HFL, illus., *Kirkus,* Sept. 23, 1937; "Juvenile with Historic Setting," review of *Chimney-sweep Tower* by Rita Kissin and HFL, illus., *LAT,* Oct. 10, 1937, III-8.

36. RHD, "Crusade of the Trail," *Newark Evening News,* Jan. 19, 1937, photocopy of clipping; Uncle Walt [pseud.], "Ozark Moon," *FD,* Oct. 13, 1936, 2; Gilstrap, "To Remembered Happiness," 16.

37. "Topics of Tucson," *ADS,* Jan. 5, 1937, 12; GWM to CR; "Dies in California," *EEN,* Nov. 9, 1940, 2.

38. William G. King, "Book of the Day," review of *Valiant Vagabonds* by CJF, *New York Sun,* Nov. 25, 1936; Jane Archer, "Books of the Moment," *Salem (OR) Capital Journal,* Dec. 12, 1936, Five Star Weekly Section, 2; Forgotten Men," *LAT,* Jan. 24, 1937, III-10; Bernice Cosulich, "Literary Lantern," *ADS,* May 30, 1937, Home News Section, 3; Locke, *Ocean,* 18; Gardner, *Reviewing the South,* 31–32.

39. RHD, "Bob Davis Reveals," *Shiner (TX) Gazette,* March 4, 1937, 2.

40. GWM to CR; CJF to WMS, Dec. 20, 1936, and Dec. 14, 1938; CJF, "Strange Folks," review of *Death Valley Prospectors* by Dane Coolidge, "Books," *NYHT,* Feb. 7, 1937, 18.

41. "Society, Church Music and Club Activities in Battle Creek," *EEN,* Aug. 20, 1937, 6; "Speaker Bankhead at Ottawa," *Montreal Gazette,* July 15, 1936, 15; "For Rent," *Ottawa Journal,* April 19, 1941, 30; Paul Harrison, "In New York," *Dunkirk (NY) Evening Observer,* Jan. 29, 1934, 6; "Woman's Realm," *Ottawa Journal,* July 20, 1934, 8; AP, "House Elects Bankhead to Succeed Byrns," *St. Louis Post-Dispatch,* June 4, 1936, 1; "Bankhead Named Speaker in US," *Ottawa Journal,* June 4, 1936, 1.

42. "Famous Artist Seeks Site for Artist Colony," *Easton (MD) Star-Democrat,* Oct. 11, 1935, 4; "Heads Elected by Collumni Club," *DFP,* Feb. 19, 1938, 10.

43. GWM to CR, undated and Dec. 8, 1935; CR to GWM, April 21, 1936, Sept. 13 and Nov. 7, 1937.

44. "Student Alumni Loan Exhibit at UA This Week," *NWAT,* Oct. 19, 1937, 3.

45. Record for death of Christopher Ferguson, San Francisco Area Funeral Home Records; record for death of Alice May Finger, Arkansas Death Index; Evans, *Grant Wood*, 297; "Mrs. Louis Steiger Leaves $22,000," *Brooklyn Daily Eagle*, Jan. 16, 1938, 13; CJF to Hubert, Jan. 29, 1938.

46. Royal L. Gard to Jose Diaz Miro, letter of introduction for CJF, Dec. 20, 1937. Richard and Elizabeth Cox led the annual cruises, and Ann Coyle Maddox was a chaperone on the 1938 cruise. ("Ann Maddox," *Tammy Howl*, May 29, 1939, 30; "Mrs. Roy Brockman and Daughter on Caribbean Cruise," *Daily Courier-Gazette [McKinney, TX]*, March 28, 1941, 2.)

47. "Personal Mention," *NWAT*, Oct. 30, 1937, 2.

48. CJF, *Give a Man*, 168, 176, 336–37.

49. "Modiste Says His Wife Made Men a Career," *Daily News (New York, NY)*, Oct. 30, 1941, Queens/Brooklyn/Long Island Section, 4.

50. Bronski, *Queer History*, 124.

51. GWM, "Ode to the Majujah."

52. Someone eventually returned this book to Gayeta. (Leflar, "Charles J. & Helen Finger Works.")

Chapter 14

1. Kenneth C. Ripley to CJF, Oct. 1, 1938; CBD, "New York Day by Day," *Bryan (TX) Daily Eagle*, Nov. 15, 1938, 4; CBD, "New York Day by Day," Jan. 20, 1941, photocopy.

2. Record for Jacob Omansky, 1930 USFC; "Newlyweds Stop in Akron on Honeymoon," *Akron (OH) Beacon Journal*, March 18, 1937, 14; CBD, "World and All," *Lansing (MI) State Journal*, April 29, 1937, 8; CBD, "High Notes from a Hog Caller," *EEN*, March 13, 1938, 18; Winchell, "On Broadway," *Democrat and Chronicle (Rochester, NY)*, June 21, 1938, 14; CBD, "New York Day by Day," *Kane (PA) Republican*, July 11, 1938, 4.

3. Record for John Stevenson, Petition for Naturalization, New York, State and Federal Naturalization Records; Testimony by John J. Crawley in Supreme Court of the State of New York, Appellate Division—First Department, William H. Wise & Co., Inc., Plaintiff-Appellant, against Doubleday Doran & Company Inc. and Literary Guild of America Inc., Defendants-Respondents, 573.

4. Stern, *Memoirs*, 224; "Stricken Riding in Park," *St. Louis Post-Dispatch*, Dec. 12, 1938, 10; AP, "Newspaper Executive Dies on Horseback Ride," *Sun (Baltimore, MD)*, Dec. 12, 1938, 2; CBD, "New York Day by Day," *Indianapolis Star*, Dec. 26, 1938, 14; CBD, "New York Day by Day," *San Bernardino Sun*, Jan. 1, 1939, 20; Stern, *Memoirs*, 250.

5. "Junior Literary Guild Books at Library," *Racine (WI) Journal-Times*, Oct. 1, 1938, 13; "Virginibus Puerisque," *SR*, Nov. 19, 1938, 21; "Verse Volume Is Frank Work," *Ogden (UT) Standard-Examiner*, Nov. 27, 1938, 13; "New Books in

Library Listed," *Santa Ana (CA) Daily Register*, Dec. 29, 1938, 4; "Calumet City Library Gets Long List of Kiddies Books," *Hammond (IN) Times*, March 27, 1939, 3; "New Books for the Children Received," *Kossuth County (IA) Advance*, April 18, 1939, 6.

6. CJF to HCP, March 1 and Oct. 31, 1939; "National PTA to Meet April 30 in Cincinnati," *Daily Messenger (Canandaigua, NY)*, March 21, 1939, 3; Ethel C. Simpson, "Charles Joseph Finger (1867–1941)," Nov. 13, 2013, retrieved July 7, 2018, from Encyclopedia of Arkansas, encyclopediaofarkansas.net.

7. AP, "Dr. Frank Luther Mott Wins Pulitzer Prize of $1,000 for His History," *Iowa City Press-Citizen*, May 1, 1939, 1.

8. "Mrs. Alice S. Bankhead," obituary, *Miami (FL) News*, Sept. 5, 1938, 14; "Fresh Off the Palette," *DFP*, March 26, 1939, Part 3, 17; CJF to JGF, April 8, 1939; CJF to JGF, May 3 and June 16, 1939; "Cecil Art Week Nov. 4–8," *Journal (Wilmington, DE)*, Oct. 19, 1939, 14; GWM to CR; AP, "Bankhead in Miami," *Palm Beach (FL) Post*, April 17, 1940, 9.

9. CJF to WMS, June 16, 1939.

10. CJF, *Golden Tales*, 1–2, 90, 109, 160, 171.

11. Alfred D. Moore to CJF, June 30 and July 28, 1937; CJF to RHD, June 6, 1939, and RHD to CJF, June 16, 1939, carbon copy, RHD Papers; CJF to WMS, June 16, 1939; "Death Comes to Author, Musician," *CE*, Jan. 9, 1941, 11, photocopy.

12. Murrow, *This Is London*, 31–33, 61–64.

13. Shores, "Library."

14. Ruth Ayers, "Blackout," *NWAT*, Jan. 5, 1940, 6.

15. Murrow, *This Is London*, 70–72.

16. "Golden Tales from Far Away," *Kirkus*, April 15, 1940.

17. CJF to JGF.

18. Robert B. Cochran, "Vance Randolph (1892–1980)," June 7, 2013, retrieved July 6, 2018, from Encyclopedia of Arkansas, encyclopediaofarkansas.net.

19. JGF to CJF, undated and May 7, 1940; CJF, "Sketch of the Arkansas Country," review of *The Arkansas* by Clyde Brion Davis, "Books," *NYHT*, May 26, 1940, 2; CJF to JGF; Clyde Brion Davis, "Something Special in Missouri," review of *An Ozark Anthology* edited by Vance Randolph, *SR*, June 22, 1940, 15.

20. Murrow, *This Is London*, 97–98, 103–04, 112–14, 116–17, 123–24.

21. CJF to JGF.

22. Haas and Lovitz, *Carl Sandburg*, 139–40.

23. "Villard Quits the Nation," *NYT*, June 28, 1940, 11; Oswald Garrison Villard to CJF, July 9, 1940.

24. David Shedden, "Today in Media History: Edward R. Murrow Describes the Bombing of London in 1940," retrieved Feb. 9, 2017, from the Poynter Institute, poynter.org; Murrow, *This Is London*, 149–50.

25. JGF, "Squire of Gayeta," *SR*, July 12, 1941, 3–4, 16.

26. West End at War, retrieved Feb. 9, 2017, from westendatwar.org.uk.

27. Record for CJF, United States of America Declaration of Intent, Nov. 26, 1940.

28. "Programs on Air," *NWAT*, Oct. 26, 1940, 4, Nov. 1, 1940, 5, and Dec. 5, 1940, 10.

29. HFL, "Autobiography," 8–16; AP, "Anglo-Spanish Financial Plan Gives Great Britain Diplomatic Victory over the Berlin Axis," *NWAT*, Dec. 2, 1940, 1; AP, "Lurid Story of Raid on Bristol Told in Letter," *NWAT*, Dec. 5, 1940, 7; AP, "British Claim to Have Cut behind Italian Army near Sidi Barrani, Farthest Invasion Point in Egypt," *NWAT*, Dec. 10, 1940, 1.

30. GWM to CR, Nov. 1, 1941.

31. GWM to RHD, April 18, 1930; GWM, "Ode to the Majujah"; GWM to CJF.

32. Gifford, *Dayneford's Library*, 83; Haley, *Wolf*, 196–97.

33. Find a Grave Index.

34. Murrow, *This Is London*, 228–30; "Radical Social," *PM*, March 14, 1889, 145; "San Angelo Music School," advertisement, *SAP*, Dec. 31, 1902, 7; "S. A. M. S.—The New Year's Reception," *SAP*, Jan. 7, 1903, 6; "Notice to the Public," advertisement, *RB*, Dec. 27, 1916, 4; CJF, "An Now, 1927," *AW* Jan. 1927 inside cover.

35. CJF, *Golden Tales*, 15–16.

36. AP, "Bomb Shelter at Savoy Where Newsmen Go for Safety Contrasts Sharply with Those They Write About," *NWAT*, Jan. 1, 1941, 4; AP, "United States Faces 'Foreign Peril' and Must 'Increase Armaments' for Defense and Use of 'Democracies,'" *NWAT*, Jan. 6, 1941, 1; notice of delivery of an oxygen tank "for Mr. Chas J Finger (coronary occlusion)" at "2:30 P.M. Jan. 7th," handwritten note; telegrams from Hubert Finger, Herbert Finger, Kitty Helbling, Mr. and Mrs. Richard G. Cox, and GWM.

37. Gilstrap, "Remembered Happiness," 18.

38. "Charles J. Finger Funeral Rites Thursday at 3," *NWAT*, Jan. 8, 1941, 1, 7; "Charles J. Finger Buried Thursday," *NWT*, Jan. 10, 1941; JGF, "Charles J. Finger," *Answers*, March 1941, 2.

39. AP, "C. J. Finger, 71, Dies; Author of Juvenile Books," *NYHT*; "Charles J. Finger, 71, Author and Editor," *NYT*, Jan. 8, 1941, 19.

40. CBD, "New York Day by Day," Jan. 20, 1941, photocopy of clipping; CBD, "New York Day by Day," *Bryan (TX) Daily Eagle*, Jan. 27, 1941, 2.

41. "Gayeta Lodge Play at Mt. Zion School Tomorrow Evening," *FD*, Nov. 28, 1924, 1; "$50 Netted by Play for Mt. Zion Piano; Players Are Praised," *FD*, Dec. 1, 1924, 1, 6; John T. Appleby, "Charles J. Finger: An Appreciation," *Washington Post*, Feb. 2, 1941, L8; Lessie S. Read, "Round about Town," *NWAT*, Nov. 26, 1941, 14.

42. "Charles J. Finger," *PM*, January 1941, 4.

43. GGB, Jan. 20, 1941.

44. "Grand View Village Historian Dies," *Journal-News (White Plains, NY)*, Feb. 4, 1982, B5.

45. Mathias, *Amazing Bob Davis*, 17, 23–24, 48, 312–22; "News of Ex-Detroiter Paul Honore in Book," *DFP*, Sept. 24, 1944, 38.

Afterword

1. "Lake and Stream Anglers Have Equal Success with Bass," *Ottawa Journal*, June 17, 1941, 19; "Some of the New Books," *Ottawa Journal*, Aug. 23, 1941, 21; GWM to CR, Dec. 13, 1941.

2. RHD, "New Old Tales of Southern Duels and Duelists," *Courier-Journal (Louisville, KY)*, Feb. 24, 1942, Sect 1, 7; AP, "Roving Writer, Bob Davis, Dies." *Capital Journal (Salem, OR)*, Oct. 12, 1942, 8.

3. "President and Mrs. Cox Pay Tribute to Bob Davis," *Tammy Howl*, Nov. 20, 1942, 3; "Robert Hobart Davis Papers," finding aid, retrieved Feb. 22, 2015, from NYPL, archives.nypl.org.

4. GGB, Nov. 27, 1949; "Personals," *NWAT*, Dec. 1, 1949, 3; GWM to CR, June 10, 1953.

5. "Paul Honore, Painter, Dies," *Philadelphia Inquirer*, April 14, 1956, 14; AP, "Col. Bankhead Dies at Home; Funeral Today," *Montgomery (AL) Advertiser*, Oct. 27, 1957, 1.

6. "Certificates Presented to 93 at Normal," *Shreveport (LA) Times*, June 22, 1941, 28; GWM to CR, Oct. 15, 1946, and Jan. 12, 1957; "Red Cross Needs Workers for Recreation Program," *Tucson Daily Citizen*, Nov. 27, 1967, 9.

7. "Funeral Notices," *Tucson Daily Citizen*, March 27, 1971, 16, March 31, 1971, 46; "Public Records," *ADS*, March 17, 1994, 11.

8. Katharine Murdoch Davis, "Interesting Arkansas People," *AG Sunday Magazine*, Dec. 10, 1939, 3, 15; "Classified Ads," *NWAT*, Jan. 6, 1941, 5.

9. "Personal Mention," *NWAT*, Aug. 3, 1943, 3; Bottoms, *World War II Records*, 1; "Help Wanted," *NWAT*, April 13, 1943, 5.

10. AP, "Merchant Ship Named for Charles Finger," *NWAT*, Jan. 29, 1944, 1; "Merchant Ship Named for Deceased Novelist," *CE*, Feb. 10, 1944, 6; "Bankheads at Sea," editorial reprinted from the *Birmingham News*, *Anniston (AL) Star*, Nov. 21, 1943, 4.

11. "Personal Mention," *NWAT*, Feb. 7, 1944, 3; "Tea to Honor John Gould Fletchers," *NWAT*, June 17, 1944, 3.

12. "Final Program at Middletown," *Chester (PA) Times*, April 10, 1941, 25; Miller, "Phyllis Reid Fenner," 66–67.

13. Leflar and Leflar, "*Recollections*," 69–70, 110–11; Revis Edmonds, "Robert Allen Leflar (1901–1997)," May 24, 2018, retrieved July 9, 2018, from Encyclopedia of Arkansas, encyclopediaofarkansas.net.

14. "Farm implements," advertisement, *NWAT*, March 18, 1947, 10; "Airedale pups," advertisement, *NWAT*, May 26, 1947, 8; "Mt. Zion Home Demonstration Club," *NWAT*, Dec. 14, 1948, 3; "Fayetteville Garden Club," *NWAT*, June 12, 1950, 2; "St. Paul's Episcopal Church," *NWAT*, April 26, 1952, 2; GGB, Aug. 8, 1949; HFL, "Guest Book," 23.

15. "Fifteen Years Ago," *NWAT*, April 20, 1972, 4; "Mrs. Finger Dies in Springdale," *NWAT*, Nov. 27, 1965, 3.

WORKS CITED

Aldrich, Robert. *Colonialism and Homosexuality*. London and New York: Routledge, 2003.

Alpern, Sara. *Freda Kirchwey, A Woman of the Nation*. Cambridge, MA: Harvard University Press, 1987.

American Battle Monuments Commission. *81st Division, Summary of Operations in the World War*. Vol. 3. Washington, DC: US Government Printing Office, 1944.

Amiel, Henri-Fréderic, and Mary Augusta Ward, trans. *Amiel's Journal: The Journal Intime of Henri-Fréderic Amiel*. New York: A. L. Burt, 1885; Project Gutenberg, 2005, unpaginated.

Anderson, Vicki. *The Dime Novel in Children's Literature*. Jefferson, NC: McFarland, 2005.

Ansel, Bernard D. "European Adventurer in Tierra del Fuego: Julio Popper." *Hispanic American Historical Review* 50, no. 1 (February 1970): 89–110.

Arreola, Daniel D. *Postcards from the Sonora Border: Visualizing Place through a Popular Lens, 1900s–1950s*. Tucson: University of Arizona Press, 2017.

Austen, Roger. *Playing the Game: The Homosexual Novel in America*. Indianapolis, IN: Bobbs-Merrill, 1977.

Austen, Roger. "Stoddard's Little Tricks in *South Sea Idyls*." In *Literary Visions of Homosexuality*, edited by Stuart Kellogg, 73–81. New York: Haworth Press, 1983.

Barkun, Michael. *Religion and the Racist Right: The Origins of the Christian Identity Movement*. Rev. ed. Chapel Hill: University of North Carolina Press, 1997.

Barrett, Robert Le Moyne, and Katharine Ellis Barrett. *A Yankee in Patagonia; Edward Chase*. Boston and New York: Houghton Mifflin Company; Cambridge, UK: Riverside Press, 1931.

Bax, E. Belfort. "A Free Fantasia on Things Divine and Human." *To-day*, no. 59 (October 1888): 101–13.

Belloc, Hilaire. *First and Last*. London: Methuen, 1911.

Belloc, Hilaire. *On Everything*. New York: E. P. Dutton, 1910.

Bender, Bert. *Sea-Brothers: The Tradition of American Sea Fiction from "Moby-Dick" to the Present*. Philadelphia: University of Pennsylvania Press, 1988.

Bergman, David. *Gay American Autobiography: Writings from Whitman to Sedaris*. Madison: University of Wisconsin Press, 2009.

Berman, Paul. Introduction to *Martin Eden*, by Jack London. New York: Modern
    Library, 2002.

Black, Barbara J. *A Room of His Own: A Literary-Cultural Study of Victorian
    Clubland*. Athens: Ohio University Press, 2012.

Blevins, Brooks. *Arkansas/Arkansaw: How Bear Hunters, Hillbillies, and Good Ol'
    Boys Defined a State*. Fayetteville: University of Arkansas Press, 2009.

Blotner, Joseph. *Faulkner: A Biography*. 3 vols. New York: Random House, 1974.

Borgeaud, Philippe, and Kathleen Atlass and James Redfield, trans. *The Cult of Pan
    in Ancient Greece*. Chicago: University of Chicago Press, 1988.

Boswell, David. "Frank Brangwyn and His Patrons." In *Frank Brangwyn, 1867–1956*,
    by Libby Horner and Gillian Naylor, 156–85. Leeds, UK: Leeds Museum and
    Galleries, 2007.

Bottoms, Daryl, comp. *World War II Records in the Cartographic and Architectural
    Branch of the National Archives*. Reference Information Paper 79. Washington,
    DC: National Archives and Records Administration, 1992.

Bozorth, Richard R. *Auden's Games of Knowledge: Poetry and the Meanings of
    Homosexuality*. New York: Columbia University Press, 2001.

Bragdon, Claude. *More Lives Than One*. New York: A. A. Knopf, 1938.

Braim, Paul F. *The Test of Battle: The American Expeditionary Forces in the Meuse–
    Argonne Campaign*. Newark: University of Delaware Press, 1987.

Brake, Laurel. "The Deaths of Heroes: Biography, Obits and the Discourse of
    the Press, 1890–1900." In *Life Writing and Victorian Culture*, edited by David
    Amigoni, 165–94. Hants, UK; and Burlington, VT: Ashgate, 2006.

Brake, Laurel. *Print in Transition, 1850–1910: Studies in Media and Book History*.
    New York: Palgrave, 2001.

Brake, Laurel, Ed King, Roger Luckhurst, and James Mussell, eds. *W. T. Stead:
    Newspaper Revolutionary*. London: British Library, 2012.

Brierton, Peggy, William J. Smith, and Steven L. Wright. "Over There, Over
    Here: Cincinnatians and the Great War." *Queen City Heritage* 56, no. 4 (Winter
    1998): 13.

Bristow, Nancy K. *American Pandemic: The Lost Worlds of the 1918 Influenza
    Epidemic*. New York: Oxford University Press, 2012.

Brodie, Fawn M. *The Devil Drives: A Life of Sir Richard Burton*. New York: W. W.
    Norton, 1967.

Bronski, Michael. *A Queer History of the United States*. Boston: Beacon Press,
    2011.

Brooks, Lindsay. *Henry Somerfield, 1867–1939*. Walsall, UK: E. M. Flint Gallery,
    1984, unpaginated.

Brown, Tony. Introduction to *Edward Carpenter and Late Victorian Radicalism*,
    edited by Tony Brown, 1–16. London: Cass, 1990.

Bruccoli, Matthew J. *The Fortunes of Mitchell Kennerley, Bookman*. San Diego:
    Harcourt Brace Jovanovich, 1986.

Bruhm, Steven. "Roderick Random's Closet." *English Studies in Canada* 19 (December 1993): 401–15.

Bryan, Ford R. *Henry's Lieutenants*. Detroit, MI: Wayne State University, 2003.

Buckton, Oliver S. *Cruising with Robert Louis Stevenson: Travel, Narrative, and the Colonial Body*. Athens: Ohio University Press, 2007.

Buckton, Oliver S. *Secret Selves: Confession and Same-Sex Desire in Victorian Autobiography*. Chapel Hill: University of North Carolina Press, 1998.

Burmeister, H. "Annals of the Museum of Buenos Ayres." *Nature* 42, no. 1082 (July 24, 1890): 293–94.

Burrow, Merrick. "Queer Clubs and Queer Trades: G. K. Chesterton, Homosociality and the City." In *G. K. Chesterton, London and Modernity*, edited by Matthew Beaumont and Matthew Ingleby, 113–34. London: Bloomsbury Academic, 2013.

Byrns, Robert E. "Tom McCloskey: The Arc Light Saloon and the McCloskey Monument." In *Historical Montage of Tom Green County*, by Tom Green County Historical Society, 52–56. San Angelo, TX: Anchor Publishing Company, 1987.

Cabell, James Branch. *Beyond Life: Dizain des Demiurges*. New York: Johnson Reprint Corp., [1927] 1970.

Cady, Harrison. "Art Comes to Cape Ann." In *Artists of the Rockport Art Association: A Pictorial Record of the Oldest Art Association on Cape Ann, with an Historical Sketch on the Rockport Art Colony by Harrison Cady*, by Kitty Parsons Recchia and Rockport Art Association, 7–12. Rockport, MA: Rockport Art Association, 1940.

Camann, Mark David. "David Guion's Vision for a Musical Americana." PhD diss. University of Texas, Austin, 2010.

Canaday, Margot. *The Straight State: Sexuality and Citizenship in Twentieth-Century America*. Princeton, NJ: Princeton University Press, 2009.

Cannadine, David. *Victorious Century: The United Kingdom, 1800–1906*. New York: Viking, 2017.

Carlson, Allan C. "Bard of the Wapsipinicon: An Assessment of Jay G. Sigmund." *Modern Age* 55, no. 4 (Fall 2013): 31–46.

Carlson, Paul H. *Texas Woollybacks: The Range Sheep and Goat Industry*. College Station: Texas A&M University Press, [1982] 2016.

Carman, Ezra Ayers, Hubert A. Heath, and John Minto. *Special Report on the History and Present Condition of the Sheep Industry of the United States*. Washington, DC: US Department of Agriculture, Bureau of Animal Industry, 1893. United States congressional serial set no. 3124, Mis. Doc., no. 105.

Carpenter, Edward, ed. *Ioläus: An Anthology of Friendship*. Boston: Goodspeed, 1902.

Carpenter, Edward. *My Days and Dreams: Being Autobiographical Notes*. New York: Charles Scribner's Sons, 1916.

Carpenter, Frank George. *South America, Social, Industrial and Political*. New York: W. W. Wilson, 1900.

Casarino, Cesare. "The Sublime of the Closet: Or, Joseph Conrad's Secret Sharing." *boundary 2*, 24, no. 2 (Summer 1997): 199–243.

Chauncey Jr., George. "Christian Brotherhood or Sexual Perversion? Homosexual Identities and the Construction of Sexual Boundaries in the World War I Era." In *Hidden from History: Reclaiming the Gay and Lesbian Past*, edited by Martin Bauml Duberman, Martha Vicinus, and George Chauncey Jr., 294–317. New York: New American Library, 1989.

Chauncey, George. *Gay New York: Gender, Urban Culture, and the Making of the Gay Male World, 1890–1940*. New York: Basic Books, 1994.

Childs, Herbert. *El Jimmy, Outlaw of Patagonia*. Philadelphia and London: J. B. Lippincott, 1936.

Chudacoff, Howard P. *The Age of the Bachelor: Creating an American Subculture*. Princeton, NJ: Princeton University Press, 1999.

Coburn, Alvin Langdon. *Men of Mark*. London: Duckworth & Co.; New York: Mitchell Kennerley, 1913.

Cocks, H. G. *Nameless Offences: Homosexual Desire in the Nineteenth Century*. London: I. B. Tauris, 2003.

Cohen, Ed. *Talk on the Wilde Side: Toward a Genealogy of a Discourse on Male Sexualities*. New York: Routledge, 1993.

Colligan, Colette. "'A Race of Born Pederasts': Sir Richard Burton, Homosexuality, and the Arabs." *Nineteenth-Century Contexts* 25, no. 1 (2003): 1–20.

Collins, Joseph. *The Doctor Looks at Literature: Psychological Studies of Life and Letters*. New York: G. H. Doran, 1923.

Conrad, Joseph. *Heart of Darkness [and] The Secret Sharer*. New York: Signet Classic, 1983.

Conroy, Carolyn. "Mingling with the Ungodly: Simeon Solomon in Queer Victorian London." In *Sex, Time and Place: Queer Histories of London, c. 1850 to the Present*, edited by Simon Avery and Katherine M. Graham, 185–202. London and New York: Bloomsbury, 2016.

Cook, Matt. *London and the Culture of Homosexuality, 1885–1914*. Cambridge, UK; and New York: Cambridge University Press, 2003.

Cook, Thomas. *Cook's Handbook for London*. London: Thos. Cook & Son, Ludgate Circus, 1882.

Cooper, Anice Page. *Authors and Others*. Garden City, NY: Doubleday, Page, 1927; Freeport, NY: Books for Libraries Press, 1970.

Copley, Antony R. H. *A Spiritual Bloomsbury: Hinduism and Homosexuality in the Lives and Writings of Edward Carpenter, E. M. Forster, and Christopher Isherwood*. Lanham, MD: Lexington Books, 2006.

Cornick, Philip H. "Land Value Taxation in the Twentieth Century." *American Journal of Economics and Sociology* 15, no. 3 (April 1956): 307–14.

Crowley, John W. Editor's introduction to *Genteel Pagan: The Double Life of Charles Warren Stoddard*, by Roger Austen, xxv–xli. Amherst: University of Massachusetts Press, 1991.

Crowther, Hal. *An Infuriating American: The Incendiary Arts of H. L. Mencken.* Iowa City: University of Iowa Press, 2014.

Cruikshank, George. *The Loving Ballad of Lord Bateman.* London: Charles Tilt, 1839.

Cullum, George Washington, and Edward Singleton Holden. *Biographical Register of the Officers and Graduates of the US Military Academy at West Point, NY.* Boston: Houghton Mifflin, 1920.

Cunninghame Graham, Jean. *Gaucho Laird: The Life of R. B. "Don Robert" Cunninghame Graham.* Glasgow, KY: Long Riders' Guild Press, 2004.

Curle, Richard, ed. *W. H. Hudson's Letters to R. B. Cunninghame-Graham.* London: Golden Cockerel Press, 1941.

Dalton, C. T. "Wagon Yards." In *Historical Montage of Tom Green County*, by Tom Green County Historical Society, 15–19. San Angelo, TX: Anchor, 1987.

David, Mildred E. "Class and Gender Aspects of Higher Education in London: The origins of London Polytechnics." In *London Higher: The Establishment of Higher Education in London*, edited by Roderick Floud and Sean Glynn, 96–121. London and Atlantic Highlands, NJ: Athlone Press, 1998.

Davies, Laurence, and Gene M. Moore. *The Collected Letters of Joseph Conrad, Vol. 8, 1923–1924.* Cambridge, UK: Cambridge University Press, 2008.

Davis, Robert Hobart. *Man Makes His Own Mask.* New York: Huntington Press, 1932.

Davis, Robert Hobart. *Over My Left Shoulder: A Panorama of Men and Events, Burlesques and Tragedies, Cabbages and Kings and Sometimes W and Y.* New York: D. Appleton, 1926.

DeGruson, Gene. Introduction to *Dust*, by Marcet Haldeman-Julius and Emanuel Haldeman-Julius, unpaginated. Topeka, KS: Washburn University Center for Kansas Studies, 1992.

Dellamora, Richard. *Masculine Desire: The Sexual Politics of Victorian Aestheticism.* Chapel Hill: University of North Carolina Press, 1990.

D'Emilio, John, and Estelle B. Freedman. *Intimate Matters: A History of Sexuality in America.* New York: Harper & Row, 1988.

Dennis, James M. "Grant Wood Works on Paper: Cartooning One Way or the Other." In *Grant Wood's Studio: Birthplace of "American Gothic,"* edited by Jane C. Milosch, 35–48. Cedar Rapids, IA: Cedar Rapids Museum of Art; Munich and London: Prestel, 2005.

Dillard, Tom. *Statesmen, Scoundrels, and Eccentrics: A Gallery of Amazing Arkansans.* Fayetteville: University of Arkansas Press, 2010.

Dixie, Florence. *Across Patagonia.* New York: R. Worthington, 1881.

Driscoll, Charles B. *The Life of O. O. McIntyre.* New York: Greystone Press, 1938.

Dubourg, George. *The Violin*. London: R. Cocks, 1878.

Dynes, Wayne. *Homolexis: A Historical and Cultural Lexicon of Homosexuality*. New York: Gay Academic Union, 1985.

Dzwonkoski, Peter, ed. *American Literary Publishing Houses, 1900–1980: Trade and Paperback*. Detroit, MI: Gale Research, 1986.

Earle, David M. "Pulp Magazines and the Popular Press." In *The Oxford Critical and Cultural History of Modernist Magazines, Vol. 2, North America 1894–1960*, edited by Peter Brooker and Andrew Thacker, 197–216. New York: Oxford University Press, 2012.

Eddy, Jacalyn. *Bookwomen: Creating an Empire in Children's Book Publishing, 1919–1939*. Madison: University of Wisconsin Press, 2006.

Edmundson, William. *A History of the British Presence in Chile: From Bloody Mary to Charles Darwin and the Decline of British Influence*. New York: Palgrave Macmillan, 2009.

Edwards, Justin D. *Exotic Journeys: Exploring the Erotics of US Travel Literature, 1840–1930*. Hanover, NH: University Press of New England, 2001.

Egira. "Imri, Or the Bride of a Star: Part II." *Southern Literary Messenger* 6, no. 5 (May 1840): 326–28.

Eidenbach, Peter L. *Alamogordo*. Charleston, SC: Arcadia, 2010.

Elias, Robert H., ed. *Letters of Theodore Dreiser: A Selection*. 2 vols. Philadelphia: University of Pennsylvania Press, 1959.

Elledge, Jim. *Masquerade: Queer Poetry in America to the End of World War II*. Bloomington: Indiana University Press, 2004.

Ellis, William E. *Irvin S. Cobb: The Rise and Fall of an American Humorist*. Lexington: University Press of Kentucky, 2017.

Evans, R. Tripp. *Grant Wood: A Life*. New York: Alfred A. Knopf, 2010.

Fairholt, F. W. *Gog and Magog: The Giants in Guildhall; Their Real and Legendary History*. London: John Camden Hotten, 1859.

Findlay, Alexander George. *A Directory for the Navigation of the South Pacific Ocean*. 4th ed. London: Richard Holmes Laurie, 1877.

Finger, Charles J. "Adventures of Andrew Lang." *Century* 108, no. 3 (July 1924): 311–324.

Finger, Charles J. *The Affair at the Inn as Seen by Philo the Innkeeper and the Taxgatherer of Rome*. Orange, NJ: Lillian Newton & Wilbur Macey Stone, 1931; Camden, NJ: Haddon Craftsmen, 1937.

Finger, Charles J., ed. *The Choice of the Crowd*. Fayetteville, AR: Golden Horseman Press, 1922.

Finger, Charles J. "Ebro." *Reedy's Mirror* 29, no. 24 (June 10, 1920): 469–473, 482–483.

Finger, Charles J. "Eric." In *The Choice of the Crowd*, edited by Charles J. Finger, 39–66. Fayetteville, AR: Golden Horseman Press, 1922.

Finger, Charles J. "Evolution in Transportation." *Nation* 109, no. 2841 (Dec. 13, 1919): 744–45.

Finger, Charles J. *Henry David Thoreau: The Man Who Escaped from the Herd* [Little Blue Book no. 339]. Girard, KS: Haldeman-Julius, 1922.

Finger, Charles J. *Hints on Writing Short Stories* [Little Blue Book no. 326]. Girard, KS: Haldeman-Julius, 1922, e-book.

Finger, Charles J. "History Hath Its Lessons." *Electric Railway Journal* 54, no. 22 (Dec. 27, 1919): 1036–38.

Finger, Charles J. "Incongruity." *Smart Set* 61, no. 1 (January 1920): 65–75.

Finger, Charles J. Introduction to *Collected Works of Joseph Conrad, Vol. 1: "Almayer's Folly" [and] "The Inheritors."* Part 2, vii–x. New York: Doubleday, Page, 1925.

Finger, Charles J. Introduction to *Collected Works of Joseph Conrad*. Vol 2: vii–x. New York: Doubleday and Page, 1925.

Finger, Charles J. "The Lizard God," *Current Opinion* 70 (May 1921): 623–30.

Finger, Charles J. "The Lizard God." In *In Lawless Lands*, by Charles J. Finger, 200–25. New York: M. Kennerley, 1924.

Finger, Charles J. "London Johnny and the Claim-Jumpers: A Story of Tierra-Del-Fuego." Part 1. *PM* (Sept. 28, 1898): 118–19.

Finger, Charles J. *Mark Twain: The Philosopher Who Laughed at the World*. Little Blue Book no. 517. Girard, KS: Haldeman-Julius, 1924.

Finger, Charles J. "My Spottgeist." *Smart Set* 69, no. 2 (October 1922): 109–18.

Finger, Charles J., *Oscar Wilde in Outline* [Little Blue Book no. 442]. Girard, KS: Haldeman-Julius, 1923.

Finger, Charles J. *Seven Horizons*. Garden City, NY: Doubleday, Doran, 1930.

Finger, Charles J. "Some Mischievous Thing." *Smart Set* 61, no. 4 (April 1920): 119–26.

Finger, Charles J. *Tales from Silver Lands*. New York: Scholastic Book Services, 1972.

Finger, Charles J. "The Tooth." *Double Dealer* 1, no. 6 (June 1921): 221–26.

Finger, Charles J. "An Unrecognized Golden Age." *American Mercury* 19, no. 76 (April 1930): 406–13.

Finger, Charles J. *Valiant Vagabonds*. New York and London: D. Appleton-Century Company, 1936.

Finger, Charles J. "A Very Satisfactory God." *Double Dealer* 2, no. 8–9 (Aug.–Sept. 1921): 70–77.

Finger, Charles J., and Helen Finger, illus. *Adventure under Sapphire Skies*. New York: William M. Morrow, 1931.

Finger, Charles J., and Helen Finger, illus. *Footloose in the West: Being the Account of a Journey to Colorado and California and Other Western States*. New York: William Morrow, 1932.

Finger, Charles J., and Helen Finger, illus. *Golden Tales from Far Away*. Philadelphia: John C. Winston, 1940.

Finger, Charles J., ed., and Paul Honoré, illus. *Heroes from Hakluyt*. New York: Henry Holt, 1928.

Finger, Charles J., and Paul Honoré, illus. *Highwaymen: A Book of Gallant Rogues.*
New York: R. M. McBride, 1923.

Finger, Charles J., and Paul Honoré, illus. *The Spreading Stain: A Tale for Boys and
Men with Boys' Hearts.* Garden City, NJ: Doubleday, Page and Company, 1927.

Finger, Charles J., and Henry C. Pitz, illus. *The Distant Prize: A Book about Rovers,
Rangers and Rascals.* New York and London: D. Appleton-Century, 1935.

Finger, Charles J., and Henry C. Pitz, illus. *Give a Man a Horse.* Philadelphia:
John C. Winston, 1938.

Finger, Charles J., and Charles Morrow Wilson, eds., and Paul Honoré, illus. *Ozark
Fantasia.* Fayetteville, AR: Golden Horseman Press, 1927.

Finger, George. "A Single Tax Town." *Land and Freedom* 28, no. 1 (January–
February 1928): 12–13.

Flanagan, John T. "Reedy of the Mirror." *Missouri Historical Review* 43, no. 2
(January 1949): 128–44.

Fletcher, John Gould. *The Autobiography of John Gould Fletcher.* Fayetteville:
University of Arkansas, [1937] 1988.

Fodor's Travel. *London.* New York: Penguin Random House, 2016.

Fone, Byrne R. S. *A Road to Stonewall: Male Homosexuality and Homophobia in
English and American Literature, 1750–1969.* New York: Twayne, 1995.

Fone, Byrne R. S. "This Other Eden: Arcadia and the Homosexual Imagination."
In *Literary Visions of Homosexuality,* edited by Stuart Kellogg, 13–34. New York:
Haworth Press, 1983.

Forgue, Guy J., ed. *Letters of H. L. Mencken.* New York: Knopf, 1961.

Foy, Jessica H. "The Home Set to Music." In *The Arts and the American Home, 1890–
1930,* by Jessica H. Foy and Karal Ann Marling, 62–84. Knoxville: University of
Tennessee Press, 1994.

Frederick, John T. *William Henry Hudson.* New York: Twayne Publishers, 1972.

Fremantle, Anne Jackson. *The Protestant Mystics.* Boston: Little, Brown, 1964.

Furneaux, Holly. *Queer Dickens: Erotics, Families, Masculinities.* New York: Oxford
University Press, 2009.

Gair, Christopher. "Gender and Genre: Nature, Naturalism, and Authority in *The
Sea-Wolf.*" *Studies in American Fiction* 22, no. 2 (Autumn 1994): 131–47.

Galbraith Jr., R. C. *The History of the Chillicothe Presbytery, from Its Organization
in 1799 to 1889.* Chillicothe, OH: Committee on Publication Appointed by the
Presbytery, 1889.

Galbreath, C. B. "Claude Meeker as Member of the Kit-Kat Club, and the Ohio
State Archaeological and Historical Society." *Ohio History Journal* 40, no. 4
(October 1931): 600–12.

Galsworthy, John. *The Little Man and Other Stories.* New York: Charles Scribner's
Sons, 1915.

Gannett, Lewis Stiles, and Ruth Chrisman Gannett, illus. *Sweet Land.* Garden City,
NY: Doubleday, 1934.

Gardner, Sarah E. *Reviewing the South: The Literary Marketplace and the Southern Renaissance, 1920–1941*. Cambridge, UK; and New York: Cambridge University Press, 2017.

Gardner, Washington. *History of Calhoun County, Michigan*. Vol. 2. Chicago and New York: Lewis, 1913.

Garrison, William H. "Walt Whitman." *McBride's* 49 (May 1892): 623–26.

Garvey, Ellen Gruber. "Ambivalent Advertising: Books, Prestige, and the Circulation of Publicity." In *Print in Motion: The Expansion of Publishing and Reading in the United States, 1880–1940*, edited by Carl F. Kaestle and Janice A. Radway, 170–89. Chapel Hill: University of North Carolina Press, 2009.

Geddes, Norman Bel. *Miracle in the Evening: An Autobiography*. Garden City, NY: Doubleday, 1960.

Gertz, Elmer. *Odyssey of a Barbarian: The Biography of George Sylvester Viereck*. Buffalo, NY: Prometheus Books, 1978.

Gifford, James. *Dayneford's Library: American Homosexual Writing, 1900–1913*. Amherst: University of Massachusetts Press, 1995.

Gilstrap, Marguerite. "To Remembered Happiness." *Flashback* 31, no. 1 (February 1981): 10–18.

Glass, Loren, *Authors, Inc.: Literary Celebrity in the Modern United States, 1880–1980*. New York: New York University Press, 2004.

Glynn, Sean. "The Establishment of Higher Education in London: A Survey." In *London Higher: The Establishment of Higher Education in London*, edited by Roderick Floud and Sean Glynn, 1–35. London and Atlantic Highlands, NJ: Athlone Press, 1998.

Goodridge, Paul F. *William Brockman Bankhead: Speaker of the House of Representatives, United States Congress, 1936–1940: The Bankhead Family Heritage*. New York: Page, 2015.

Goodway, David. *Anarchist Seeds beneath the Snow: Left-Libertarian Thought and British Writers from William Morris to Colin Ward*. Liverpool, UK: Liverpool University Press, 2006.

Graham, Ian. *Herbert Brenon: An American Cinema Odyssey*. Kindle edition, 2016, unpaginated.

Green, Roger Lancelyn. *Mrs. Molesworth*. London: Bodley Head, 1961; New York: Walck, 1964.

Greene, Harlan. *The Damned Don't Cry, They Just Disappear: The Life and Works of Harry Hervey*. Columbia: University of South Carolina Press, 2018.

Gregory, Horace, and Marya Zaturenska. *A History of American Poetry, 1900–1940*. New York: Harcourt, Brace, [1942] 1946.

Guion, David W. "Sail Away for the Rio Grande." Four-part chorus, Octavo no. 9460. New York: G. Schirmer, [1925] 1945.

Gunn, Drewey Wayne. *Gay American Novels, 1870–1970: A Reader's Guide*. Jefferson, NC: McFarland, 2016.

Gunn, John W. "John W. Gunn Visits Charles J. Finger." *Life and Letters* 1, no. 9 (May 1923): 1–4.

Gunn, John. "Recent Exploration in Tierra del Fuego." *Scottish Geographical Magazine* 4, no. 6 (June 1888): 319–26.

Gunther, Gerald. *Learned Hand: The Man and the Judge.* New York: Alfred A. Knopf, 1994.

Haas, Joseph, and Gene Lovitz. *Carl Sandburg: A Pictorial Biography.* New York: Putnam, 1967.

Hagen, Lyman B. "*The New Yorker.*" In *American Literary Magazines: The Twentieth Century,* edited by Edward E. Chielens, 214–20. Westport, CT: Greenwood Press, 1992.

Haldeman-Julius, E. *The First Hundred Million.* New York: Arno Press, 1928.

Haldeman-Julius, E. *My Second Twenty-Five Years: Instead of a Footnote, An Autobiography.* Girard, KS: Haldeman-Julius Publications, 1949; New York: Arno Press, 1974.

Haley, James L. *Wolf: The Lives of Jack London.* New York: Basic Books, 2010.

Hall, Clayton Colman. *Baltimore: Biography.* Baltimore: Lewis, 1912.

Hamburger, Robert. *Two Rooms: The Life of Charles Erskine Scott Wood.* Lincoln: University of Nebraska Press, 1998.

Hamilton, Sharon. "American Manners: *The Smart Set* (1900–29); *American Parade* (1926)." In *The Oxford Critical and Cultural History of Modernist Magazines, Vol. 2, North America 1894–1960,* edited by Peter Brooker and Andrew Thacker, 224–48. New York: Oxford University Press, 2012.

Hansen, Harry. "These Literary Lobbies." *North American Review* 230, no. 2 (August 1930): 162–68.

Harpham, Geoffrey Galt. *One of Us: The Mastery of Joseph Conrad.* Chicago: University of Chicago Press, 1996.

Harrison, Barbara. "May Massee." In *Notable American Women: The Modern Period: A Biographical Dictionary,* edited by Barbara Sicherman, 462–64. Cambridge, MA: Harvard University Press, 1980.

Hart-Davis, Rupert. *Hugh Walpole, A Biography.* New York: Macmillan, 1952.

Hart-Davis, Rupert. *The Letters of Oscar Wilde.* New York: Harcourt, Brace & World, 1962.

Hatcher, John Bell, and William Berryman Scott. *Reports of the Princeton University Expeditions to Patagonia, 1896–1899, Vol. 3, Zoology.* Princeton, NJ: Princeton University, 1911.

Herder, Dale M. "American Values and Popular Culture in the Twenties: The Little Blue Books." *Historical Papers* 6, no. 1 (1971): 289–99.

Herring, Scott. "Regional Modernism: A Reintroduction." Abstract. *MFS Modern Fiction Studies* 55, no. 1 (Spring 2009): 1–10.

Hill, Luther B. *A History of the State of Oklahoma.* Vol. 2. Chicago and New York: Lewis, 1909.

Hilton, George Woodman, and John F. Due. *The Electric Interurban Railways in America*. 2nd printing. Stanford, CA: Stanford University Press, 1960, 1964.

Hoag, J. J. *San Francisco Blue Book and Club Directory*. San Francisco, CA: Smith-Hoag, 1919.

Hobson Jr., Fred C. *Serpent in Eden: H. L. Mencken and the South*. Baton Rouge: Louisiana State University Press, 1974.

Hodges, R. R. "Deep Fellowship: Homosexuality and Male Bonding in the Life and Fiction of Joseph Conrad." *Journal of Homosexuality* 4, no. 4 (Summer 1979): 379–93.

Hodgins, Bruce W., and Gwyneth Hoyle. *Canoeing North into the Unknown: A Record of River Travel, 1874–1974*. Toronto: Natural Heritage/Natural History, 1994.

Hodgson, J. B., and G. Stamp. *Guide to the Philip H. Cornick Papers, 1922–1971*. Ithaca, NY: Cornell University Library, Division of Rare and Manuscript Collections, 1974.

Hodowanec, George V., ed. *The May Massee Collection: Creative Publishing for Children, 1923–1963: A Checklist*. Emporia, KS: William Allen White Library, Emporia State University, 1979.

Hoffman, Frederick J., Charles Allen, and Carolyn F. Ulrich. *The Little Magazine: A History and Bibliography*. Princeton, NJ: Princeton University Press, 1946.

Hogg, Ethel Mary. *Quintin Hogg: A Biography*. London: Archibald Constable, 1906.

Holditch, W. Kenneth. "William Faulkner and Other Famous Creoles." In *Faulkner and His Contemporaries*, edited by Joseph R. Urbo and Ann J. Abadie, 21–39. Jackson: University Press of Mississippi, 2004.

Hommerding, Christopher. "As Gay as Any Gypsy Caravan: Grant Wood and the Queer Pastoral at the Stone City Art Colony." *Annals of Iowa* 74, no. 4 (Fall 2015): 378–412.

Horner, Libby. "Biography." In *Frank Brangwyn, 1867–1956*, by Libby Horner and Gillian Naylor, 24–49. Leeds, UK: Leeds Museum and Galleries, 2007.

Horner, Libby, and Gillian Naylor. *Frank Brangwyn, 1867–1956*. Leeds, UK: Leeds Museum and Galleries, 2007.

Howard Payne College. *Twelfth Annual Catalogue, 1901–1902*. Brownwood, TX: Howard Payne College, 1901.

Howe, M. A. DeWolfe. *Memoirs of the Harvard Dead in the War against Germany*. Vol. 2. Cambridge, MA: Harvard University Press, 1921.

Humes, Dollena Joy. *Oswald Garrison Villard, Liberal of the 1920s*. Syracuse, NY: Syracuse University Press, 1960.

Huneker, James Gibbons. *Ivory, Apes, and Peacocks*. New York: Sagamore Press, 1957.

Hurley, Natasha. *Circulating Queerness: Before the Gay and Lesbian Novel*. Minneapolis: University of Minnesota Press, 2018.

Hurley, Natasha. "The Queer Traffic in Literature; or, Reading Anthologically." *ESC* 36, no. 1 (March 2010): 81–108.

Hyde, H. Montgomery. *The Cleveland Street Scandal*. New York: Coward, McCann & Geoghegan, 1976.

Hyde, H. Montgomery. *The Love That Dared Not Speak Its Name: A Candid History of Homosexuality in Britain*. Boston: Little, Brown, 1970.

Hydrographic Office [of the] Admiralty. *The South American Pilot*. Part II, 9th ed. London: Hydrographic Office, 1895.

Hynes, Samuel. "The Art of Telling: An Introduction to Conrad's Tales." In *The Complete Short Fiction of Joseph Conrad: The Stories*, edited by Samuel Hynes, III: xi–xviii. Hopewell, NJ: Ecco, 1992.

Illinois College. *Catalogue of Illinois College*. Jacksonville: Illinois College, 1905.

Imko, Victor. "Pan and 'Homosexual Panic' in Turn of the Century Gothic Literature." *Chrestomathy: Annual Review of Undergraduate Research* 12 (2013): 1–29.

Insight Guides. *England*. London: APA, [2000] 2010.

Izbicki, John. "The London Polytechnics." In *London Higher: The Establishment of Higher Education in London*, edited by Roderick Floud and Sean Glynn, 199–222. London and Atlantic Highlands, NJ: Athlone Press, 1998.

Jack, Zachary Michael. "America's Forgotten Regionalist: Jay G. Sigmund." In *The Plowman Sings: The Essential Fiction, Poetry, and Drama of America's Forgotten Regionalist, Jay G. Sigmund*, edited by Zachary Michael Jack, 1–16. Lanham, MD: University Press of America, 2008.

Jeffs, W. P. "'Man's Words' and Manly Comradeship: Language, Politics, and Homosexuality in Walt Whitman's Works." *Journal of Homosexuality* 23, no. 4 (1992): 19–41.

Johnson III, Ben F. *Fierce Solitude: A Life of John Gould Fletcher*. Fayetteville: University of Arkansas Press, 1994.

Johnson, David R. *Conrad Richter: A Writer's Life*. University Park: Pennsylvania State University Press, 2001.

Jones, Geoffrey. *Merchants to Multinationals: British Trading Companies in the Nineteenth and Twentieth Centuries*. New York: Oxford University Press, 2000.

Joselyn, Sister M. "Edward Joseph O'Brien and the American Short Story." *Studies in Short Fiction* 3, no. 1 (Fall 1965): 1–15.

Joshi, S. T., ed. *From Baltimore to Bohemia: The Letters of H. L. Mencken and George Sterling*. Rutherford, NJ: Fairleigh Dickinson University Press, 2001.

Joyner, Arista Arnold. "Sketches." Unpublished manuscript. UA Libraries Special Collections.

Kaestle, Carl F., and Janice A. Radway. "Reading in Situ: Introduction." In *Print in Motion: The Expansion of Publishing and Reading in the United States, 1880–1940*, edited by Carl F. Kaestle and Janice A. Radway, 471–75. Chapel Hill: University of North Carolina Press, 2009.

Kaplan, Morris B. *Sodom on the Thames: Sex, Love, and Scandal in Wilde Times*. Ithaca, NY: Cornell University Press, 2005.

Keddie, James. *Shady Corner in Paradise*. Chicago and Boston: Bellows-Reeve, 1936.

Kellner, Bruce. *Carl Van Vechten and the Irreverent Decades*. Norman: University of Oklahoma Press, 1968.

Kellner, Bruce, ed. *Letters of Carl Van Vechten*. New Haven, CT: Yale University Press, 1987.

Kellogg, Stuart. "Introduction: The Uses of Homosexuality in Literature." In *Literary Visions of Homosexuality*, edited by Stuart Kellogg, 1–12. New York: Haworth Press, 1983.

Kelvin, Norman, ed. *The Collected Letters of William Morris, 1885–1888*. Princeton, NJ: Princeton University Press, [1987] 2014.

Kershen, Anne J. "Higher Education in the London Community." In *London Higher: The Establishment of Higher Education in London*, edited by Roderick Floud and Sean Glynn, 77–95. London and Atlantic Highlands, NJ: Athlone Press, 1998.

Kitton, Frederic G. *The Minor Writings of Charles Dickens: A Bibliography and Sketch*. London: Elliot Stock, 1900.

Kluger, Richard, and Phyllis Kluger. *The Paper: The Life and Death of the New York Herald Tribune*. New York: Alfred A. Knopf, 1986.

Knighton, Mary A. "William Faulkner's Illustrious Circles: Double-Dealing Caricatures in Style and Taste." In *Faulkner and Print Culture: Faulkner and Yoknapatawpha, 2015*, edited by Jay Watson, Jaime Harker, and James G. Thomas Jr., 28–50. Jackson: University Press of Mississippi, 2017.

Knuth, Rebecca. *Children's Literature and British Identity: Imagining a People and a Nation*. Lanham, MD: Scarecrow Press, 2012.

Koestenbaum, Wayne. *Double Talk: The Erotics of Male Literary Collaboration*. New York: Routledge, 1989.

Korte, Barbara. *English Travel Writing from Pilgrimages to Postcolonial Explorations*. Basingstoke, UK; and New York: Palgrave, [1996] 2000.

Koszarski, Richard. *Fort Lee: The Film Town*. Bloomington: Indiana University Press, 2004.

Koven, Seth. *Slumming: Sexual and Social Politics in Victorian London*. Princeton, NJ: Princeton University Press, 2004.

Kunitz, Stanley J., and Howard Haycraft, eds. *Twentieth Century Authors: A Biographical Dictionary of Modern Literature*. New York: H. W. Wilson, 1942.

Labor, Earle. *Jack London: An American Life*. New York: Farrar, Straus & Giroux, 2013.

Lang, John H. *History of Harrison County, Mississippi*. Gulfport, MS: Dixie Press, 1936.

Larson, Edward J. *Summer for the Gods: The Scopes Trial and America's Continuing Debate over Science and Religion*. New York: Basic Books, 1997.

Larson, Orville K. *Scene Design in the American Theatre from 1915 to 1960*. Fayetteville: University of Arkansas Press, 1989.

Laurie, Clayton D., and Ronald H. Cole. *The Role of Federal Military Forces in Domestic Disorders, 1877–1945.* Washington, DC: Center of Military History, United States Army, 1997.

Leap, W. L., and T. Boellstorff, eds. *Speaking in Queer Tongues: Globalization and Gay Language.* Urbana: University of Illinois Press, 2004.

Leflar, Charles Joseph Finger, ed. "The Memories of Helen Grace Finger Leflar." Unpublished manuscript, 1999.

[Leflar], Helen Finger. "My Autobiography." Unpublished manuscript, 1931.

Leflar, Helen Finger. "The Guest Book." *Flashback* 31, no. 1 (February 1981): 19–23.

Leflar, Robert B, and Robert A. Leflar. "Recollections of Robert A. Leflar." Bound manuscript, October 1992. Courtesy of Robert B Leflar.

Levin, James. *The Gay Novel: The Male Homosexual Image in America.* New York: Irvington, 1983.

Lewis, David L. *The Public Image of Henry Ford: An American Folk Hero and His Company.* Detroit, MI: Wayne State University Press, 1976.

Lewis, Oscar. *Silver Kings: The Lives and Times of Mackay, Fair, Flood, and O'Brien, Lords of the Nevada Comstock Lode.* New York: Alfred A. Knopf, 1947, unpaginated.

Locke, John, ed. *The Ocean: 100th Anniversary Collection.* Castroville, CA: Off-Trail Publications, 2008.

London, Jack. *The Little Lady of the Big House.* New York: Macmillan, 1916.

London, Jack. *Revolution and Other Essays.* New York: Macmillan, 1910.

London, Jack, and Daniel J. Wichlan, ed. *The Complete Poetry of Jack London.* New London, CT: Little Red Tree, 2007.

Lonely Planet. *England.* Lonely Planet, 2013.

Loving, Jerome. *The Last Titan: A Life of Theodore Dreiser.* Berkeley: University of California Press, 2005.

Lundquist, James. *Jack London: Adventures, Ideas, and Fiction.* New York: Continuum, 1990.

Maclaren, James Malcolm. *Gold: Its Geological Occurrence and Geographical Distribution.* London: Mining Journal, 1908.

Mallios, Peter Lancelot. *Our Conrad: Constituting American Modernity.* Stanford, CA: Stanford University Press, 2010.

Marcus, Leonard S. *Minders of Make-Believe: Idealists, Entrepreneurs, and the Shaping of American Children's Literature.* Boston: Houghton Mifflin, 2008.

Martin, Robert K. *Hero, Captain, and Stranger: Male Friendship, Social Critique, and Literary Form in the Sea Novels of Herman Melville.* Chapel Hill: University of North Carolina Press, 1986.

Martin, Robert K. *The Homosexual Tradition in American Poetry.* Austin: University of Texas Press, 1979.

Masefield, John. *The Story of a Round House and Other Poems.* Rev. ed. New York: Macmillan, [1912] 1916.

Massee, May. Introduction to *Children's Stories and How to Tell Them*, by Woutrina Agatha Bone, xv–xviii. New York: Harcourt, Brace and Company, 1924.

Massee, May. "The Reminiscences of May Massee." Transcript of interviews. New York: Columbia University Oral History Collection, 1966.

Mathias, Fred S. *The Amazing Bob Davis: His Last Vagabond Journey*. New York: Longmans, Green, 1944.

Matson, Elizabeth Anna. "The Birth of Children's Book Reviews, 1918–1929." Thesis. University of North Carolina, Chapel Hill, April 2008.

Mayfield, Sara. *The Constant Circle: H. L. Mencken and His Friends*. New York: Delacorte Press, 1968; Tuscaloosa: University of Alabama Press, 2003.

McKinney, Nancy E. "William Marion Reedy." In *Dictionary of Midwestern Literature*, edited by Philip A. Greasley, I: 430–41. Bloomington: Indiana University Press, 2001.

Mencken, H. L., and Jonathan Yardley. *My Life as Author and Editor*. New York: Vintage, 1992, unpaginated e-book.

Menikoff, Ed. *Robert Louis Stevenson and "The Beach of Falesá."* Stanford, CA: Stanford University Press, 1984.

Meyers, Jeffrey. *Joseph Conrad*. New York: Charles Scribner's Sons, 1991.

Miller, Corinne. "Swiftness, Vigour and Exuberance." In *Frank Brangwyn, 1867–1956*, by Libby Horner and Gillian Naylor, 98–125. Leeds, UK: Leeds Museum and Galleries, 2007.

Miller, Louise. "Phyllis Reid Fenner (1899–1982)." In *Pioneers and Leaders in Library Services to Youth: A Biographical Dictionary*, edited by Marilyn Lea Miller, 66–67. Westport, CT: Libraries Unlimited, 2003.

Milne-Smith, Amy. *London Clubland: A Cultural History of Gender and Class in Late-Victorian Britain*. New York: Palgrave Macmillan, 2011.

Mitchell, Mark, and David Leavitt. *Pages Passed from Hand to Hand: The Hidden Tradition of Homosexual Literature in English from 1748 to 1914*. Boston and New York: Houghton Mifflin, 1997.

Mjagkij, Nina. *Men and Women Adrift: The YMCA and the YWCA in the City*. New York: New York University Press, 1997.

Molesworth, Richard Bevil. "A Ghost of the Pampas." In *The Wrong Envelope and Other Stories*, by Mary Louisa Molesworth, 227–48. London: Macmillan, 1906.

Moore, Anne Carroll. *My Roads to Childhood: Views and Reviews of Children's Books*. New York: Doubleday, Doran, 1939.

Moskowitz, Sam. *Under the Moons of Mars: A History and Anthology of "The Scientific Romance" in the Munsey Magazines, 1912–1920*. New York: Holt, Rinehart & Winston, 1970.

Moss, Chris. *Patagonia: A Cultural History*. Andrews UK Limited, 2011.

Mullins, Maire. "Stopping History in Walt Whitman's 'Drum-Taps.'" *Walt Whitman Quarterly Review* 17, no. 1 (Summer 1999): 4–14.

Murrow, Edward R. *This Is London*. New York: Simon and Schuster, 1941.

Musselwhite, David E. *Partings Welded Together: Politics and Desire in the Nineteenth-Century English Novel.* London: Methuen, 1987.

National Civil Liberties Bureau. *The Outrage on Rev. Herbert S. Bigelow.* New York: National Civil Liberties Bureau, 1918.

Newlin, Keith, ed. *A Theodore Dreiser Encyclopedia.* Westport, CT: Greenwood, 2003.

Nissen, Axel. *Manly Love: Romantic Friendship in American Fiction.* Chicago: University of Chicago Press, 2009.

Niven, Penelope. *Carl Sandburg: A Biography.* New York: Charles Scribner's Sons, 1991.

Noel, Joseph. *Footloose in Arcadia: A Personal Record of Jack London, George Sterling, Ambrose Bierce.* New York: Carrick & Evans, 1940.

Oberlin College. *General Catalogue of Oberlin College, 1833–1908.* Oberlin, OH: Oberlin College, 1909.

Office of the Adjutant General of the Army. *A List of Awards of the Congressional Medal of Honor, the Distinguished-Service Cross, and the Distinguished-Service Medal Awarded under Authority of the Congress of the United States, 1862–1926.* Washington, DC: US Government Printing Office, 1927.

Ohmann, Richard. "Diverging Paths: Books and Magazines in the Transition to Corporate Capitalism." In *Print in Motion: The Expansion of Publishing and Reading in the United States, 1880–1940,* edited by Carl F. Kaestle and Janice A. Radway, 102–15. Chapel Hill: University of North Carolina Press, 2009.

Orens, John Richard. "Christ, Communism, and Chorus Girls: A Reassessment of Stewart Headlam." *Historical Magazine of the Protestant Episcopal Church* 49, no. 3 (September 1980): 233–48.

Osborne, Roger. "The Publication of *Victory* in *Munsey's Magazine* and the London *Star*." *Conradiana* 41, no. 2–3 (Summer–Fall 2009): 266–87.

Oskison, John Milton. *Tales of the Old Indian Territory and Essays on the Indian Condition.* Lincoln: University of Nebraska Press, 2012.

Paddock, B. B. *A History of Central and West Texas.* Vol. 1. Chicago: Lewis, 1911.

Paul, Doris A. "Life and Works of Paul Honoré." Unpublished manuscript, 12 pp. East Lansing, MI: People's Church, 1988.

Peer, C. J. "Social and Educational Centers of London." *Altruistic Review* 1, no. 2 (August 1893): 70–73.

Penrose Jr., R. A. F. "The Gold Regions of the Strait of Magellan and Tierra del Fuego." *Journal of Geology* 16, no. 8 (November–December 1908): 683–97.

Peterson, Theodore. *Magazines in the Twentieth Century.* Urbana: University of Illinois Press, 1956.

Popper, Julius. *The Popper Expedition [to] Tierra del Fuego: A Lecture Delivered at the Argentine Geographical Institute, March 5, 1887.* Buenos Aires, Argentina: L. Jaacobsen & Co., n.d.

Pratt, John, and Nick Richards. "Higher Education and the London Economy 1830–1914." In *London Higher: The Establishment of Higher Education in*

London, edited by Roderick Floud and Sean Glynn, 36–76. London and Atlantic Highlands, NJ: Athlone Press, 1998.

Price, Kenneth M. "Whitman in Selected Anthologies: The Politics of His Afterlife." *Virginia Quarterly Review* 81 (Spring 2005): unpaginated.

Prince, Cathryn J. *American Daredevil: The Extraordinary Life of Richard Halliburton, the World's First Celebrity Travel Writer*. Chicago: Chicago Review Press, 2016.

Putzel, Max. *Genius of Place: William Faulkner's Triumphant Beginnings*. Baton Rouge: Louisiana State University Press, 1985.

Putzel, Max. *The Man in the Mirror: William Marion Reedy and His Magazine*. Cambridge, MA: Harvard University Press, 1963.

Quinan, Jack. "Elbert Hubbard's Roycroft." In *Head, Heart, and Hand: Elbert Hubbard and the Roycrofters*, by Marie Via and Marjorie B. Searl, 1–18. Rochester, NY: University of Rochester Press, 1994.

Radway, Janice A. *A Feeling for Books: The Book-of-the-Month Club, Literary Taste, and Middle Class Desire*. Chapel Hill: University of North Carolina Press, 1997.

Radway, Janice A. "Learned and Literary Print Cultures in an Age of Professionalization and Diversification." In *Print in Motion: The Expansion of Publishing and Reading in the United States, 1880–1940*, by Carl F. Kaestle and Janice A. Radway, 197–233. Chapel Hill: University of North Carolina Press, 2009.

Raitt, Suzanne. *May Sinclair: A Modern Victorian*. Oxford: Clarendon Press, 2000.

Raitz, Karl, and Nancy O'Malley. *Kentucky's Frontier Highway: Historical Landscapes along the Maysville Road*. Lexington: University Press of Kentucky, 2012.

Rawson, Robert. "Gottfried Finger's Christmas Pastorellas." *Early Music* 33, no. 4 (November 2005): 591–608.

Ray, Robert C. *The West Coast of South America*. Washington, DC: United States Naval Oceanographic Office, 1890.

Reade, Brian. *Sexual Heretics: Male Homosexuality in English Literature from 1850 to 1900*. New York: Coward-McCann, [1970] 1971.

Recchia, Kitty Parsons, and Rockport Art Association. *Artists of the Rockport Art Association: A Pictorial Record of the Oldest Art Association on Cape Ann, with an Historical Sketch on the Rockport Art Colony by Harrison Cady*. Rockport, MA: Rockport Art Association, 1940.

Rector, John L. *The History of Chile*. Westport, CT: Greenwood Press, 2003.

Reed, John Shelton. *Dixie Bohemia: A French Quarter Circle in the 1920s*. Baton Rouge: Louisiana State University Press, 2012.

Riggio, Thomas P., ed. *Dreiser–Mencken Letters: The Correspondence of Theodore Dreiser & H. L. Mencken, 1907–1945*. 2 vols. Philadelphia: University of Pennsylvania Press, 1986.

Riggio, Thomas P., ed. *Theodore Dreiser: Letters to Women; New Letters*. Vol. 2. Champaign: University of Illinois Press, 2008.

Riskin, Marci L. *The Train Stops Here: New Mexico's Railway Legacy*. Albuquerque: University of New Mexico Press, 2005.

Robbins, Fred W. "*The Double Dealer.*" In *American Literary Magazines: The Twentieth Century*, edited by Edward E. Chielens, 86–92. Westport, CT: Greenwood, 1992.

Robson, F. T. (Maj.) "Administrative and Supply Functions of the 82nd Division." In *Official History of the 82nd Division American Expeditionary Forces, 1917–1919*, 246–58. Indianapolis: Bobbs-Merrill, 1919.

Roell, Craig H. "The Piano in the American Home." In *The Arts and the American Home, 1890–1930*, by Jessica H. Foy and Karal Ann Marling, 85–110. Knoxville: University of Tennessee Press, 1994.

Rose, Jonathan. *The Intellectual Life of the British Working Classes*. New Haven, CT: Yale University Press, 2001.

Rothman, Sheila M. *Living in the Shadow of Death: Tuberculosis and the Social Experience of Illness in American History*. New York: Basic Books, 1994.

Rowbotham, Sheila. *Edward Carpenter: A Life of Liberty and Love*. London: Verso, 2008.

Rubin, Joan Shelley. "Making Meaning: Analysis and Affect in the Study and Practice of Reading." In *Print in Motion: The Expansion of Publishing and Reading in the United States, 1880–1940*, edited by Carl F. Kaestle and Janice A. Radway, 511–27. Chapel Hill: University of North Carolina Press, 2009.

Rubin, Joan Shelley. *The Making of Middlebrow Culture*. Chapel Hill: University of North Carolina Press, 1992.

Ruppell, Richard J. "'Girl! What? Did I Mention a Girl?' The Economy of Desire in *Heart of Darkness*." In *Imperial Desire: Dissident Sexualities and Colonial Literature*, edited by Philip Holden and Richard J. Ruppell, 152–71. Minneapolis: University of Minnesota Press, 2003.

Ruppell, Richard J. *Homosexuality in the Life and Work of Joseph Conrad: Love between the Lines*. New York: Routledge, 2008.

Rusch, Frederic E., and Donald Pizer. *Theodore Dreiser: Interviews*. Urbana: University of Illinois Press, 2004.

Sandburg, Carl. *Abraham Lincoln: The Prairie Years*. 2 vols. New York: Harcourt, Brace, 1926.

Sandburg, Carl. *The American Songbag*. New York: Harcourt, Brace, 1927; San Diego: Harcourt, Brace, 1990.

Schmidt, Gary D. *Making Americans: Children's Literature from 1930 to 1960*. Iowa City: University of Iowa Press, 2013.

Schults, Raymond L. *Crusader in Babylon: W. T. Stead and the Pall Mall Gazette*. Lincoln: University of Nebraska Press, 1972.

Schultz, David E., and S. T. Joshi, eds. *The Shadow of the Unattained: The Letters of George Sterling and Clark Ashton Smith*. New York: Hippocampus, 2005.

Scott, John W. *Natalie Scott: A Magnificent Life*. Gretna, LA: Pelican, 2008.

Sedgwick, Eve Kosofsky. *Between Men: English Literature and Male Homosexual Desire*. New York: Columbia University Press, [1985] 1993.

Sedgwick, Eve Kosofsky. *Epistemology of the Closet*. Berkeley: University of California Press, 1990.

Shapiro, Herbert. "The Herbert Bigelow Case: A Test of Free Speech in Wartime." *Ohio History* 81, no. 2 (Spring 1972): 108–21.

Sheehan, Murray. *Half-gods*. New York: E. P. Dutton, 1927.

Sheehy, Donald, Mark Richardson, Robert Bernard Hass, and Henry Atmore, eds. *The Letters of Robert Frost, Vol. 2: 1920–1928*. Cambridge, MA: Harvard University Press, 2016.

Shores, Elizabeth Findley. "Charles J. Finger's Library at Gayeta, Fayetteville, Arkansas." Unpublished manuscript, 2017. This inventory is available in Special Collections, University of Arkansas Libraries.

Shores, Elizabeth Findley. "Published Works of Charles J. Finger and Helen Finger Leflar." Unpublished manuscript. 2018. This list is available in Special Collections, University of Arkansas Libraries.

Showalter, Elaine. *Sexual Anarchy: Gender and Culture at the Fin de Siècle*. New York: Viking, 1990.

Simonis, H. *The Street of Ink: An Intimate History of Journalism*. New York: Funk & Wagnalls, 1917.

Simpson, Colin, Lewis Chester, and David Leitch. *The Cleveland Street Affair*. Boston: Little, Brown, 1976.

Simpson, Ethel C. "C. J. Finger in Fayetteville: The Last Horizon." *Arkansas Historical Quarterly* 72, no. 3 (Autumn 2013): 222–41.

Slide, Anthony. *Lost Gay Novels: A Reference Guide to Fifty Works from the First Half of the Twentieth Century*. New York: Routledge, 2013, unpaginated.

Smith, Alson J. *Chicago's Left Bank*. Chicago: Henry Regnery, 1953.

Smith, Herbert F. "Michael Monahan and His Little Known Little Magazine." *Journal of the Rutgers University Library* 24, no. 1 (1960): 24–28.

Smith, Irene. *A History of the Newbery and Caldecott Medals*. New York: Viking, 1957.

Smollett, Tobias, and James G. Basker, Paul-Gabriel Boucé, Nicole A. Searcy, and O. M. Brack Jr., eds. *The Adventures of Roderick Random*. Athens: University of Georgia Press, 2012.

Spears, John R. *The Gold Diggings of Cape Horn: A Study of Life in Tierra del Fuego and Patagonia*. New York: G. P. Putnam's Sons, 1895.

Starrett, Vincent. "Starrett's Chicago Letter," *Double Dealer* 1, no. 2 (February 1921): 66–68.

Stern, J. David. *Memoirs of the Maverick Publisher*. New York: Simon and Schuster, 1962.

Stevenson, Robert Louis. "The Beach of Falesá." In *Robert Louis Stevenson and "The Beach of Falesá,"* edited by Barry Menikoff, 115–86. Stanford, CA: Stanford University Press, 1984.

Strong, Michele. *Education, Travel and the "Civilisation" of the Victorian Working Classes*. New York: Palgrave Macmillan, 2014.

Summerall, Charles Pelot, and Timothy K. Nenninger, ed. *The Way of Duty, Honor, Country: The Memoir of General Charles Pelot Summerall*. Lexington: University Press of Kentucky, 2010.

Sutton, William A. *Carl Sandburg Remembered*. Metuchen, NJ: Scarecrow, 1979.

Symonds, John Addington. *Walt Whitman, A Study*. London: John C. Nimmo, 1893.

Taliaferro, John. *Tarzan Forever: The Life of Edgar Rice Burroughs, Creator of Tarzan*. New York: Scribner, 1999.

Tebbel, John William, and Mary Ellen Zuckerman. *The Magazine in America, 1741–1990*. New York: Oxford University Press, 1991.

Thompson, E. P. *William Morris: Romantic to Revolutionary*. New York: Pantheon, [1955] 1977.

Tolppanen, Bradley P. *Churchill in North America, 1929: A Three Month Tour of Canada and the United States*. Jefferson, NC: McFarland, 2014.

Tolstoy, Leo. *The Kreutzer Sonata*. New York: Modern Library, 2003.

Tom Green County Historical Preservation League. *Tom Green County: Chronicles of Our Heritage*, I. San Angelo, TX: Tom Green County Historical Preservation League, 2003.

Tsuzuki, Chushchi. *Edward Carpenter, 1844–1929: Prophet of Human Fellowship*. Cambridge, UK: Cambridge University Press, 1980.

Turner, Catherine. *Marketing Modernism between the Two World Wars*. Amherst: University of Massachusetts Press, 2003.

Ulrich, Carolyn F., ed. *Periodicals Directory*. New York: R. R. Bowker, 1938.

United States Ordnance Department. *The Big Gun*. Aberdeen Proving Ground, MD, 1918.

University of Arkansas. *Razorback*. Yearbook. Fayetteville: University of Arkansas, 1922.

University of Arkansas. *Razorback*. Yearbook. Fayetteville: University of Arkansas, 1927.

Updike, John, and Katrina Kenison. *The Best American Short Stories of the Century*. Boston: Houghton Mifflin Harcourt, 2000.

Van Vechten, Carl. *Peter Whiffle: His Life and Works*. New York: Alfred A. Knopf, 1922.

Viereck, George Sylvester. *The Candle and the Flame*. New York: Moffat, Yard, and Company, 1912.

Vining, Elizabeth Gray. "May Massee: Who Was She?" In *The May Massee Collection: Creative Publishing for Children, 1923–1963: A Checklist*, edited by George V. Hodowanec, v–xi. Emporia, KS: William Allen White Library, Emporia State University, 1979.

Wald, Alan M. *The Revolutionary Imagination: The Poetry and Politics of John Wheelwright and Sherry Mangan*. Chapel Hill: University of North Carolina Press, 1983.

Wappell, Anthony J., and Ethel C. Simpson. *Once upon Dickson: An Illustrated History, 1868–2000*. Fayetteville: University of Arkansas Press, 2008.

Weeks, Jeffrey. *Coming Out: Homosexual Politics in Britain, from the Nineteenth Century to the Present*. London: Quartet, 1977.

Wetzsteon, Ross. *Republic of Dreams: Greenwich Village, the American Bohemia, 1910–1960*. New York: Simon & Schuster, 2002.

Whitman, Walt. *Democratic Vistas*. 1871, unpaginated, retrieved Feb. 24, 2018, from xroads.virginia.edu.

Whitman, Walt. *Selected Poems, 1855–1892*. New York: St. Martin's Press, 2013.

Wigginton, Caroline. *In the Neighborhood: Women's Publication in Early America*. Amherst: University of Massachusetts Press, 2016.

Wilde, Oscar. *Collected Poems of Oscar Wilde*. Ware, UK: Wordsworth, 2000.

Wilson, A. N. *Hilaire Belloc*. London: Gibson Square, 2003.

Woeste, Victoria Saker. *Henry Ford's War on Jews and the Legal Battle against Hate Speech*. Stanford, CA: Stanford University Press, 2012.

Wood, Charles Erskine Scott, Art Young, and Hugo Gellert, illus. *Heavenly Discourse*. New York: Vanguard, 1927.

Woods, Gregory. *A History of Gay Literature: The Male Tradition*. New Haven, CT: Yale University Press, 1998.

Woods, Gregory. *Homintern: How Gay Culture Liberated the Modern World*. New Haven, CT: Yale University Press, 2016.

Wright, J. B. "'The Valiant Dead': William Morris and the Paris Commune of 1871." *Journal of the William Morris Society* 13, no. 2 (Spring 1999): 34–38.

Young, Elizabeth. *Disarming the Nation: Women's Writing and the American Civil War*. University of Chicago Press, 1999.

Young, Gwenda. "Herbert Brenon." In *Ireland and the Americas*, edited by James Patrick Bryne, Philip Coleman, and Jason Francis King, 118–19. Santa Barbara, CA: ABC-CLIO, 2008.

Young, Paul. "The Underground Railroad: A Summing Up." *Ohio Southland* 3, no. 1 (1991): 2–13.

Young, Walter H. *A Merry Banker in the Far East (and South America)*. New York: John Lane, 1916.

Youngs, Tim. *The Cambridge Introduction to Travel Writing*. Cambridge, UK: Cambridge University Press, 2013.

Zachman, Richard E. *Historical Homes of Ripley*. Photographs by David Rice. Ripley, OH: 1976.

INDEX